Norfolk
THROUGH TIME

AMY WATERS YARSINSKE

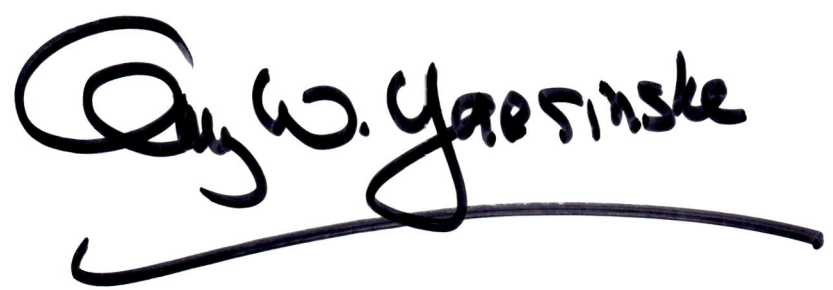

AMERICA THROUGH TIME®
ADDING COLOR TO AMERICAN HISTORY

About the Author

To those who know Amy Waters Yarsinske, it's no surprise that this award-winning Renaissance woman became a writer. She learned at an early age that self-expression had to be forceful, accurate and relevant. This drive to document and investigate history-shaping stories and people has already led to over 60 nonfiction books, most of them spotlighting current affairs, the military, history and the environment. She is the 2014 recipient of the Next Generation Indie Book Award for General Non-fiction for *An American in the Basement* (Trine Day, 2013). Yarsinske received her Bachelor of Arts in Economics and English from Randolph-Macon Woman's College and her Master of Planning from the University of Virginia School of Architecture, where she was a DuPont Fellow. Publication of *America Through Time: Norfolk* marks the twentieth anniversary since Yarsinske wrote her first book on the city.

AMERICA THROUGH TIME is an imprint of Fonthill Media LLC

First published 2015

Copyright © Amy Waters Yarsinske 2015

Unless otherwise indicated in the caption, the pictures in
this book are courtesy of the author.

ISBN 978-1-63500-001-6

All rights reserved. No part of this publication may be reproduced, stored in
a retrieval system or transmitted in any form or by any means, electronic,
mechanical, photocopying, recording or otherwise, without prior permission
in writing from Fonthill Media LLC

Typeset in Mrs Eaves XL Serif Narrow
Printed in the United States of America

Published by Arcadia Publishing by arrangement with Fonthill Media LLC

For all general information, please contact Arcadia Publishing:
Telephone 843-853-2070
Fax 843-853-0044
E-mail sales@arcadiapublishing.com
For customer service and orders:
Toll-Free 1-888-313-2665

Visit us on the internet at www.arcadiapublishing.com

Introduction

Photographs chosen for this volume are testament to the power of "a picture is worth a thousand words." Each photograph tells a story of Norfolk through time, starting with the city center—the downtown—before going down to the river, revisiting the significance of the streetcar and the horseless carriage on the city's development, moving into the wards, and, finally, a journey to the Chesapeake Bay on the city's north shore. With over three centuries of rich history, and with so little intact of the city's historic built environment, photographs are a priceless record of Norfolk, the "sunrise city by the sea."

The way we see the city "now" may not be how we remember it "when." This harks back to an old way of seeing the past as part of the present. The razing of many of the city's most historically and architecturally significant buildings during post-Second World War redevelopment, a practice that continues, even today, has detached people from the past, from an appreciation for what was and connectivity with a sustainable, historically significant built environment, and therefore, from a sense of place. There was a time when one could walk down any Norfolk street and find buildings that fit together harmoniously, but, more than that, the buildings were alive in their surroundings as much as the people moving in and out, and around them. The streets of Norfolk stopped being joyfully alive after the Second World War. Gone is the appreciation for history, tradition, and Southern culture that tourists and residents alike find so appealing in destinations like Charleston, South Carolina, or Annapolis's charming streets, tucked intimately close to the water.

Context is only part of it. There is certainly something intrinsically wrong with the siting of new buildings in an old city when they wipe their aged neighbor off the block. In trying to make the city come alive again, there is a tendency to make buildings that are about other places, and not about who we are and where we live. Many buildings can be put down in metropolitan areas but if they lack any component, style, color, scale, historical accuracy to the place, and craftsmanship, observed architect and author Jonathan Hale, they lack rhythm with the environment, including people. They do not add to the sense of place. Norfolk fell into this trap in the 1950s and 1960s when it traded a historic downtown in favor of an entirely new one. In the process Norfolk lost old traditions and sacrificed the city's original footprint. Today, we replicate old styles as symbols to invoke the "lost magic" of the past. We cannot go back and make it right, but we can resist the impulse to destroy what is left and remember what our history, interpreted through our buildings, streetscapes and riverbanks signify in the life, and sense of place, of this old port city.

The impact of the automobile on the city was so significant that Norfolk had its own "Auto Row," an area in which dozens of buildings were built for the purpose of selling or servicing motor cars at the start of the twentieth century. An extraordinary example of this is the fact that every parcel in the 700-block of Granby Street at one time or another contained a building related to the auto industry, including dealerships, repair shops, parts suppliers and even a few small light industrial manufacturers. The district was also dotted with important retail development as businesses moved north from downtown looking for cheaper land and proximity to newly developed residential areas of the city; much of this land speculation and construction occurred on Granby Street north of Brambleton Avenue, along Brambleton (formerly Queen Street) itself, and on Monticello Avenue (formerly James Street). In fact, most of the city's significant retail growth just prior to the First World War was on Granby Street. Prosperity drove up and down the streets of Norfolk courtesy of Henry Ford.

Though Norfolk fared well during the Great Depression and social downturn following the Second World War, the ultimate decline of the city can be traced to three major factors that occurred between 1947 and 1965: "white flight" from the city center and early city suburbs; the increased mobility and growing affluence of African Americans, impacted by opportunities brought about during the peak of the civil rights movement, and African Americans' growing acceptance of living in outlying suburbia; and the last, the severance of lower Church Street with the construction of the Downtown Plaza Shopping Center, a decision that effectively halved the street and cut it off from its southern end that terminated at the Elizabeth River. As the city's first phase of redevelopment got underway on December 11, 1951, the date the first slum structure was demolished and a date that is now recognized as the start of redevelopment in the United States, no one could foresee today (without photographic evidence) the gravity of what was lost. Norfolk was the first city in the country to implement wholesale urban redevelopment. Many of the properties declared blighted were historically and architecturally significant structures condemned because they sat next to beside a dilapidated neighbor or sat in the path of a private development project. The city's first redevelopment project, which was not phased out until 1964, cleared 127 acres of downtown and cleared land for thirty new commercial buildings built by private developers; the Golden Triangle Motor Hotel was one of them. The project to follow, on the northwest boundary of downtown, occurred in Atlantic City and involved the extension of Hampton Boulevard to the Midtown Tunnel; creation of a medical center complex around Norfolk General Hospital; provided land for Eastern Virginia Medical School, and made property available to private developers for apartment buildings and commercial storefronts. Demolition started in Atlantic City on September 26, 1957, and cleared 140 acres, razing 361 structures. With the exception of two homes, all the dwellings in the bounds of the Atlantic City area were built prior to the First World War.

There was further a laundry list of projects which, in their planning, were not intended to end the important contribution of East Main and Church Streets, and Commercial Place, but did. The completion of the Norfolk–Portsmouth Downtown Tunnel and new Berkley Bridge enabled the city's commuters to bypass Norfolk's east-end commercial corridor. Urban renewal projects in the 1950s and early 1960s cleared over 200 acres of downtown Norfolk, thus eliminating the connection between the city center and Church Street. In July 1956 a master plan for Norfolk's central business district was announced that initiated Downtown Redevelopment Project–North and –South, which contained 838 residential and commercial structures. Norfolk Redevelopment and Housing Authority (NRHA) started demolition on July 30, 1958, starting with the old National Hotel that stood on an East Main Street lot that was set aside for a new public safety building. On June 27, 1961, the Norfolk City Council added Downtown Redevelopment Project–East. Bulldozers moved in to clear twenty-one acres for the Downtown Shopping Center. Old streets were rerouted, others cut off or eliminated to facilitate traffic between downtown and new facilities, including the medical center complex and Eastern Virginia Medical School, thus Saint Paul's Boulevard was laid down; Brambleton Avenue extended to Hampton Boulevard, and Waterfront, later Waterside, Drive was constructed.

Despite Norfolk's expansive redevelopment program, the city center continued to struggle until the late twentieth century, when an infusion of investor capital led to permanent changes, including new residential and commercial buildings that brought an influx of downtown residents and new businesses. All of this, of course, followed on the heels of grassroots initiatives like Harborfest, which brought Hampton Roads citizens back to Norfolk with a lively waterfront festival started in 1976, and the establishment of Town Point Park, soon after. Evident today is the attempt to recreate what was, to design and build condominiums, apartment buildings, single-family homes, and a festival marketplace reminiscent of the city's old ferry terminal building, all bearing architectural features that take us back to the glory days of old Norfolk, and streetscapes that revive the appearance of the same. Norfolk revived passenger rail with a new light rail system in the twenty-first century, but it had passenger rail a half-century ago—and a magnificent station at Union Street—before the building was razed and track pulled up during the rush to make everything old new again at the peak of postwar redevelopment. Today's downtown Norfolk is a wall of steel, glass and concrete office towers that give the appearance the city did not exist until modern times. There are few remaining buildings that tether Norfolk to its roots as one of the East Coast's oldest and most important seaport cities.

On the Cover

Front cover photographs:

Above: This 1980 Carroll H. Walker picture of the east end of Main Street and reoriented Commercial Place demonstrates the postwar transformation of downtown Norfolk. The only structure that is familiar is the Confederate Monument, but it was moved 150 feet northeast of its original position at the head of old Commercial Place. The dark glass building (center) at 500 East Main Street (also 5 Main Plaza East) belonged to United Virginia Bank until it closed on December 31, 1979, when it was acquired by Crestar. First Virginia Bank, at 555 East Main Street, occupied the building on the right.

Below: Looking east on Main Street from Commerce Street in 1910, left foreground, is Saks & Company, a popular men's clothier and outfitter, at 234-238 Main Street, and down the street, the white columned building is Norfolk National Bank at 248 Main Street, organized on August 1, 1885, and which was the oldest bank in eastern Virginia, at that time; Caldwell Hardy was president, and Edwin T. Lamb and Albert B. Schwarzkopf, vice presidents. Down from this bank, rising in the center of this Harry C. Mann postcard, is the National Bank of Commerce, completed in 1905.

Back cover photographs:

Above: By 1910, animals, including monkeys, ducks, sea lions and a bear were housed in outdoor exhibits separated by paved roads that allowed visitors to drive through the park. That year, a main building was built for the zoo, and it was this building that would be used until 1950. Harry C. Mann took this picture, turned into a postcard also made available in 1910, of visitors watching the feeding of the park's sea lions.

Below: The Virginia Zoo's summer safari campers get a lesson on the zoo's two South African bush elephants—Lisa and Cita—in this photograph by David Totten. Both female, the zoo's elephants can be easily identified. Lisa's tusks are symmetrical and she also is the hairier of the two. Cita, who was born in 1968 and is one of the zoo's oldest animals, is smaller and her tusks are asymmetrical. Lisa has lived at the Virginia Zoo for most of her life. Cita is a movie star—having appeared in films including *The Color Purple*, *Sheena Queen of the Jungle*, and *Pee Wee's Big Adventure*. *Virginia Zoo.*

The City Center

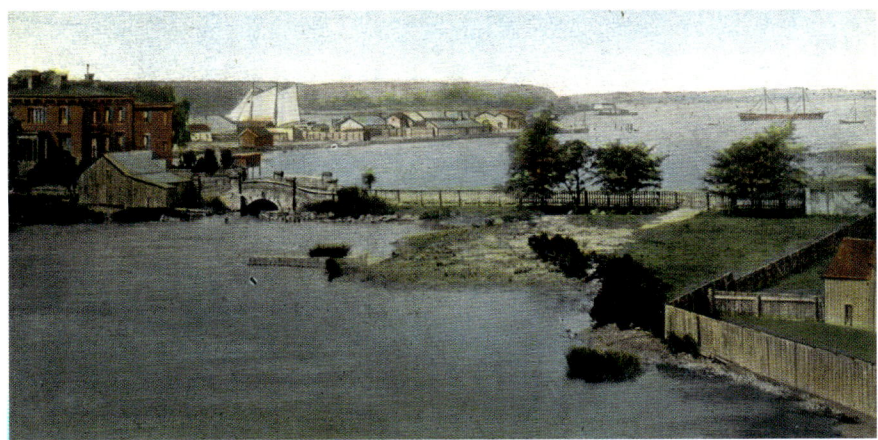

MARITIME NORFOLK: The stone bridge over Town Back Creek is shown in this photograph, taken about 1870. The brick home to the left of the bridge was the residence of Cincinnatus W. Newton; it was built in the early 1800s, but torn down in 1905, when the Law Building was constructed on its site. The buildings to the right of the Newton home, the sails of merchant vessel visible in the background, are the piers and warehouses of the Merchants and Miners Transportation Company. After the creek was filled in, the Haddington Building was built in 1890 roughly on the site of the wooden building to the immediate left of the bridge. To the right of the bridge the Royster Building was erected in 1912, and to the extreme right, the Monticello Hotel in 1898.

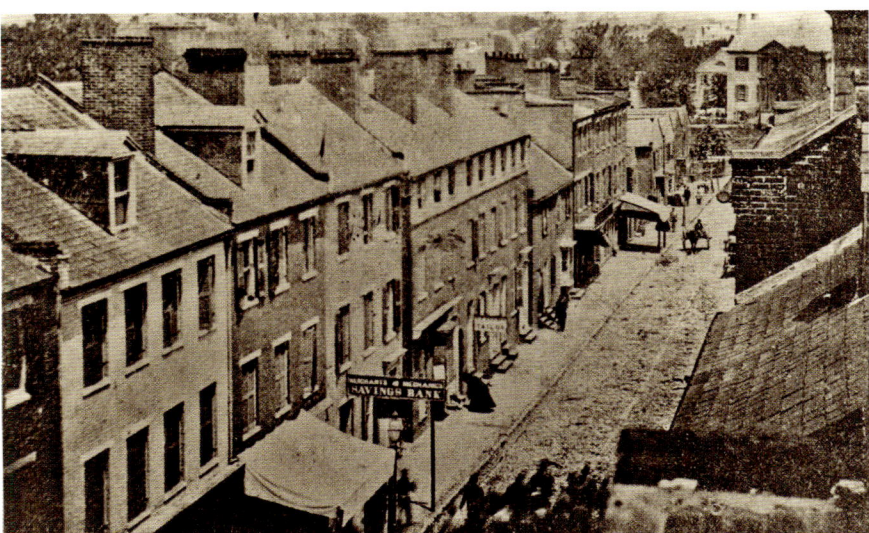

BANK STREET: This picture may well be the oldest, or one of the oldest, existing photographs of Norfolk; it was taken from the top of a building near the corner of Bank and Main Streets, sometime in the middle of the 1860s. The picture shows that part of Bank Street running between Main Street and what is today known as City Hall Avenue. The latter was just a creek at that time and was known as Town Back Creek, which was gradually filled in after the Civil War. The Merchants & Farmers Bank, chartered in 1849, is shown in the picture. What is believed to a squad of Union soldiers can be seen in the lower right hand corner of the picture.

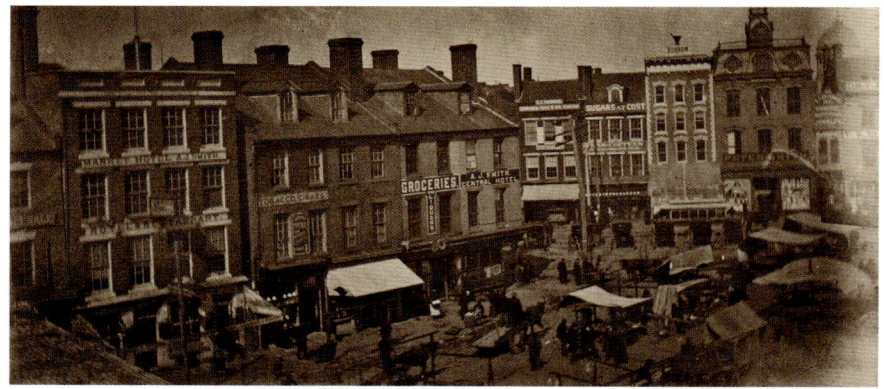

MARKET SQUARE: Perhaps one of the rarest of rare photographs of Norfolk's Market Square (later Commercial Place) and Main Street, this image was taken from the top of the market building in 1885. The buildings on the west side of Market Square (left) include the Market Hotel, Andrew J. Smith, proprietor, 30–32 Market Square, whose establishment offered "a splendid dinner" for thirty cents, Charles J. Holland, cigar manufacturer, 34 Market Square, and on Main Street (facing the square, left to right) are E. T. Thomas Confectioner, owned by Edward T. Thomas, at 138 Main Street; C. D. Kenny, teas and coffees, 140 Main Street; John W. Burrow's drug store at 142 Main Street; Peter Smith & Company (Peter and Cosmos F. Smith) dry goods and notions, 144 Main Street, and Arthur C. Freeman, jewelry and watches, 144½ Main Street. Beyond the roof line of Peter Smith's dry goods store, the dome of Norfolk's 1850 City Hall is visible.

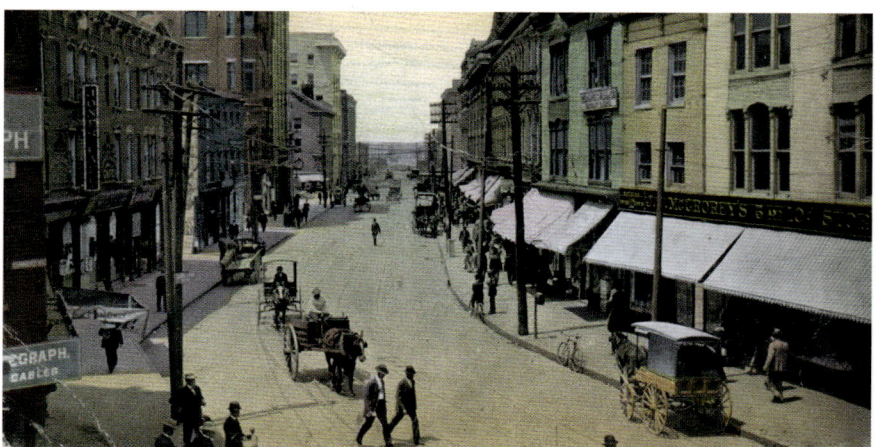

DOWNTOWN RETAIL: Main Street was the principal retail street in the city and ran east from the Elizabeth River, first north and then parallel to Water Street. This view, looking west, offers a view of the street as it looked in 1906, dated by the establishments identifiable in the image. From the left, starting foreground, there is the Postal Telegraph-Cable Company; the Virginia Dairy Lunch Room; Jones Café Welcome Restaurant; Norfolk Landmark, home of the newspaper; McKevitt's Saloon; Virginia Bank & Trust Company; the 1888 Young Men's Christian Association Building (YMCA) (with the turret); the Citizens' Bank Building (later known as the Wheat Building); the United States Custom House (out of view); Talbot Building, and the Atlantic Trust and Deposit Company Building. On the right, starting foreground, there is J. G. McCrorey's 5¢ & 10¢; Rudolph & Wallace Tailors; Smith & Welton dry goods; Academy of Music Building; Lowenberg Building; D. P. Paul, a jewelry store, and Watt, Rettew & Clay, a department store that sat prominently at the corner of Main and Granby streets.

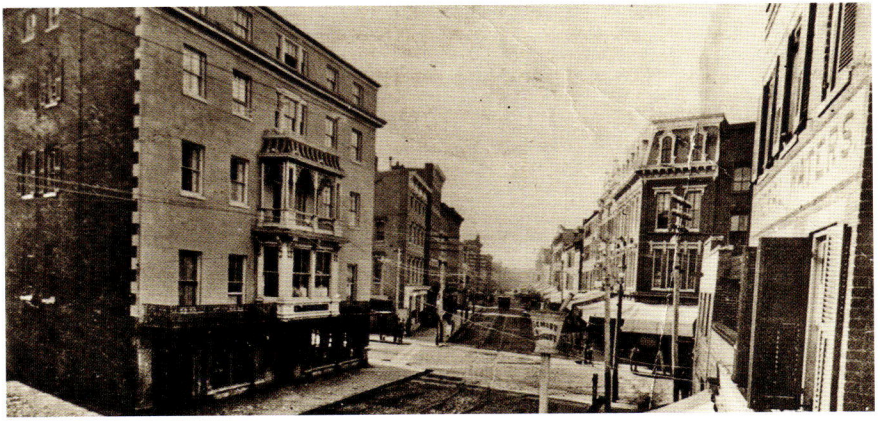

FRENCH'S HOTEL: The hotel (left foreground), looking west from Church and East Main Streets, opened April 19, 1837; its first guest was France's Prince Charles Louis Napoleon Bonaparte, who returned home from exile as Emperor Louis Napoleon in 1852. French's became the National Hotel in 1846, and on August 25, 1860, Stephen A. Douglass made a speech from its balcony. Named Purcell House from 1881 to 1897, it became Hotel Norfolk from 1897 to 1900. John Willis Jr. Furniture moved into the building in 1901; by then it was called the Eclipse Building. A succession of furniture businesses followed, including Willis-Smith-Crall from 1906 to 1913; Forrest-Hall Furniture, 1914; Norfolk Furniture Manufacturing Company, 1915; and Forrest Furniture, 1916. Many tenants and periods of vacancy would follow. French's was razed by Norfolk Redevelopment and Housing Authority in 1961 and with it went the place that had welcomed a cross section of American history, from an emperor, Presidents of the United States John Tyler and Grover Cleveland to General Winfield Scott and Mark Twain.

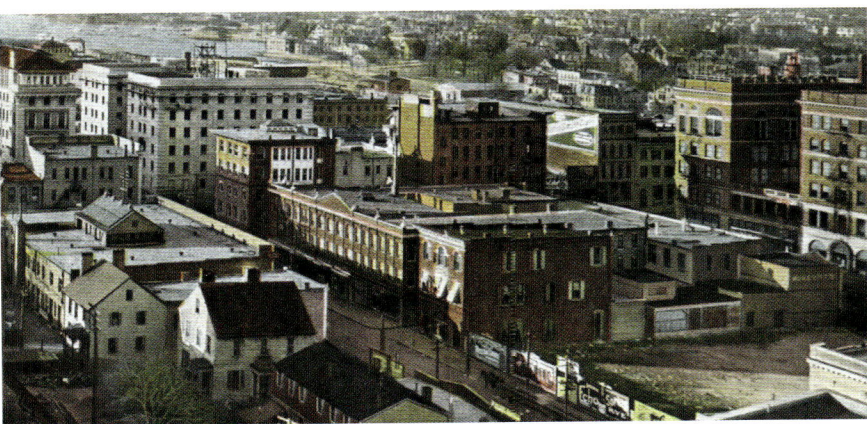

HARBOR VIEW: This bird's-eye view of downtown Norfolk and the harbor dates to 1905. Upper left, the building with the rust-colored roof is the Virginia Club Building, which was built on the southwest corner of Granby and Plume streets, and across from the club is the first two sections of the Law Building, completed that year; a third section was added in 1922. On the northeast corner of this intersection, facing the Law Building, was the Chamberlain Building and behind it, facing Plume, is the Neddo Hotel. The empty lot in the foreground is the future site of the Monticello Arcade, which was not completed until late 1907. In the right foreground is the Monticello Hotel at the corner of City Hall Avenue and Granby Street. The dirt patch in the center of the picture is the end of Botetourt Street (just right of the Law Building). Atlantic City is center, just a bit beyond the Freemason section, upper right.

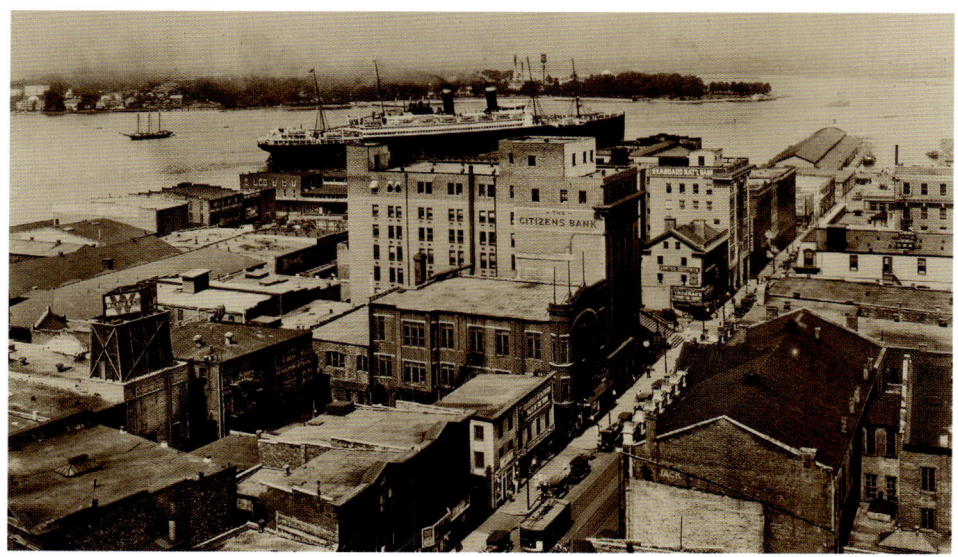

MAIN STREET: Taken in 1925 of Main Street looking west to the harbor, this photograph demonstrates the powerful presence of vehicular traffic that shared the road with the streetcar. The tall building center is the Citizens' Bank Building and out of view next to it is the United States Custom House. The buildings beyond Fayette Street (on the other side the custom house), which include the Seaboard National Bank Building, are no longer standing; the 367,000-square-foot World Trade Center, built in two phases, the first completed in 1983 and the second in 1986, occupies the footprint of the buildings razed from Fayette to Water streets in this picture. Gone, too, is Water Street, which ran parallel to and south of Main Street along the waterfront; the closest approximation today of Water Street is Waterside Drive as it curves around and meets Boush Street. The large steamship in the background is the 723-foot steamship SS *George Washington*, Norddeutscher German Lloyd Shipping Company's largest pre-First World War ship.

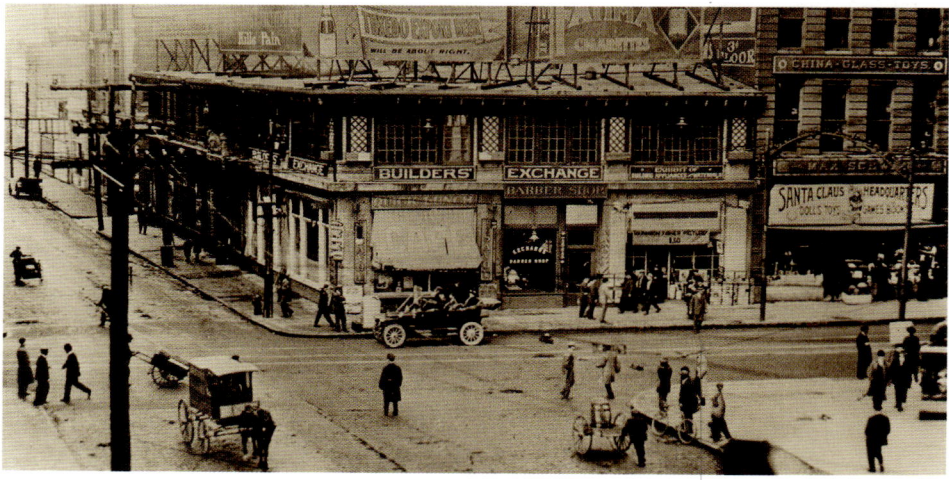

NORFOLK BUILDERS' EXCHANGE: This photograph of the long gone landmark appeared in the December 24, 1911 *Virginian-Pilot*, in an article announcing that the buildings on the northwest corner of Granby Street and City Hall Avenue would be razed and the new twelve-story F.S. Royster Building would be built there the following year. Demolition was quick. By January 1, 1912, the first of more than 1,700 piles were being driven for the F. S. Royster Building; it was finished by the end of that year.

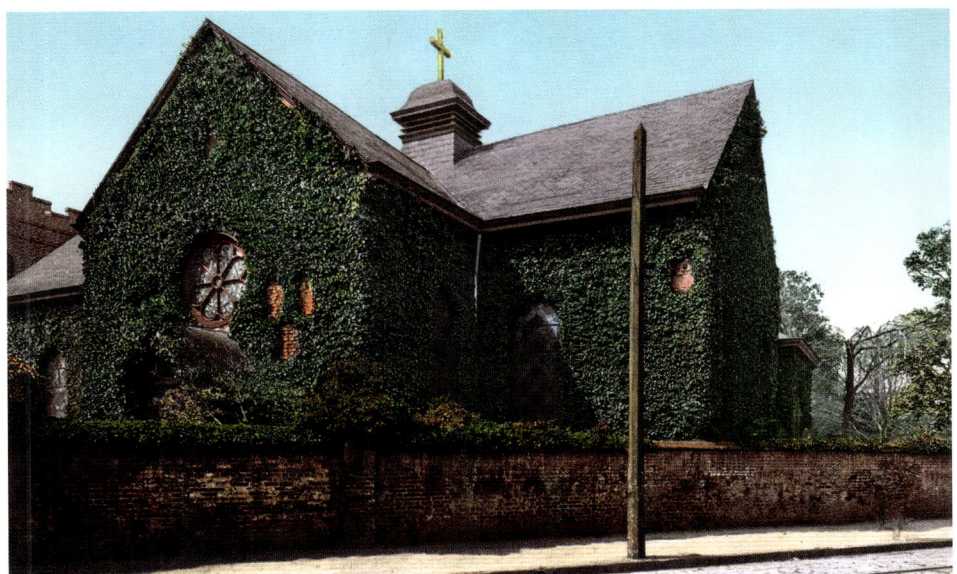

SAINT PAUL'S EPISCOPAL CHURCH: The southern gable of Saint Paul's from Church Street was photographed in 1902 (shown here). A cannonball fired in the direction of the church on January 1, 1776, by attacking British forces under the command of John Murray, Earl of Dunmore, and later mounted to the wall of Saint Paul's that it purportedly struck, is visible far right, to the right of the utility pole. *Detroit Publishing Company, Library of Congress.*

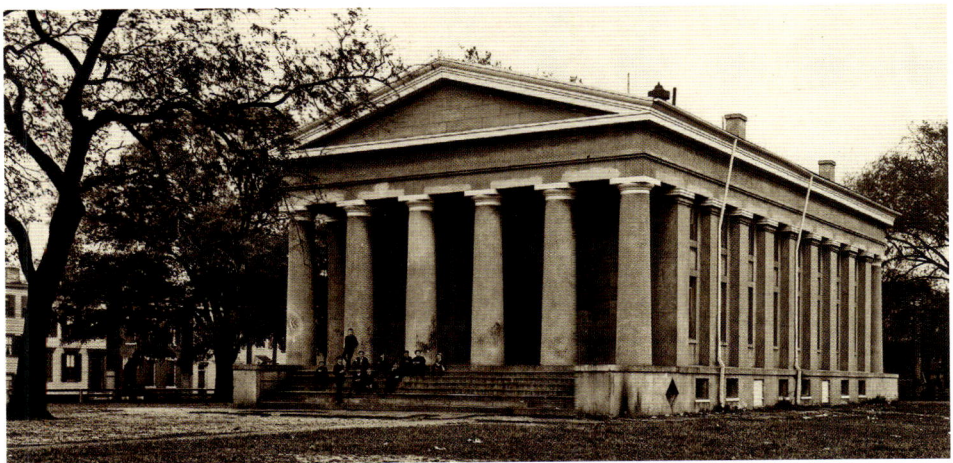

NORFOLK ACADEMY: The school, chartered in 1728, has occupied several locations in the city, among them the site shown here in 1900, on Bank Street. In 1806 the school's trustees purchased former Saint Paul's Episcopal Church glebe land from the Overseers of the Poor. The area, bounded by Catherine (later Bank), Charlotte and Cumberland Streets, and the former Grigsby Place, sat empty until 1840, when the cornerstone of this Greek Revival Doric temple was built to accommodate Norfolk Academy's boys' school. Thomas Ustick Walter, of Philadelphia, architect of the U.S. Capitol, designed it. Norfolk Academy vacated this building in 1915. Of note, Edgar Allan Poe started what would be his last lecture series in Virginia in the summer of 1849, starting with his acclaimed "The Poetic Principle" in Richmond on August 17 and Norfolk—at the Norfolk Academy—on September 14 and then back to Richmond on September 24; he was dead two weeks later.

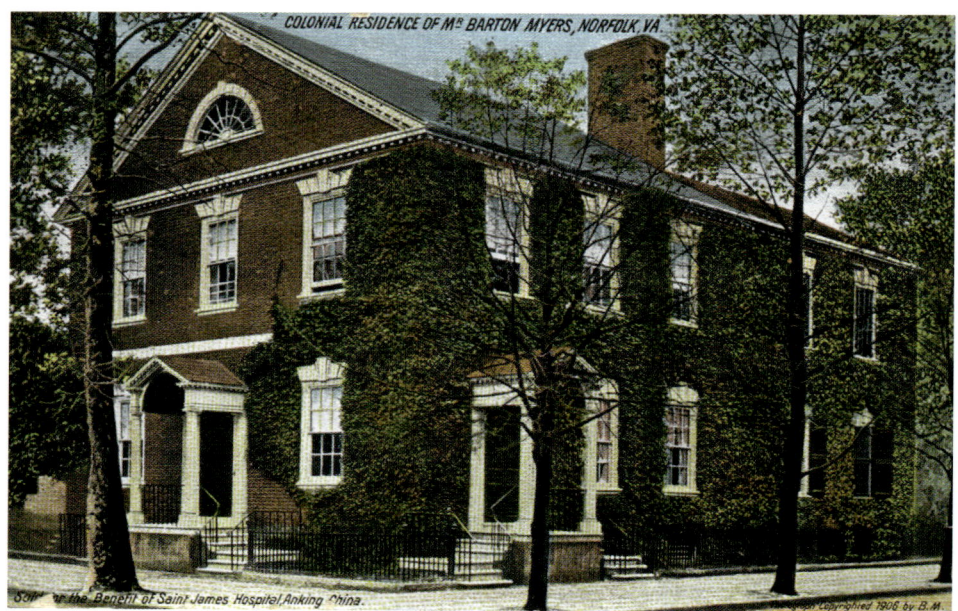

MOSES MYERS HOUSE: The 1792 residence, built for the wealthy New York born importer and most prominent Jewish resident of the city in its nascent years, was eventually, as the postcard indicates, the residence of his ancestor, Barton Myers, when this picture was taken of the home in 1906.

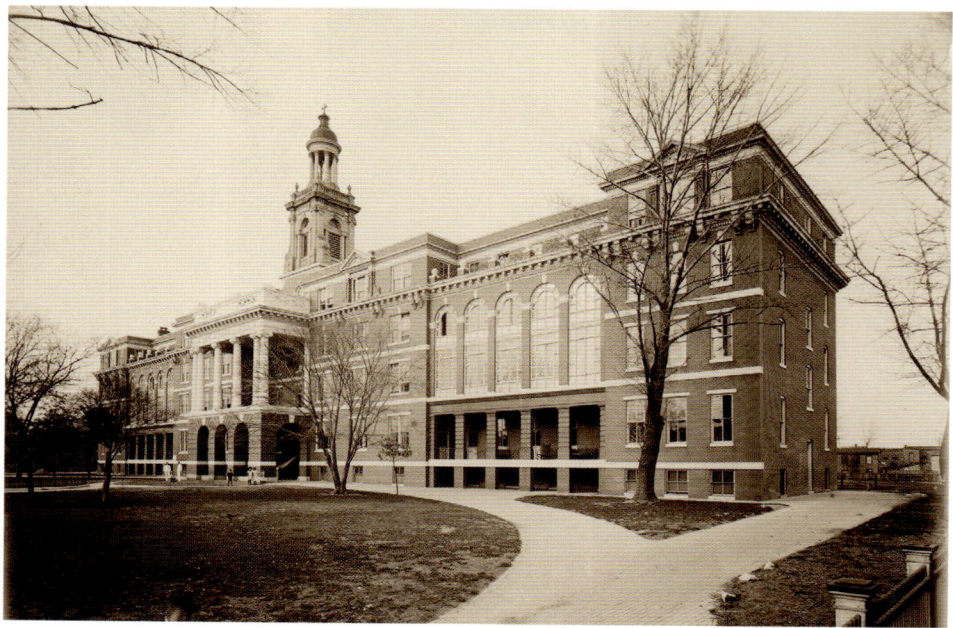

SAINT VINCENT DEPAUL HOSPITAL: The hospital, located at the corner of Wood and Church streets, is shown in this 1905 photograph. This was the second DePaul hospital on this site, the first burned to the ground on September 21, 1899. The land on which this hospital and its predecessor were built was the location of Walter Herron's residence. The Herron family transferred the property to Bishop John McGill of the Catholic Diocese of Richmond for the construction of a hospital. *Detroit Publishing Company, Library of Congress.*

THE BASILICA OF SAINT MARY OF THE IMMACULATE CONCEPTION: The basilica (shown here, 1910) is located on Chapel Street in downtown Norfolk; it is the oldest parish community in the Catholic Diocese of Richmond and often referred to as "The Mother Church of Tidewater Virginia." Today's basilica came into existence in 1791 as Saint Patrick's Church, two years before the establishment of Roman Catholic hierarch in the United States and 29 years before the institution of the Richmond Diocese. The church's first parishioners were French Catholics, who had abandoned France in the wake of the French Revolution. In a matter of years, it received some of the earliest Irish Catholic immigrants to the United States. The original church was built in 1842, but was destroyed by fire in 1856 rendering the building useable as a sanctuary. In 1858, the present church building was completed and dedicated to Mary of the Immaculate Conception. Further, it was the first church to bear the name after the dogma of the Immaculate Conception by Pope Pius IX. On December 8, 1991, the date that marked the 200th anniversary of the church, Saint Mary became a minor basilica.

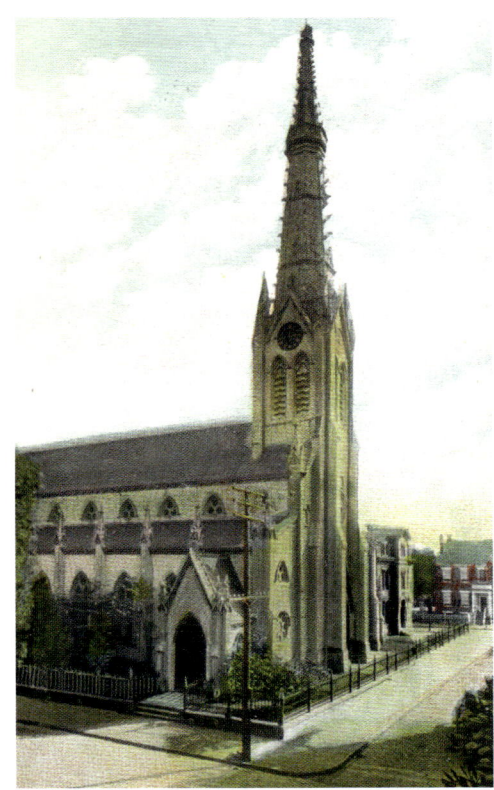

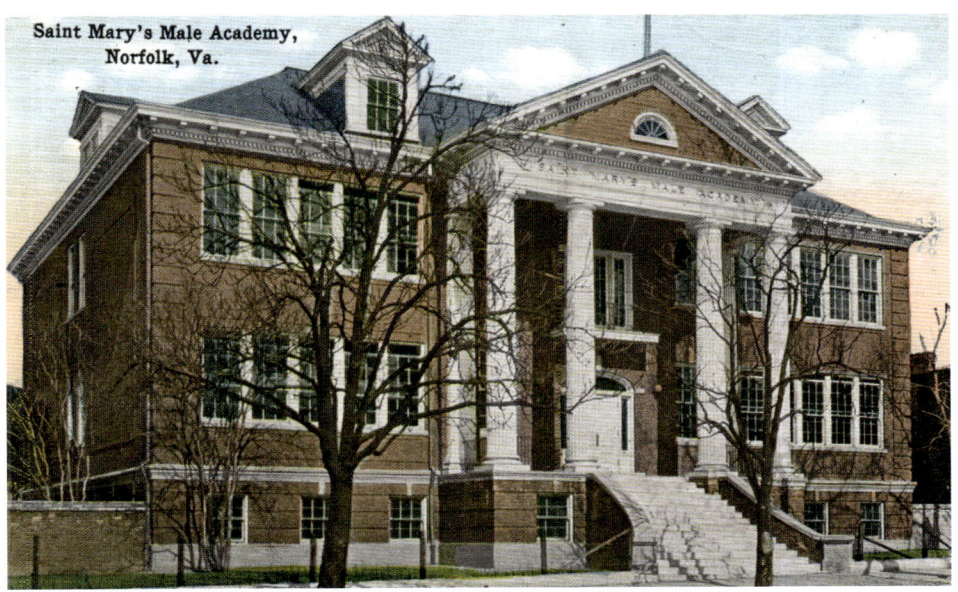

SAINT MARY'S MALE ACADEMY: When Father John J. Doherty arrived at Saint Mary of the Immaculate Conception in 1887, his first priority was construction of a larger school; he brought in the Xaverian Brothers Order and established the academy, shown here on a 1910 period postcard. The building faced Holt Street to the rear of the church and opened in 1889.

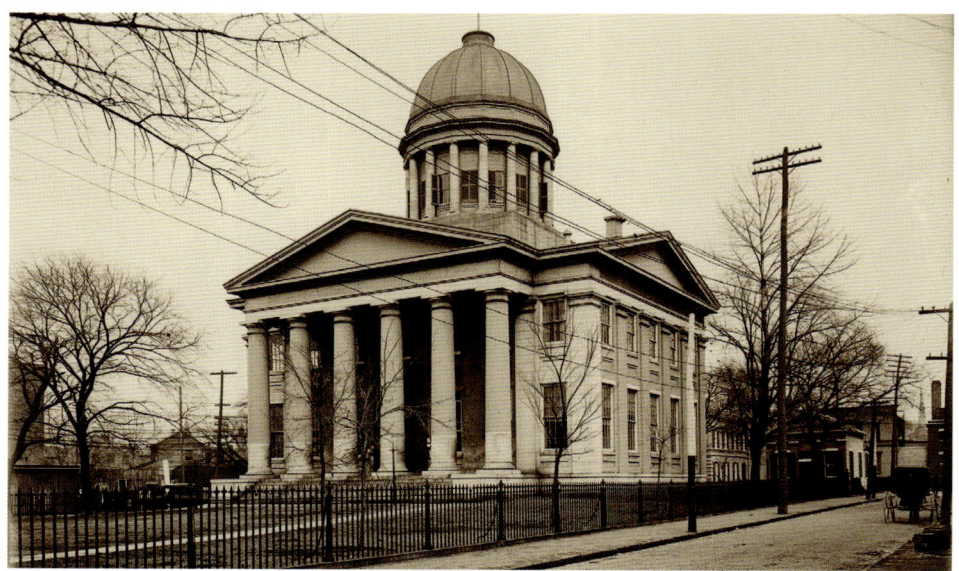

CITY HALL: Norfolk became an independent city by Act of Assembly on February 13, 1845 and almost immediately thereafter, the select council appointed a committee of three to find a suitable location for a new city hall building and courthouse that would house new municipal offices and, simultaneously, symbolize Norfolk's new status and prosperity. This building, shown here as it looked in 1905, served as city hall from 1850 until 1918, and as a courthouse only until 1960. In 1961, the interior was substantially remodeled to provide a future memorial and tomb for General Douglas A. MacArthur. The structure was originally designed by William R. Singleton, a Portsmouth native and Saint Louis architect, with assistance from Philadelphia architect Thomas Ustick Walter, who designed the dome and two wings of the United States Capitol. The old Norfolk City Hall has been described as one of Virginia's best remaining Classical Revival buildings. The site of the old city hall as bounded by Court, Plume and Bank streets and City Hall Avenue. *Detroit Publishing Company, Library of Congress.*

MACARTHUR MEMORIAL: In 1960, General Douglas MacArthur agreed to house his papers and memorabilia in Norfolk, and the city offered the soon-to-be vacated courthouse for the purpose (shown in this contemporary Carol M. Highsmith photograph). Though MacArthur was born in Little Rock, Arkansas, on January 26, 1880, the son of Arthur MacArthur, a lieutenant in the United States Army, and Mary Pinkney Hardy of Norfolk, he always felt close to Norfolk and felt it appropriate for his final resting place. MacArthur was Supreme Commander of the Allied Powers in the Pacific and on December 19, 1944, he became a five-star General of the Army. He later became a commander of United Nations Forces in Korea, from which position he was dismissed by President Harry Truman in 1951. The memorial opened informally in January 1964 and was to have been officially dedicated by MacArthur in May 1964, but he died on April 5, 1964; he was subsequently interred under the dome

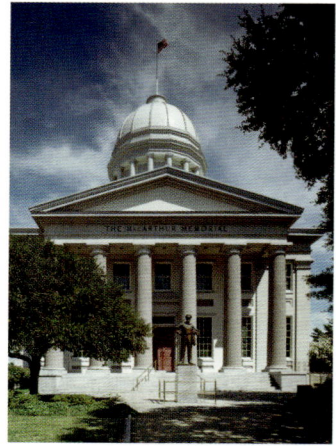

of the rotunda. In 1970, a bronze statue of MacArthur was erected in front of the main building; it was executed by sculptor Walter Hancock of Gloucester, Massachusetts, and is a duplicate of Hancock's statue for the Military Academy at West Point. The statue, which weighs 900 pounds, portrays MacArthur in his uniform of the 1942-1945 period. *Carol M. Highsmith Archive, Library of Congress.*

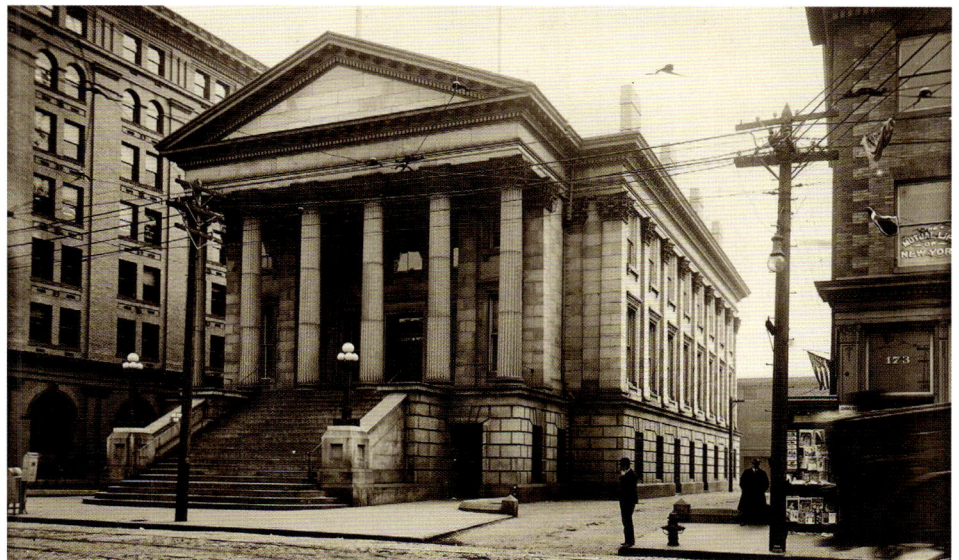

CUSTOM HOUSE: A prominent site in downtown Norfolk at Main and Granby streets was purchased in 1852 to replace the city's first custom house but also to accommodate a larger United States Post Office. Supervising architect of the Treasury Ammi B. Young produced a design based on precepts of classical Roman architecture. Historians of the period anticipated that when completed, Norfolk's new custom house would be "one of the most imposing and showy buildings in the city." Construction began in 1853 with John H. Sale in the role as construction superintendent for the United States Treasury Department. The post office moved into the building in 1857, a few months ahead of its completion in 1858. The 1858 United States Custom House was designed by architect Ammi B. Young (1798–1874), who was then the supervising architect of the Department of the Treasury. The custom house is shown here in 1905. *Detroit Publishing Company, Library of Congress.*

ACADEMY OF MUSIC: New York native, resident and financier Henry Dubois Van Wyck's academy (also called the Van Wyck Academy of Music) at 210–212 Main Street is shown (second building, left) in this 1897 Alfred S. Campbell stereoview. The academy's interior included a frescoed ceiling decorated with the portraits of William Shakespeare, Ludwig van Beethoven, Johann Wolfgang von Goethe, Joseph Hayden, and many others. Performers Sarah Bernhardt, Oscar Wilde, Robert B. Mantell, Ignacy Jan Paderewski, Maude Adams and Lillian Russell played there. The academy later hosted notable vaudevillians and silent and sound motion pictures. Van Wyck, who speculated in properties in the South after the Civil War, first came to the city in 1869 and owned several Norfolk buildings and outlying county properties; his first purchase was the Mallory family plantation and four adjacent estates for truck farming. Van Wyck bought the academy property in 1882 and developed it into a "temple of the dramatic and lyric arts," one that could seat 1,600 and

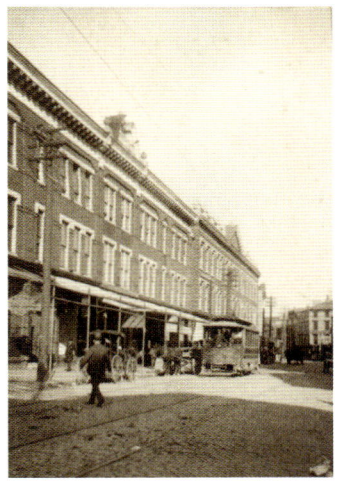

standing room for 700–800 more. The academy building burned down in 1930, and the Selden Arcade now occupies this site. The building, left foreground, is the Lowenberg Building (the Adams Express Company occupies the storefront far left), and in a few short years, it would be home (albeit briefly) of Cosmos F. Smith and Richard F. Welton's Smith & Welton's dry goods store. *Library of Congress.*

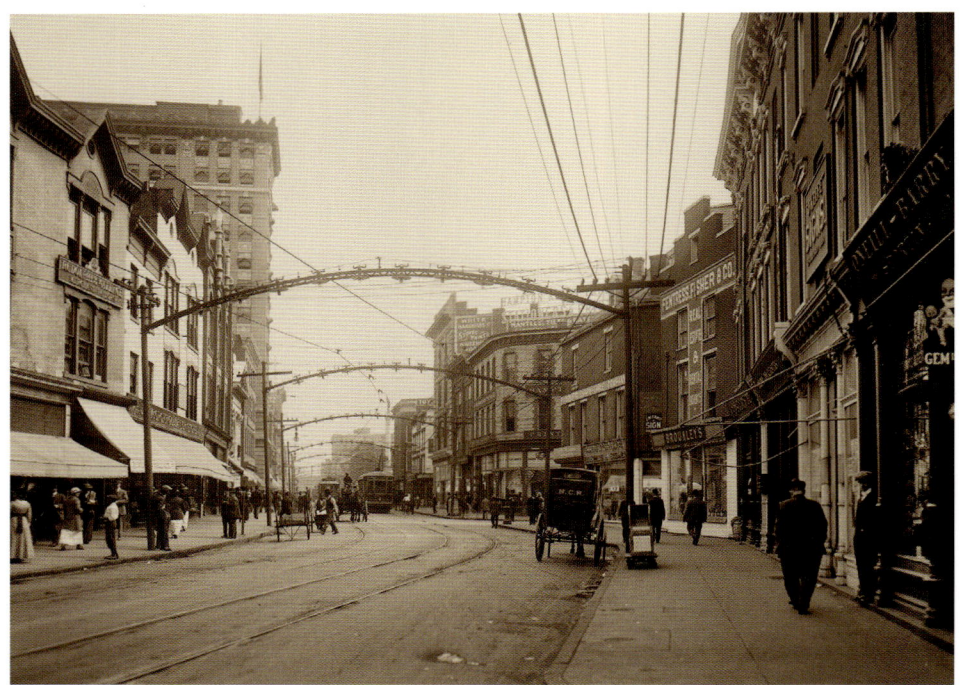

DOWNTOWN LIGHTING: This view looking east on Main Street dates to 1910 and is the flip view of the prior image looking west in 1906. Note that there are no motor vehicles on the street at this time. On the night of September 10, 1909, James H. Brownley, president of Ames, Brownley and Hornthal, a popular department store, pulled the switch that lit up Norfolk's new arch lighting system. The fixed arches with incandescent lamps were first installed to increase the efficiency of the lighting, to give the streets a gala appearance and to reduce lamp maintenance costs from Charlotte to Granby streets, and Main to Church streets, then up Church Street to Queen Street (later Brambleton Avenue); they were removed completely by 1925. *Detroit Publishing Company, Library of Congress.*

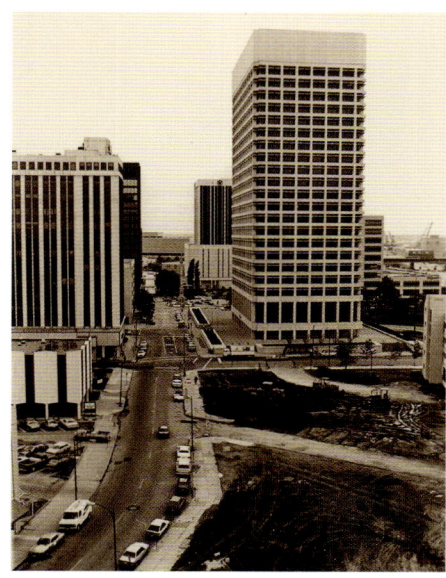

NEW DOWNTOWN: This photograph, taken from the roof of the Citizens' Bank Building by Carroll H. Walker in 1985, shows the last of old Main Street being cleared away (right) to make way for new development; it is today the site of the Marriott Hotel and Conference Center. The large striped office tower just behind it was occupied by First and Merchants Bank Building, which took over the National Bank of Commerce Building when the latter changed its name to Virginia National Bank and moved across the street to a new building. In 1968, First and Merchants clad the building with a façade, and in June 1988, it was imploded. The office tower to the right was occupied by Sovran Bank, the product of a merger between First and Merchants Bank and Virginia National Bankshares, from 1983 to 1990. Subsequent mergers produced the building's current occupant—Bank of America.

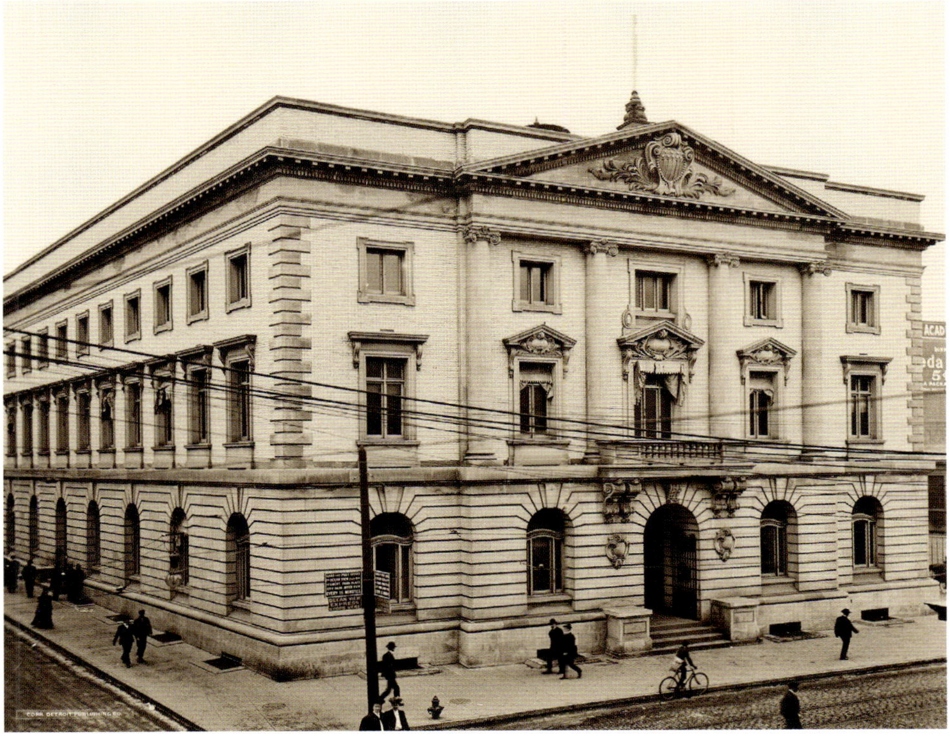

OLD POST OFFICE AND FEDERAL COURTS BUILDING: The building shown here, which also served at one time as city hall, is located at 235 East Plume Street, and is presently the Slover Memorial Main Branch, Norfolk Public Library. During the extensive building boom that occurred in the city center as well as surrounding Norfolk County from 1880 to 1917, the federal government commissioned the firm of James B. Wyatt and William G. Nolting to design a new building for the city's post office and federal courts. Initial construction began in 1898–1900, and this is the exterior of the finished building in 1905 (top, *Detroit Publishing Company, Library of Congress*). The architectural firm of Wyatt and Nolting was responsible for a number of historical landmarks in the Baltimore and Washington, D.C. areas, and their Norfolk post office and federal court project stands as an important and rare example of Neo-Palladian Revival. Neo-Palladianism draws upon the architecture of Palladio and his followers for its composition and detailing. The style, while popular in Europe at the end of the nineteenth century, was overshadowed in the United States by the Greek- and Roman-influenced Neoclassical Revival. This is an interior, second floor view of the former Post Office and Federal Courts Building, later called the Seaboard Building, on Plume Street photographed in August 1981 by Charles Ansell (bottom, *Library of Congress*).

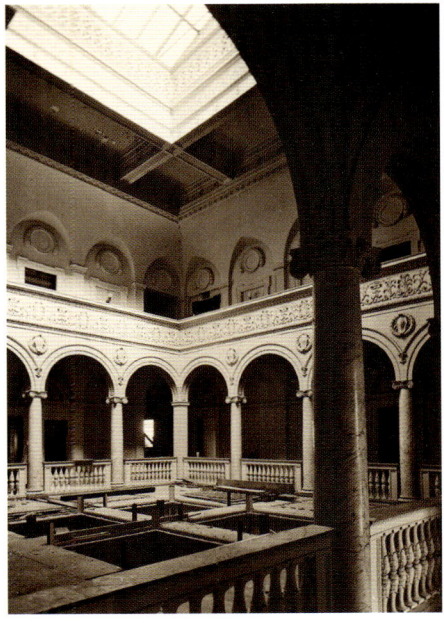

17

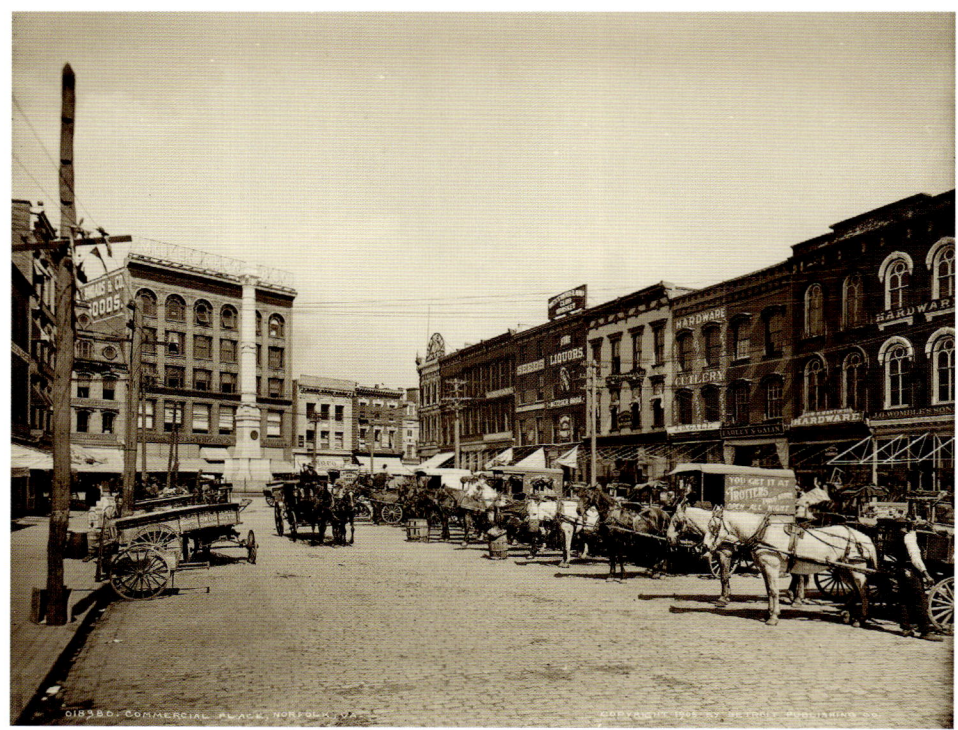

COMMERCIAL PLACE: These two views of Commercial Place looking toward Main Street show the dramatic difference between horse and cart and the growing use of automobiles and trucks. The top photograph, which was taken in 1905, is dated by the incomplete Confederate Monument and a number of the businesses occupying storefronts on the east side of the old market square. Miller, Rhoads & Swartz dry goods store is located behind the monument, facing Commercial Place (top, *Detroit Publishing Company, Library of Congress*). In the bottom picture, a 1920 postcard, horse-drawn carts and carriages that once dominated the square had given way to dozens of automobiles and delivery trucks.

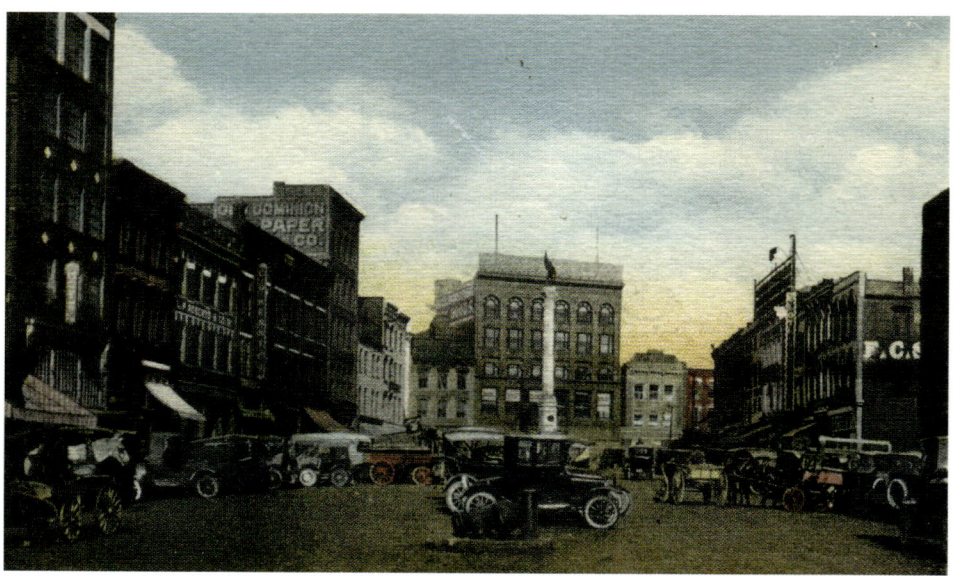

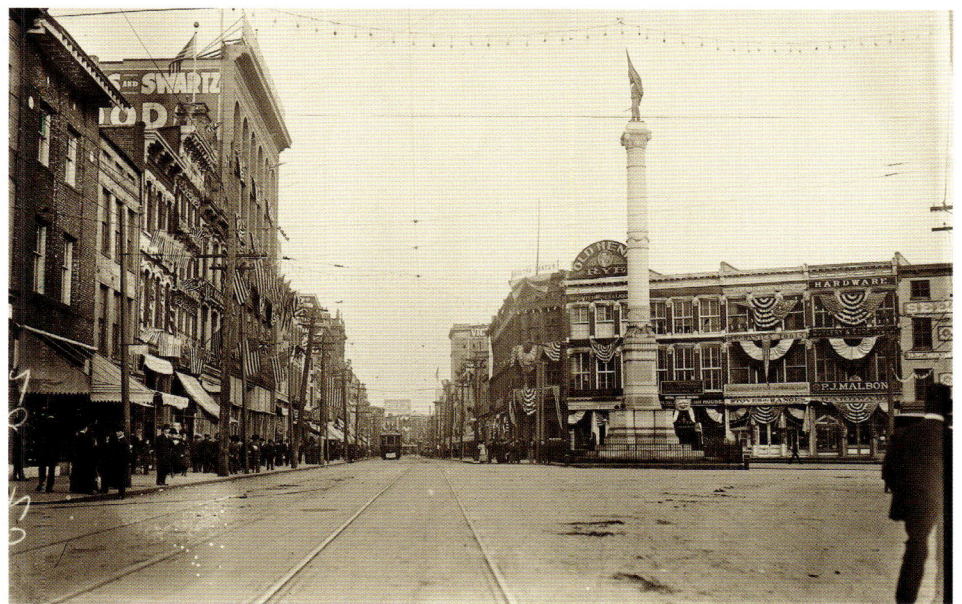

FIRST WORLD WAR ARMISTICE: When this picture was taken of Main Street looking east toward Commercial Place and the Confederate Monument, the buildings were decked out in celebration of the nation's First World War victory, declared by armistice on November 11, 1918. *Bain News Service, Library of Congress.*

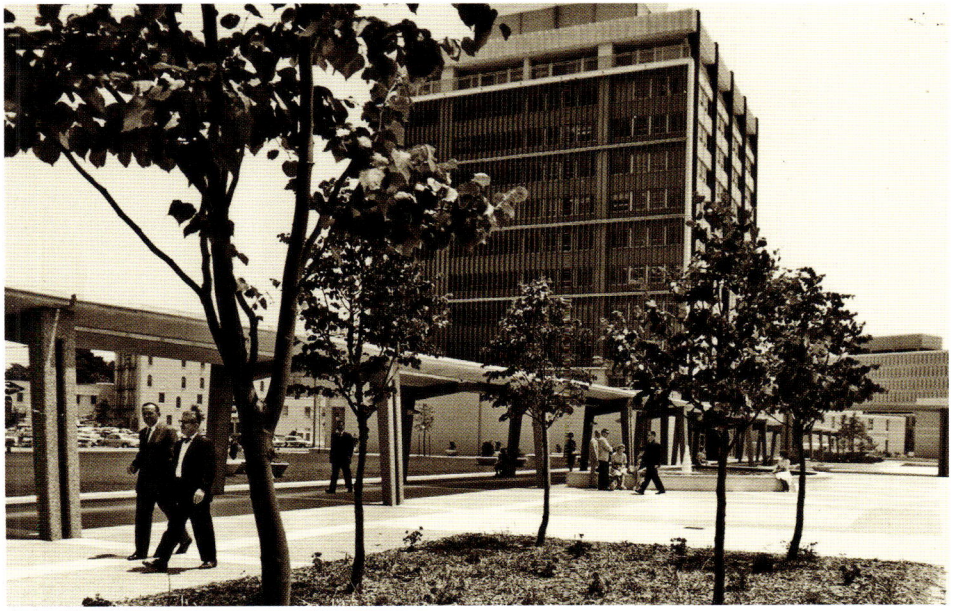

MAIN STREET REDEVELOPMENT: The new plaza walkway and office building in this R. V. Fischbeck photograph, taken on June 18, 1964, was part of Norfolk's expansive post-Second World War redevelopment program that rose from the rubble of what had been old East Main Street, an area redevelopment advocates called the city's "honky-tonk," an eclectic mix of burlesque houses, tattoo parlors and bars that populated the street at that time.

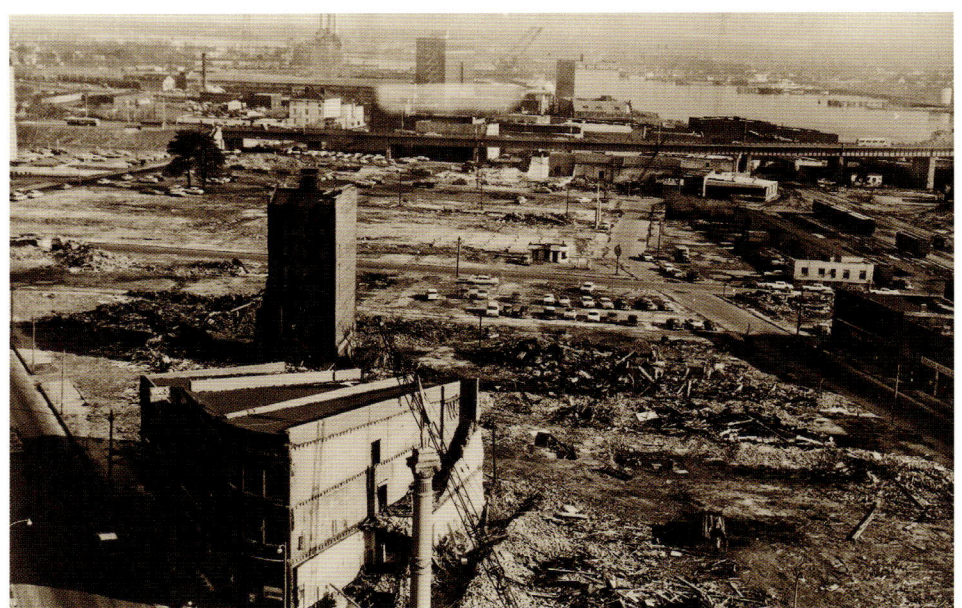

DOWNTOWN RAZED: When this picture was taken by Carroll H. Walker on February 1, 1962, it showed all that was left of the east end of Main Street and Commercial Place, and above the Confederate Monument (still in its original location), the intersection of Union and Church streets, also razed of dozens of buildings as part of the city's massive post-Second World War redevelopment. With exception of the monument, all of the buildings in this picture are gone.

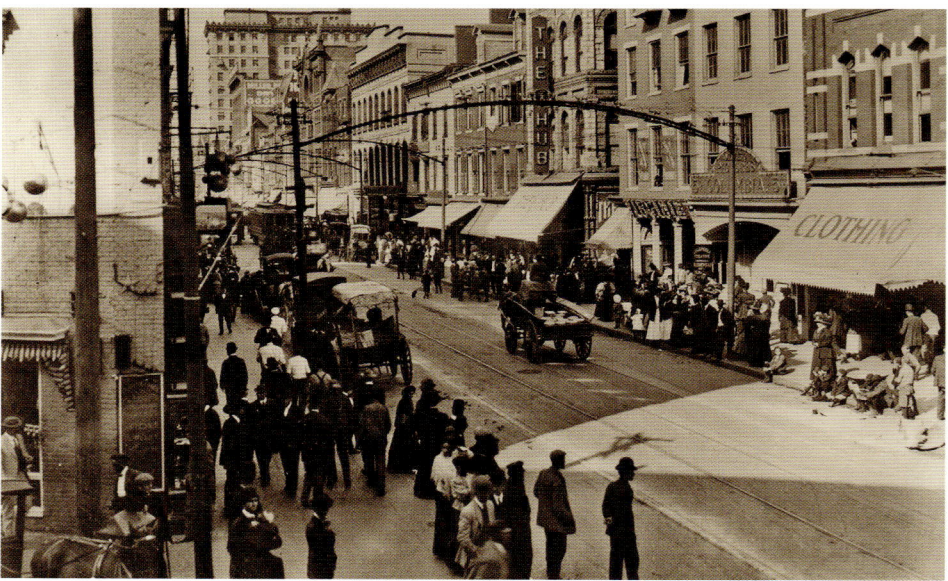

HUB OF ACTIVITY: Harry C. Mann took this picture looking west on Main Street from Church Street in 1911. From this perspective, it is easy to see how Church Street was the center of activity in old Norfolk. The National Bank of Commerce Building is off in the distance left but in the foreground, directly right of the horse-drawn cart on the right are The Hub, a clothier, and the Columbia Theater, a popular vaudeville and movie house.

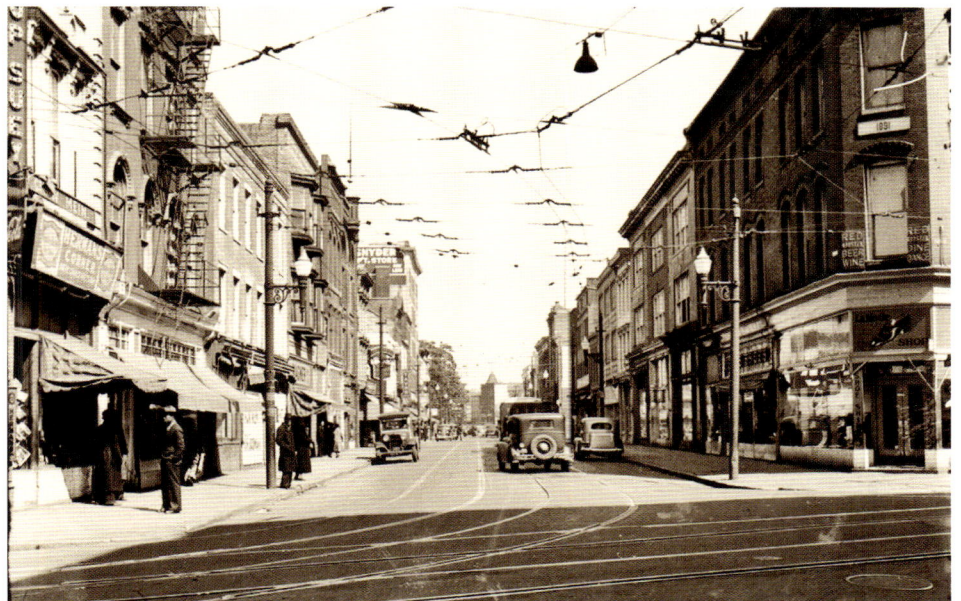

CHURCH STREET: Charles Borjes took this picture of Church Street looking north from East Main Street on November 21, 1938, at Herman's Corner. While mainstays like Matthew Tavss's children's clothier, L. Snyder Department Store, and Altschul's were still there, most of Church Street's favorite establishments were already gone, some driven away with the closure of key thoroughfares—the price of progress. The mass of trees (left) in the background of the picture marks the location of Saint Paul's Episcopal Church.

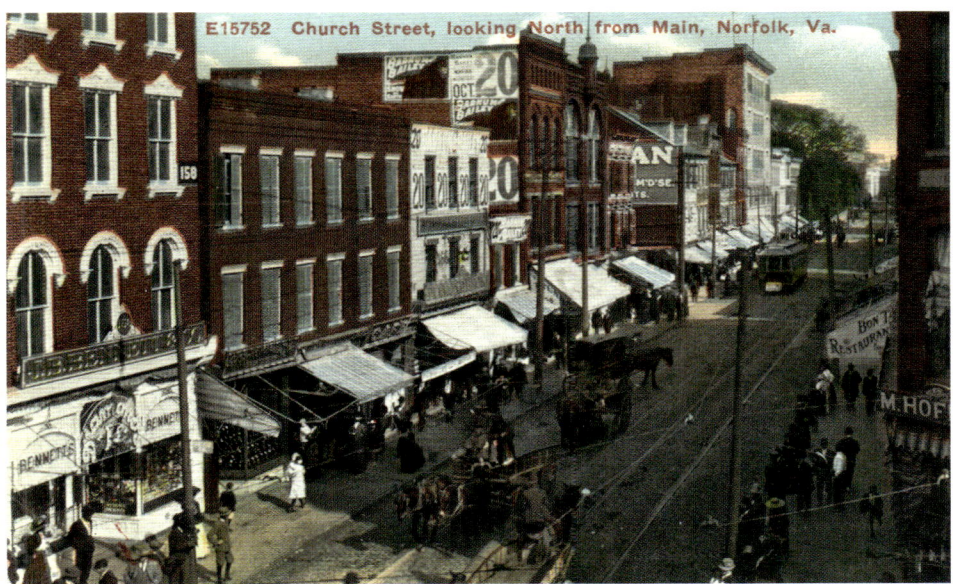

THOSE WERE THE DAYS: Harry Mann took this photograph of Church Street looking north from East Main Street in 1910. The building rising tall above the streetcar is the L. Snyder Department Store, adapted from the old Odd Fellows Hall and Church Street Opera House. Left foreground is J. B. Bennett & Company, a jewelry store at 158 Church Street. Saint Paul's Episcopal Church is hidden in the mass of trees down the street.

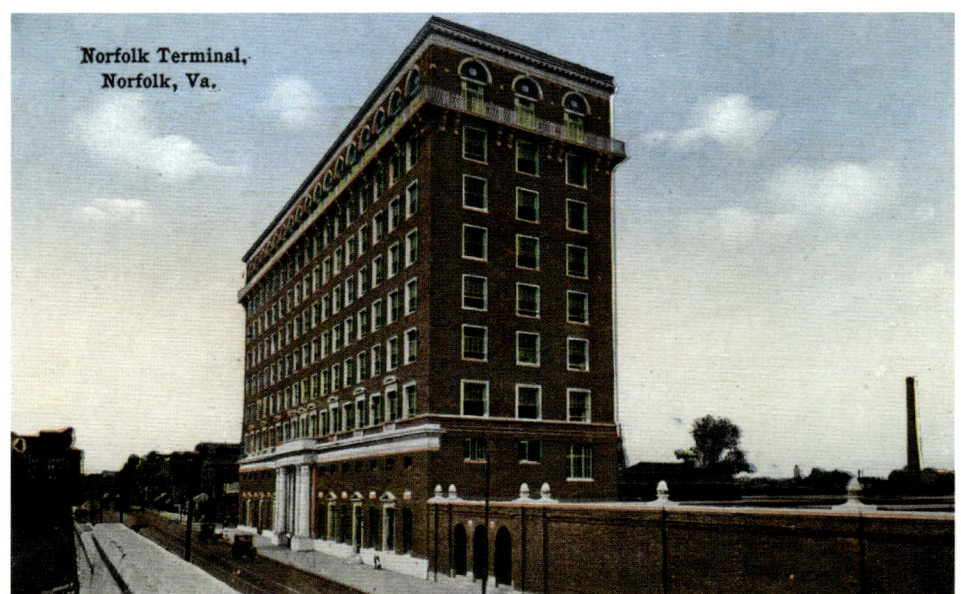

NORFOLK TERMINAL STATION: The station (top) was opened on May 31, 1912 (when this picture was taken); it was designed by Reed and Stem, architects, and built by J. Henry Miller Inc. The "Union" station was located at the foot of the eastern end of Main Street and Lake (Lovitt) Avenue in vicinity of Union Street. The station was torn down in March of 1963. Harry C. Mann took the picture (bottom) of the interior of the Norfolk Terminal Station in 1915. This waiting area was the most beautiful feature of the building with its magnificent marble columns and ornamental stucco ceiling. During its heyday, this station was one of three busiest passenger stations in Virginia.

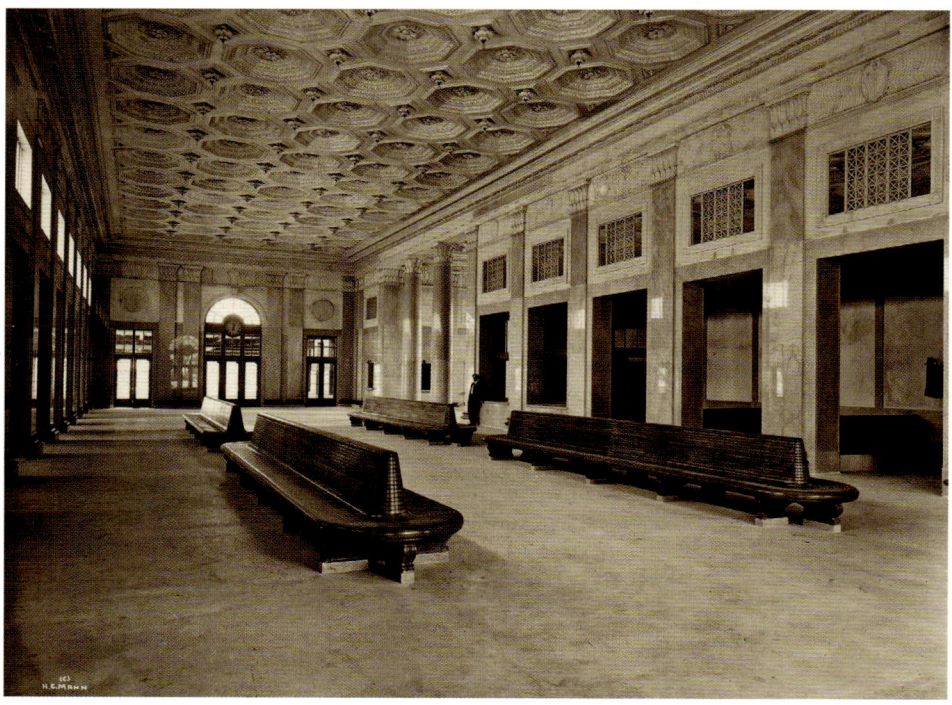

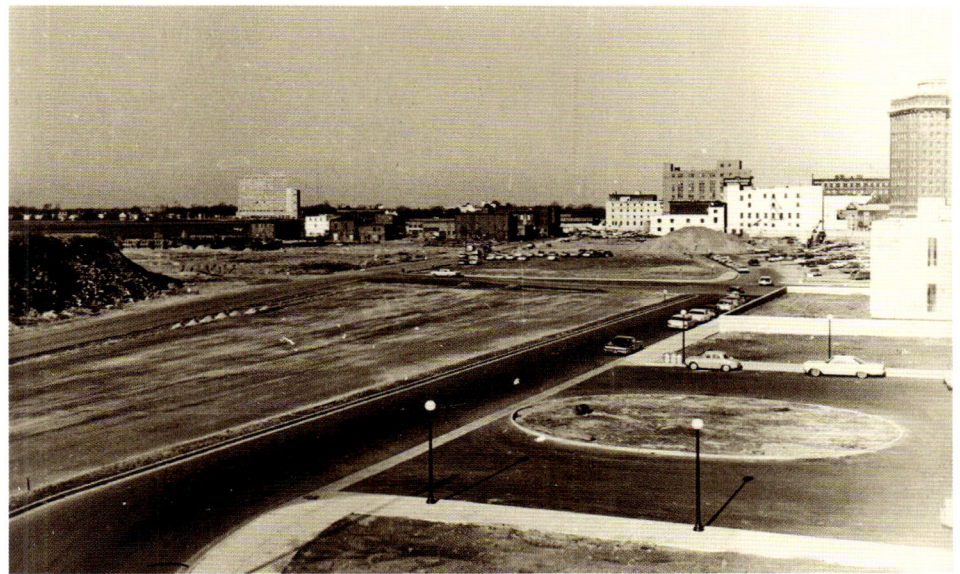

UNION STREET RAZED: This is the last of Union Street in 1962, documented by Carroll H. Walker, who carefully followed the razing of the city post-Second World War. Urban renewal wiped away Norfolk's early history with the push of a bulldozer and, often, the swing of a wrecking ball.

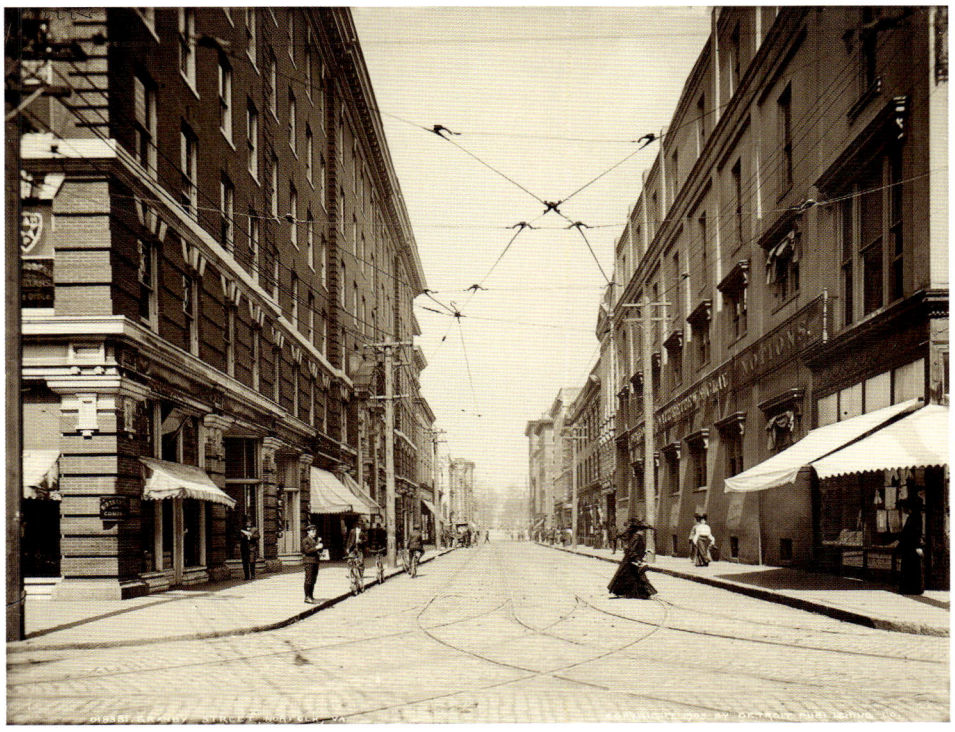

GRANBY AT MAIN: Granby Street looking north from Main Street in 1905 is a dramatic scene. To the left is the third Atlantic Hotel and on the right is Watt, Rettew & Clay, a prominent department store, both establishments on the corner of Main and Granby streets. *Detroit Publishing Company, Library of Congress.*

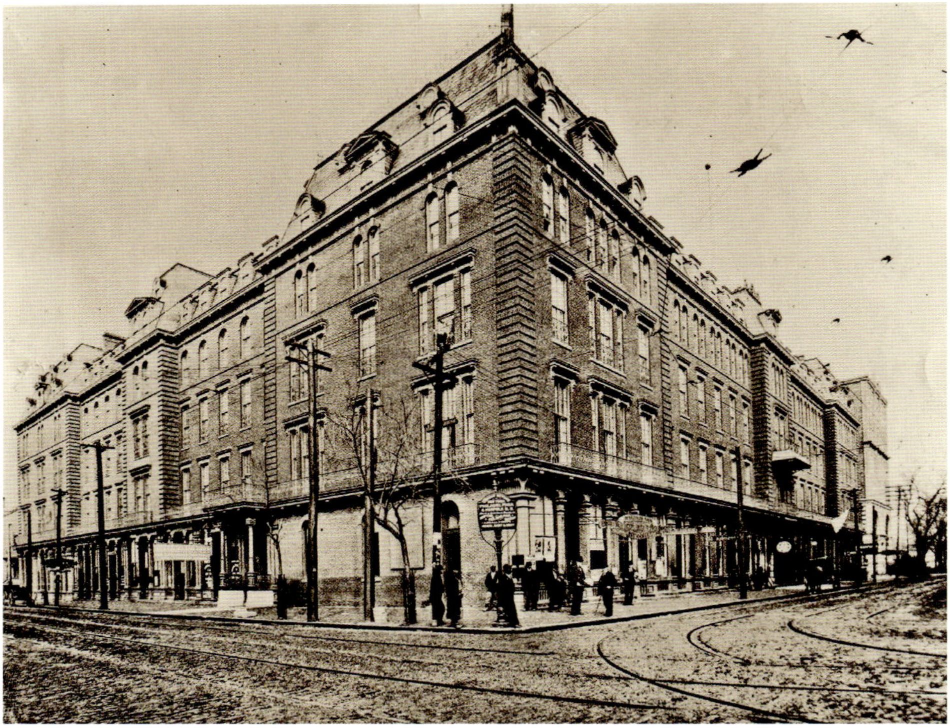

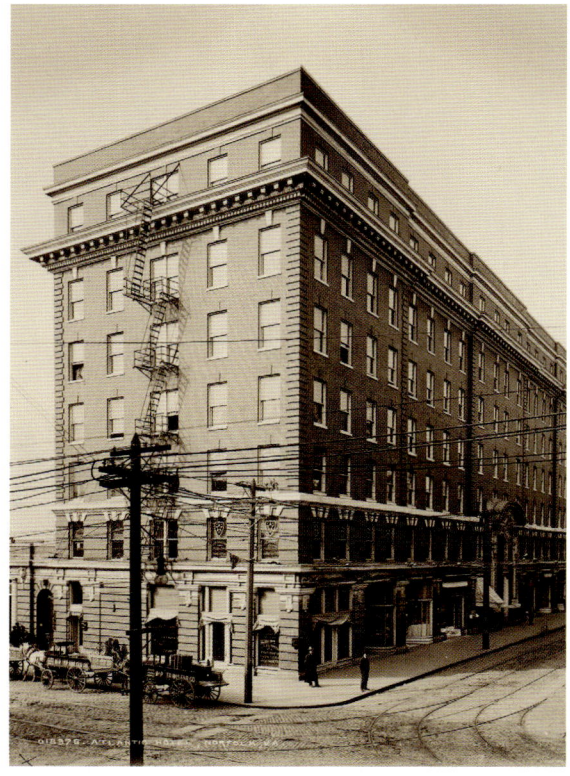

ATLANTIC HOTEL: The second and the third hotels to have that name anchored the northwest corner of Main and Granby streets. The foundation of the second Atlantic Hotel (shown here, top) was laid in August 1867. The second Atlantic Hotel was several blocks over from the first hotel by this name that had been destroyed earlier that year by fire. The first hotel had been situated at Main and Gray (later Atlantic) streets. Like its predecessor, the second Atlantic Hotel burned to the ground on January 31, 1902; it was replaced by a third Atlantic Hotel on the same site. This picture (of the second Atlantic) was taken in 1896. Built in 1903 to replace the second Atlantic Hotel and predecessor on this site (bottom, *Detroit Publishing Company, Library of Congress*), this iteration of the hotel is shown as it looked in 1905 at the corner of Main and Granby streets; it was demolished for redevelopment in 1978.

VIRGINIA CLUB: The seven-story Virginia Club building, shown here on this 1907 postcard (top), opened in March 1904 on the northwest corner of Granby and Plume Streets. The club had owned another building on this site, but it burned in January 1902. New York architect Kenneth M. Murchison Jr., best known for his railroad terminals, commercial buildings, hospitals and hotels, was hired to design a new home for the city's premier gentlemen's club. This is the only such club building of its era still standing in Norfolk. When Carroll H. Walker took this picture (bottom) of the former Virginia Club building on July 6, 1980, it was modified to a point almost unrecognizable as the building designed by Kenneth Murchison.

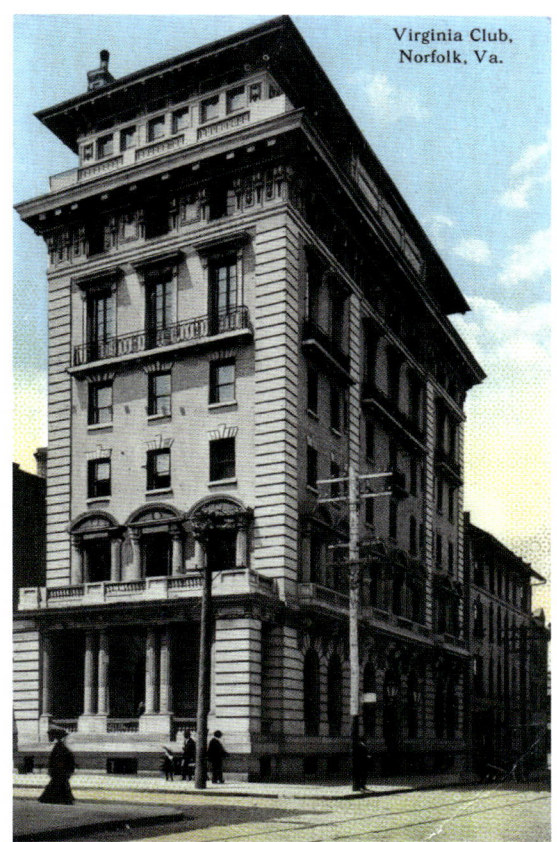

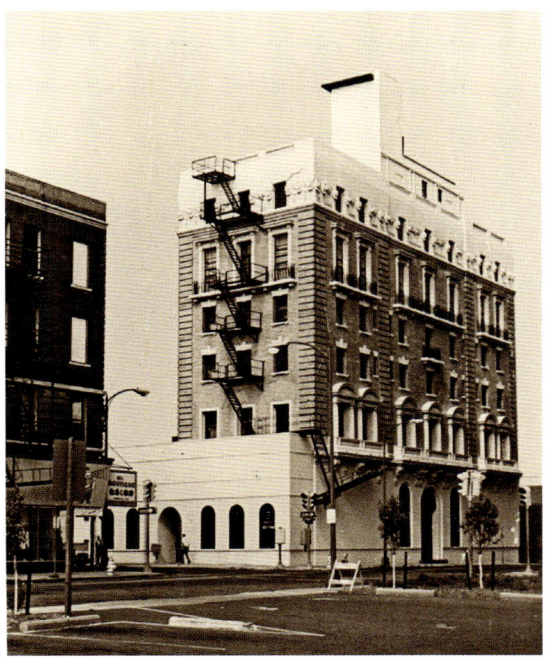

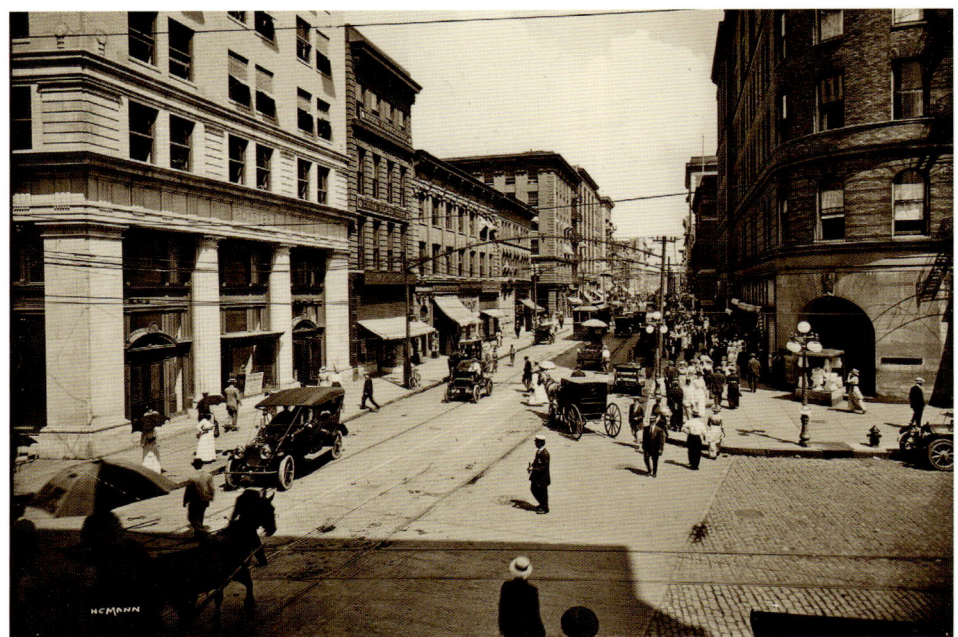

GRANBY AT CITY HALL: Granby Street at City Hall Avenue was photographed by Harry C. Mann (top) a little after 11 o'clock in the morning on a warm summer's day in 1912. Take note of the plethora of parasols, the newly constructed Frank S. Royster Building left foreground, and the grand curves of the Monticello Hotel right. Also notable is the outdoor display case at the corner entrance to the hotel. In the second picture, from a 1910 postcard looking north, Granby Street at City Hall Avenue was evolving quickly (bottom). The Royster Building is left and the Monticello Hotel to the right. The street is crowded with shoppers, buggies, wagons, and streetcars. The popular Max Schwan's is at 205 Granby Street, next-door to the Royster Building. Schwan's, a wholesale and retail establishment, was a purveyor of china, glassware, house furnishings, toys and confections.

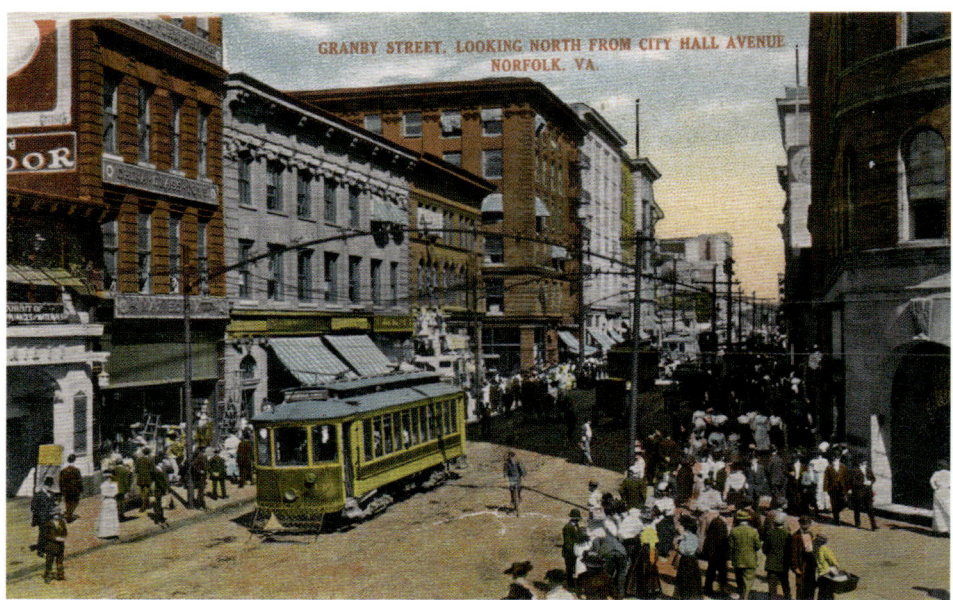

CITY CENTER CHANGES: Fast forward to 1950 (top) and 1965 (bottom) and the scene at the intersection of Granby Street and City Hall Avenue looking north has changed dramatically. In the 1950 photograph, the view is slightly beyond the Royster Building and Monticello Hotel. The Kodachrome photograph was taken by Clark A. Brandenburg. Carroll H. Walker took the 1965 picture; in it is the historic Withers Building, next to Max Schwan's (later Roxy), and it is unrecognizable after a modern facelift.

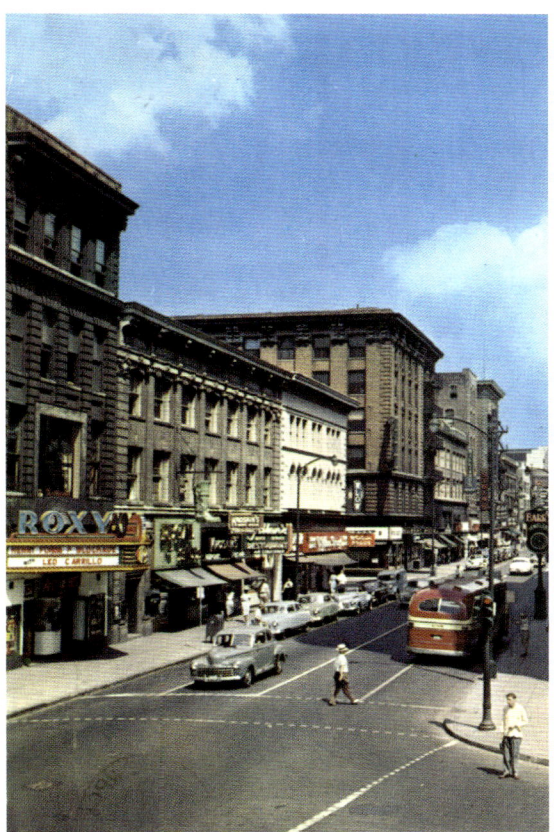

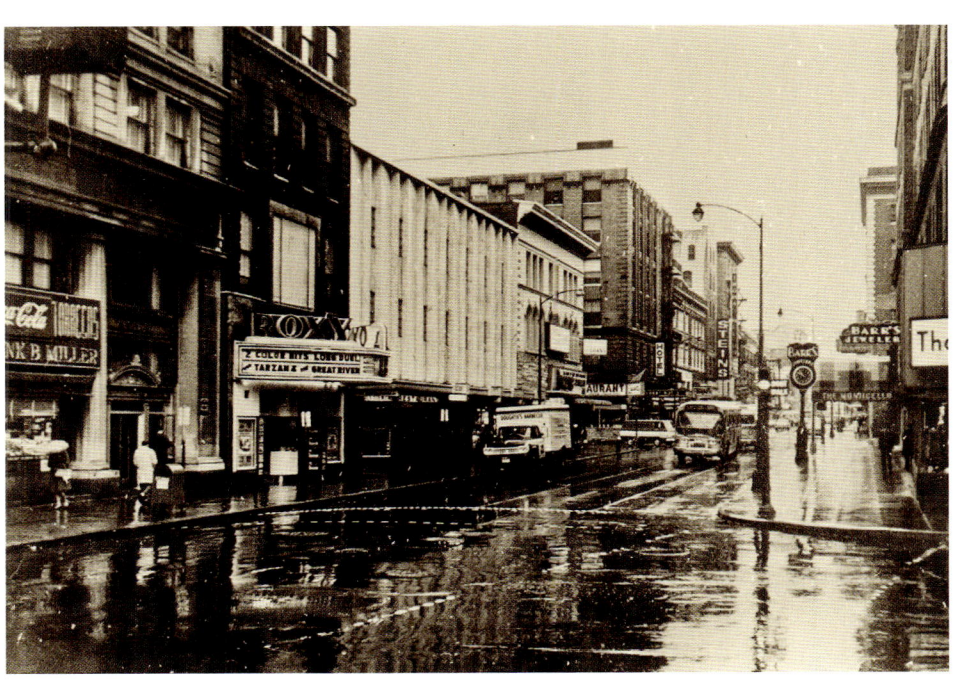

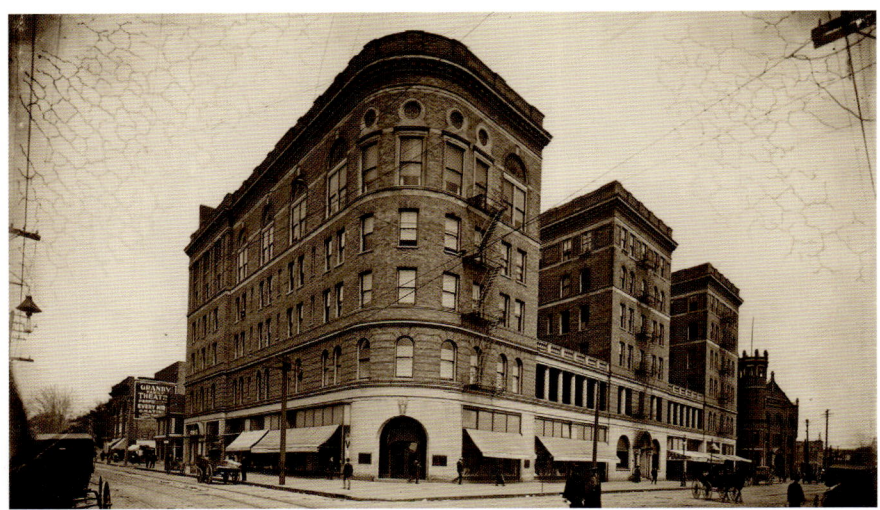

MONTICELLO HOTEL: William Henry Jackson took this picture of the iconic hotel in 1902, just four years after it opened. Originally the site of a creek that extended almost to Church Street in the vicinity of Saint Paul's Boulevard, it had finally been filled in to Granby Street. There were just a few small buildings on the west and east side of Granby Street looking north and the rest were private residences. After the hotel opened, everything changed and the street quickly developed. *Detroit Publishing Company, Library of Congress.*

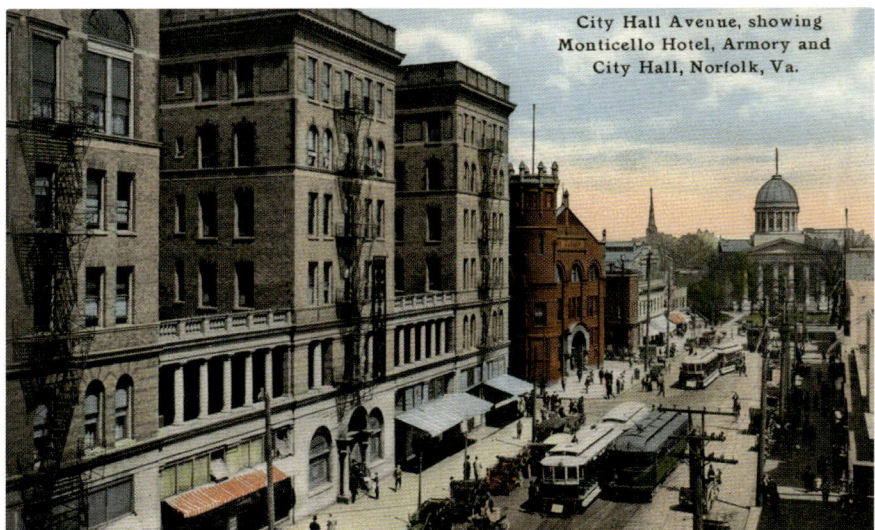

CITY HALL AVENUE: Before 1919 the passenger terminal for Norfolk Southern Railway's electric division was on City Hall Avenue at the Monticello Arcade (out of view right in this image that dates to 1912). The railway had the track rights up Monticello Avenue (the street between the Monticello Hotel and the city market and armory) over the Norfolk and Atlantic Terminal Company at Eleventh Street. The latter line then took passengers to Pine Beach, located at what is today the western edge of the Norfolk Naval Station. Norfolk Southern discontinued use of the City Hall terminal and moved to the Norfolk Terminal Station at the foot of East Main Street. Today, the left side of City Hall Avenue from the site of the armory east is occupied by the MacArthur Center Mall. The spire of the Basilica of Saint Mary of the Immaculate Conception is visible left of the old City Hall.

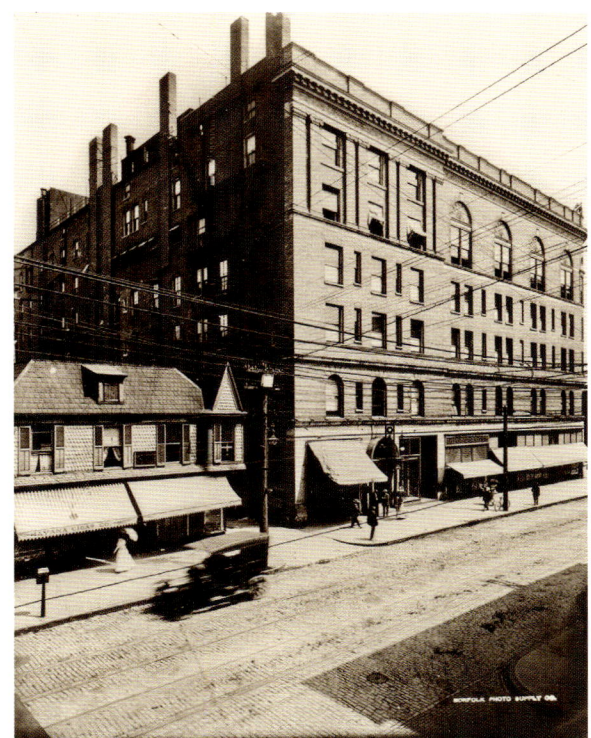

BEFORE AND AFTER: The Monticello Hotel is shown (top) from the Granby Street side in this photograph by Harry C. Mann taken in 1909. Shulman's fine men's clothier store occupied the first floor corner of the hotel. The Havana Cigar Company opened in the building just behind the hotel in 1907. The Monticello Hotel was imploded on January 26, 1976, to accommodate construction of a new federal building, shown here, in a photograph (bottom) taken on April 15, 1982, by Carroll H. Walker.

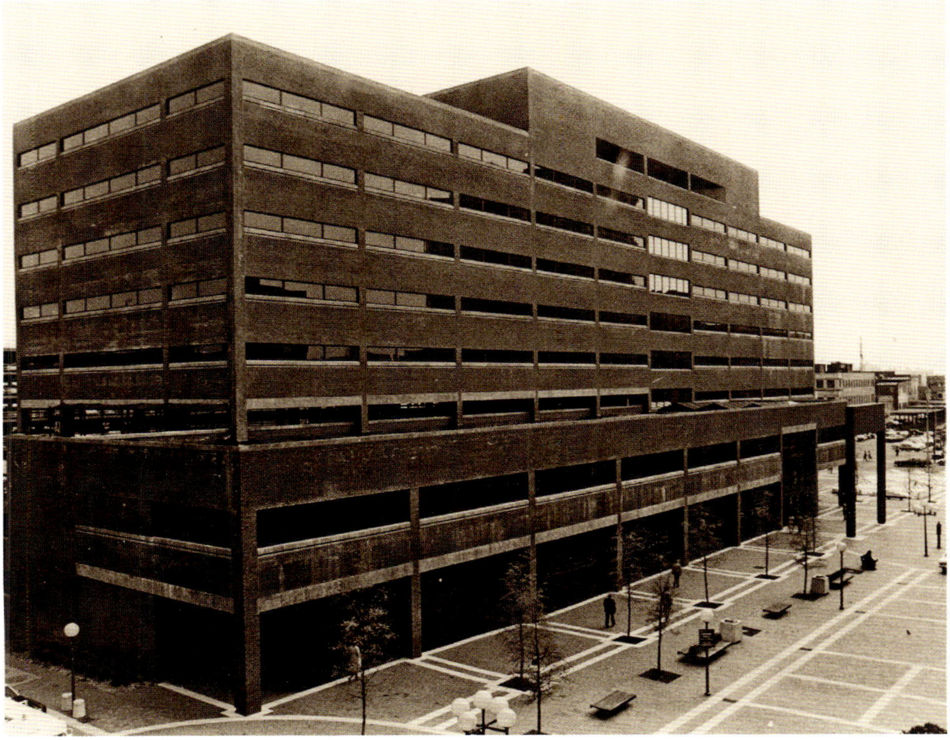

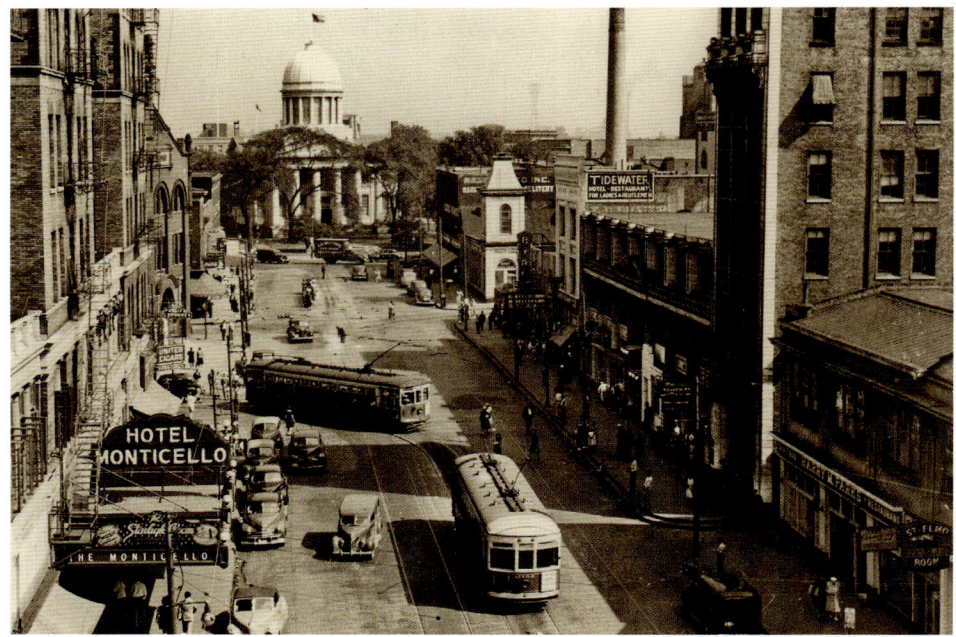

ROOM WITH A VIEW: Carroll H. Walker took these pictures of City Hall Avenue looking east many years apart. In the first (top), Walker took his photograph from the fourth floor of the F. S. Royster Building in September 1939 at the beginning of a nor'easter. By day's end the street, once a creek extending nearly all the way to Church Street, flooded quickly, becoming impassable to automobiles, streetcars and pedestrians. The second picture (bottom), taken in 1987, is looking east to MacArthur Memorial (formerly Norfolk's city hall). In addition the former city hall, the structures that remain from Walker's 1939 photograph are the Beaux Arts-style Monticello Arcade, one of Norfolk's finest and most unusual buildings completed in 1907 and often called "a perfect work of art," and the six-story McKevitt Building (now the Anders-Williams Building), named for saloon owner Michael McKevitt and built in 1916 to replace a smaller McKevitt saloon. McKevitt's Saloon operated on the first floor of the new building with offices on the remaining five. Legend has it that McKevitt placed a silver dollar on top of every pile driven to support the building for good luck.

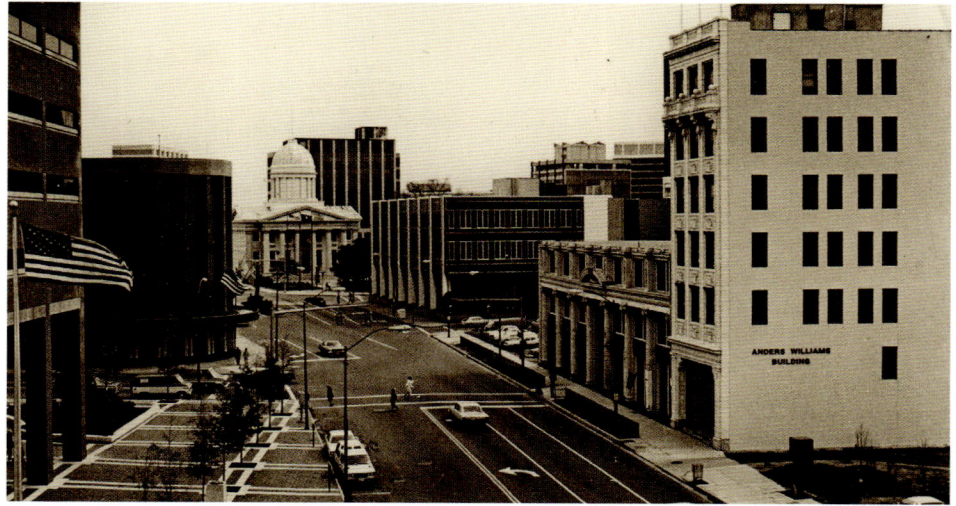

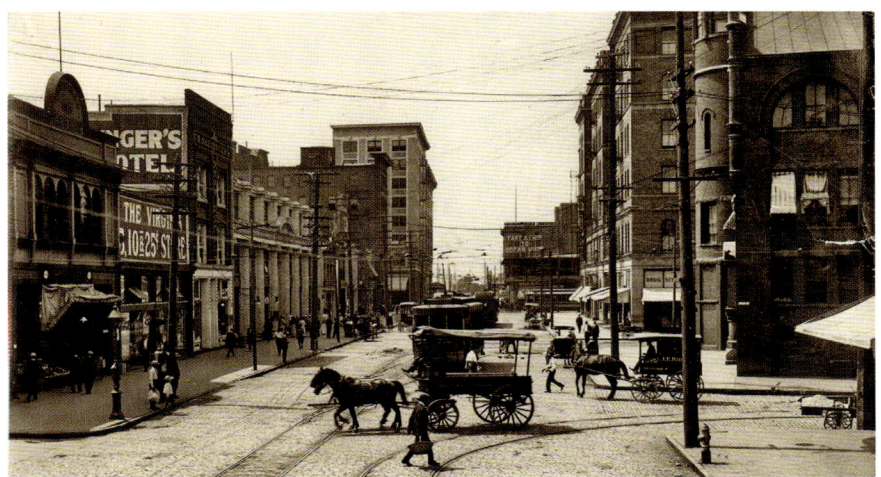

A RARE VIEW: Taken from the intersection of Atlantic Street and City Hall Avenue looking west during the peak of summer 1910, this Harry C. Mann photograph is bustling with activity and important buildings. Starting with the right foreground is the foot of old Brewer Street. Norfolk's City Market and Armory Building is on the corner, and beyond it is the Monticello Hotel, built by David B. Lowenberg and operated by him until Colonel Charles H. Consolvo acquired it in 1905. Granby Street runs between the hotel and Norfolk Builders' Exchange; the sign atop the exchange reads "Take a Trip to Ocean View." Along the left side of City Hall Avenue, foreground, is the Terminal Arcade, built in 1901. Next to the arcade is the Virginia 5, 10 & 25¢ Store; Henry Seelinger's Star Hotel, opened at 39–41 City Hall Avenue in 1906, and the Monticello Arcade, finished in 1907. Next to the Monticello Arcade is Michael McKevitt's Saloon, a fine sample room and cigar store opened in 1903 at 23 City Hall Avenue, directly across the street from the Monticello Hotel. The electric streetcars shown here belonged to Norfolk Southern Railway, and ran to Virginia Beach and Cape Henry as well as Ocean View.

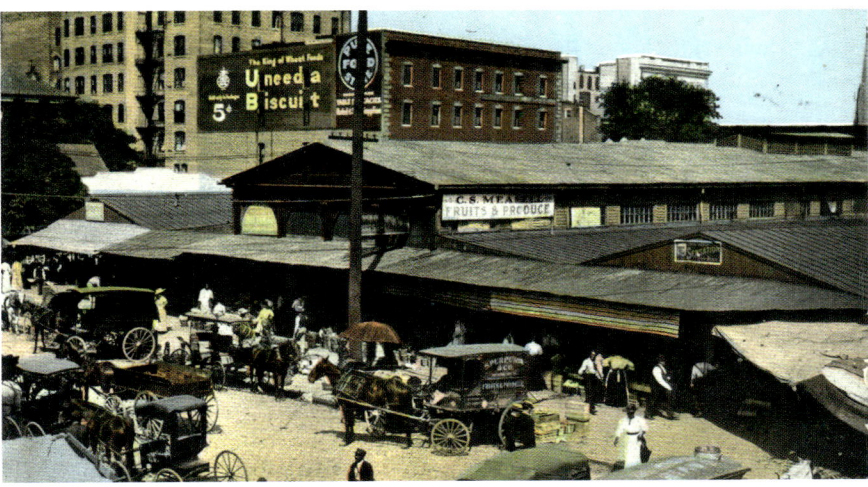

C. S. MEASELL'S FRUITS & PRODUCE: Measell's operated out of an open air storefront at the City Market on Tazewell Street between Monticello Avenue and Brewer Street from 1899 to 1911; Clarence Samuel Measell, its owner, died August 2, 1915, at age 52. The Pure Food Store, the brick building center on the corner of Washington Street (later Market Street) and Monticello Avenue, was in business from 1907 to 1910. Harry C. Mann took this picture in 1907.

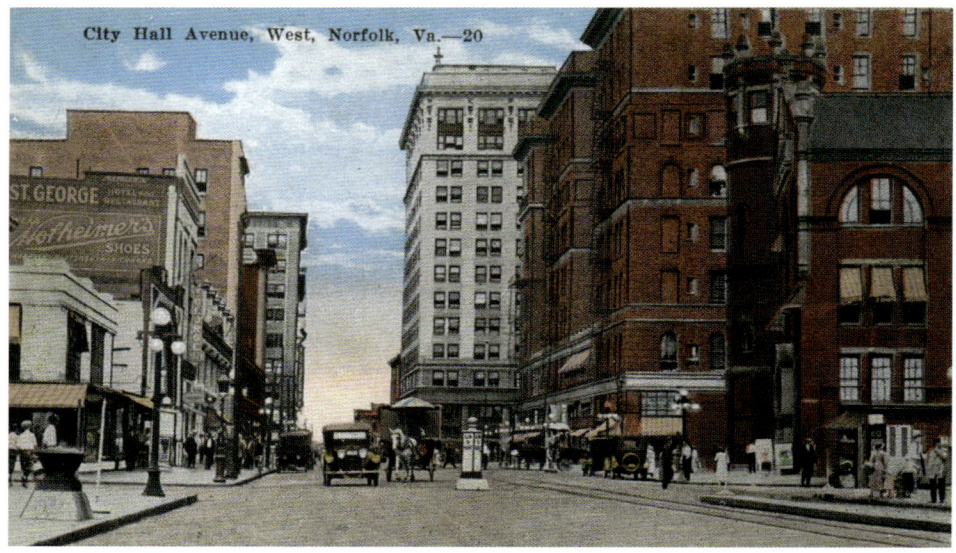

TRANSITION: Downtown Norfolk experienced a new era of construction and expansion in the 1920s. At the time the picture (top) was taken in 1920, City Hall Avenue looking east from Atlantic Street was transitioning to automobiles; note the traffic signal in the center of the intersection. Norfolk had gone to all-bus public transportation when the picture (bottom) was taken of City Hall Avenue looking east in 1952. The 1950s marked another period of great transition in downtown Norfolk as post–Second World War redevelopment took hold. Additionally, the transition from streetcar to bus had begun in September 1947, and by late November that year, there remained only 31 rail route miles in the city. By the time this picture was taken, all would be gone.

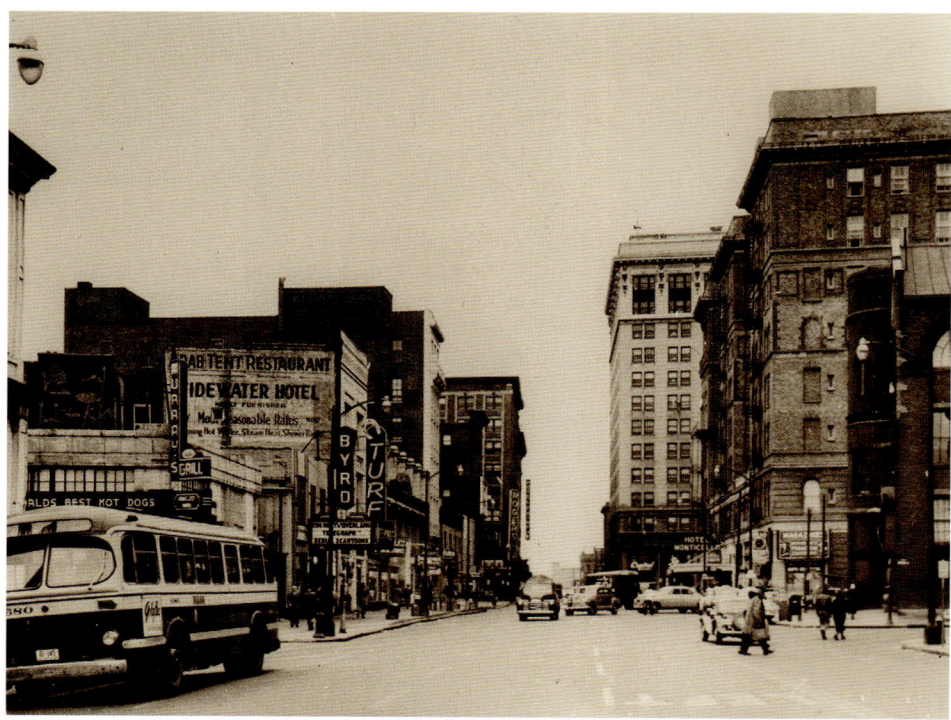

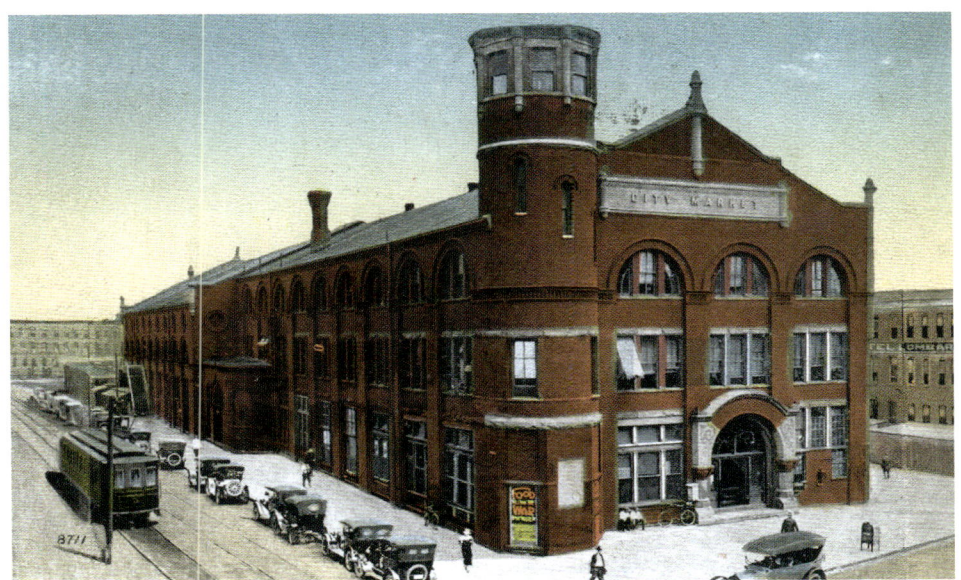

CITY MARKET AND ARMORY BUILDING: The market and armory, which included the Red Circle Theatre when this picture (top) was taken in 1920, was one of the most significant buildings in the history of the city. The cornerstone for this iconic building was laid on October 28, 1890. By 1940, the old market and armory had fallen on hard times; Norfolk residents patronized the "new" city market completed in 1923 on the site of what had been a partially open-air market that had been moved from Market Square in 1894 to a location north of the armory on Monticello Avenue. But the new city market would fair no better than the building it replaced (shown here); it was torn down in 1955, as was everything on the block, to make room for the construction of the Rennert Building (the Maritime Tower). The Rennert Building (the Maritime Tower) photograph (bottom) was taken shortly after the Rennert's completion in 1960. Today, this site is occupied by the west side of the 1.1 million square foot MacArthur Center Mall that opened in the center of downtown Norfolk on March 12, 1999.

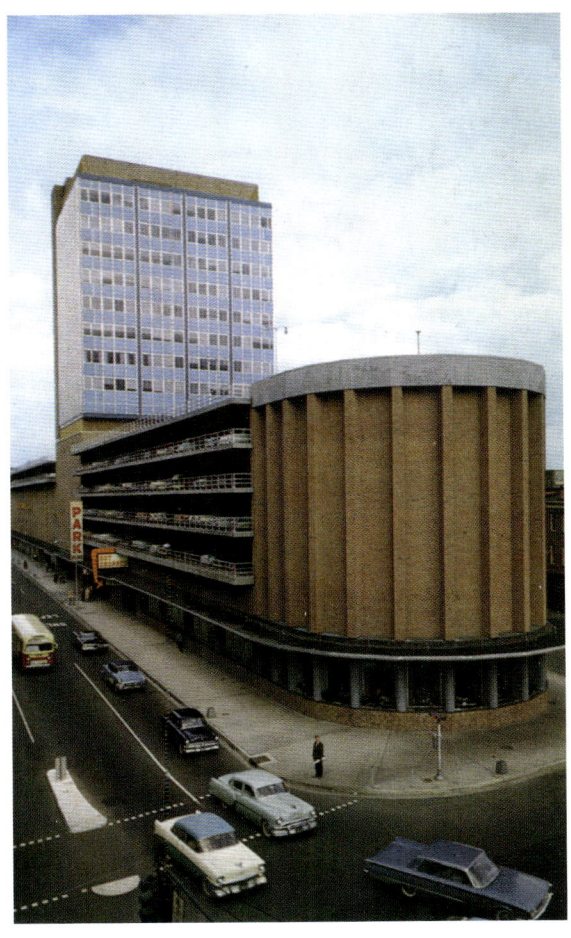

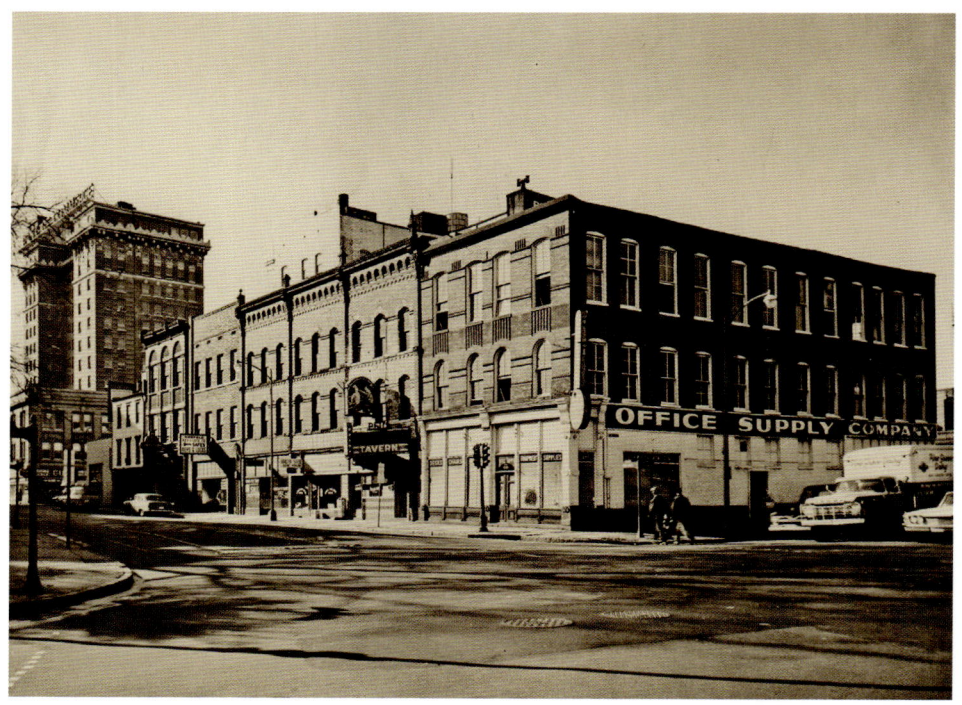

KIRN MEMORIAL LIBRARY: The library site's before and after views are remarkably telling. The first photograph shows mid-nineteenth century buildings in Norfolk's downtown redevelopment area on the site of what was planned as the city's new municipal library (shown here as it looked in 1965). The building nearest foreground was once the A. C. Cox Grocery Company, and was situated on the corner of Bank Street and East City Hall Avenue in 1930. A. C. Cox ceased operations in 1955. Kirn Memorial Library, which closed for good on December 31, 2008, on this site, was demolished over a period of several months in 2009 to make way for a light-rail station; it had served as the city's main library for 47 years.

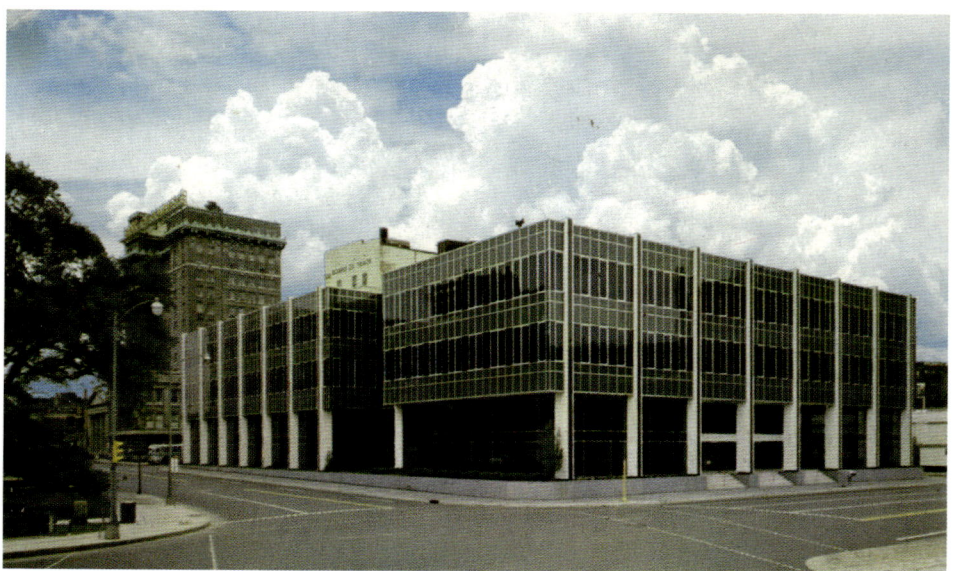

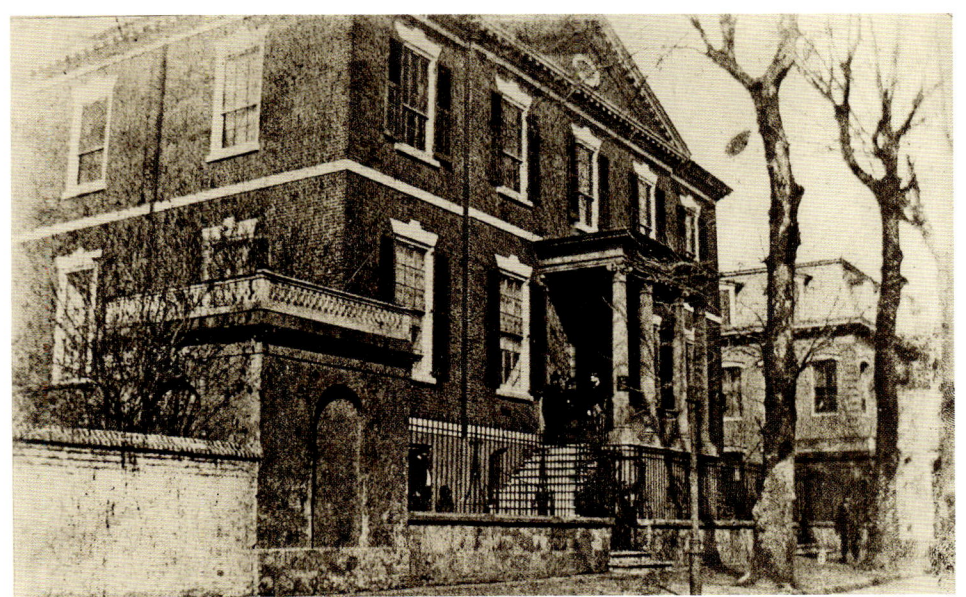

NEWTON RESIDENCE: The home of George Newton, which stood on the southwest corner of College Place and Granby Street, was built on what had been part of the original estate of Samuel Boush. The land was conveyed in 1801 by Conway Whittle to Thomas Willing, who subsequently sold the lot for one dollar to the Bank of the United States at Norfolk, who Willing represented, on March 25, 1802. Construction was begun almost immediately, and on September 7, 1803, the bank opened for business in the building. This was Norfolk's first and only bank at that time. Two brick guardhouses for bank sentries were also built on either side of the front entrance (these are visible in the photograph, top). The bank closed in 1811. George Newton, from a leading Norfolk family and a former mayor of the borough, did not purchase the property until 1826. The property remained in the Newton family until 1893, when it was sold to Charles Wesley Fentress for commercial purposes. The picture was taken in 1883. The second photograph (bottom) was taken by Harry Mann and run in the July 10, 1910 *Virginian-Pilot* that announced the house would soon be razed.

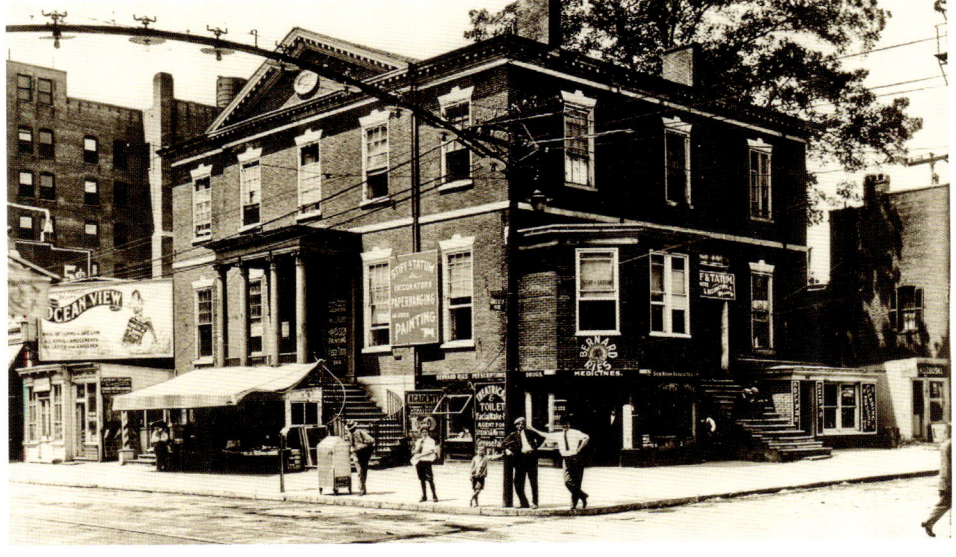

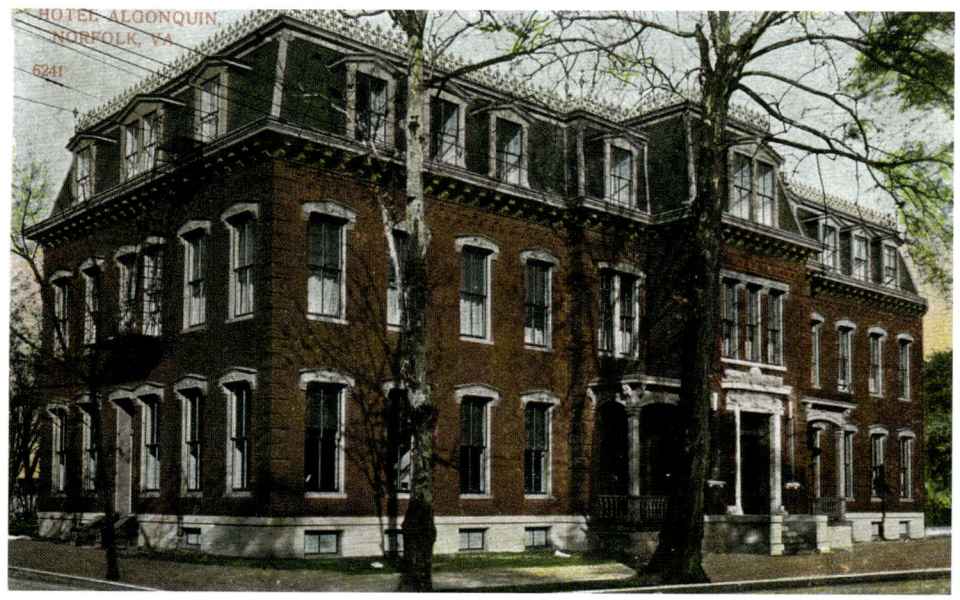

NORFOLK COLLEGE FOR YOUNG LADIES: Though labeled as the Algonquin Hotel (shown here on a 1905 postcard, top), this beautiful building at the corner of Granby Street and College Place started out as the Norfolk College for Young Ladies, chartered February 20, 1880, and which opened that year with 125 students. John L. Roper was president of the college's board. The school closed in 1899 and the Algonquin Hotel opened in its place. Looking north on Granby Street in 1916 (bottom), Smith & Welton department store is on the right (foreground) and the former Norfolk College for Young Ladies (later Algonquin Hotel) has been converted on the lower level to storefronts.

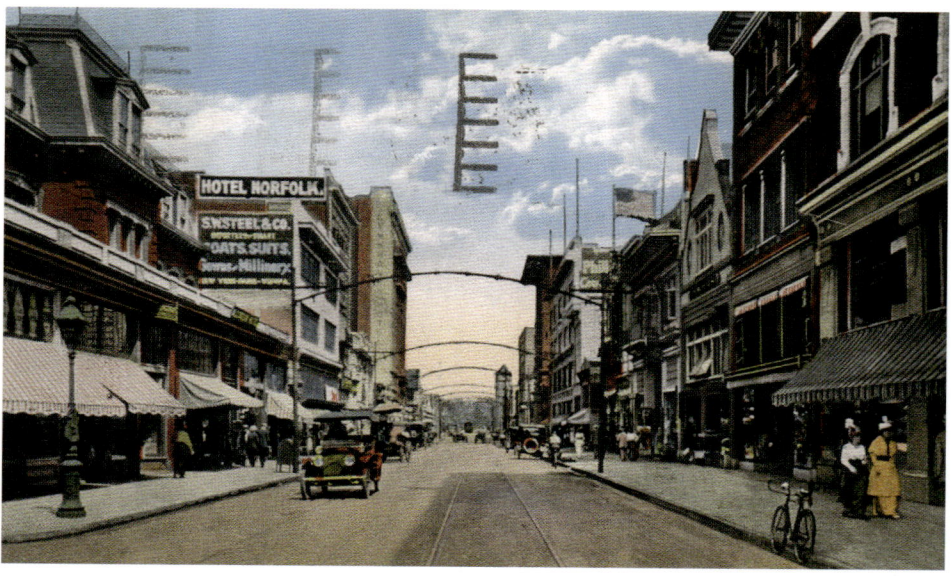

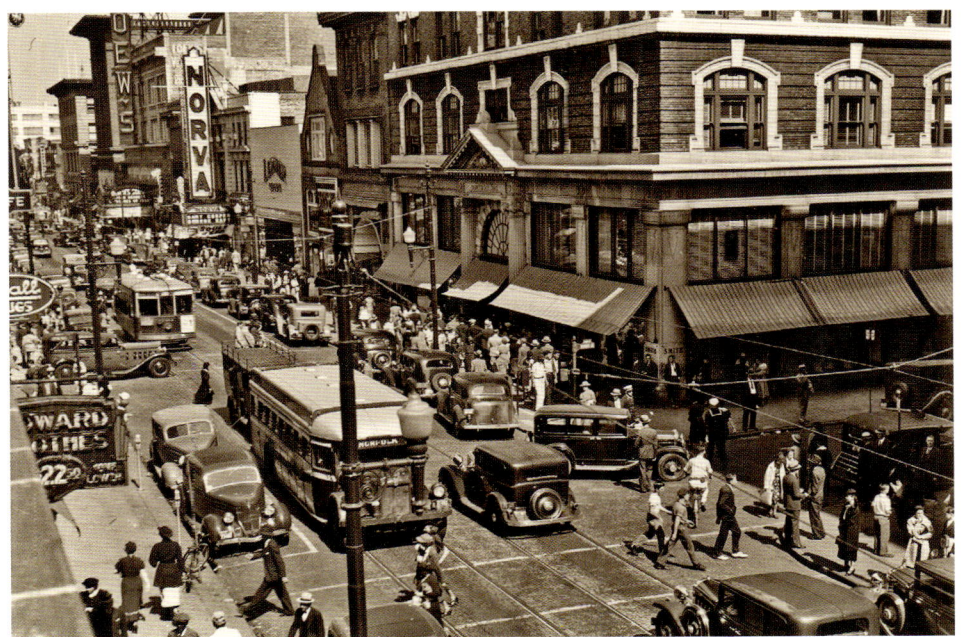

BOOM AND BUST: The evolution of Granby Street from retail mecca to retail decline is evident in these photographs, taken more than twenty years apart. In the first (top), Charles S. Borjes took his picture of Granby Street at Market Street on September 2, 1937. Smith & Welton department store (right foreground, in the Martin Building) is bustling with activity. Down the street are the Norva and Loew's State theaters (top, *Sargeant Memorial Room, Norfolk Public Library*). The second photograph (bottom) is Granby Street looking north from Market Street, and is dated by the Norva's marquee: Audrey Hepburn was starring in *The Nun's Story* (1959). The street changed dramatically over two decades; there far fewer people patronizing the many stores and restaurants that still dotted the street. Note that Granby Street at this time was a one-way street southbound. The streetcar has been replaced by the bus.

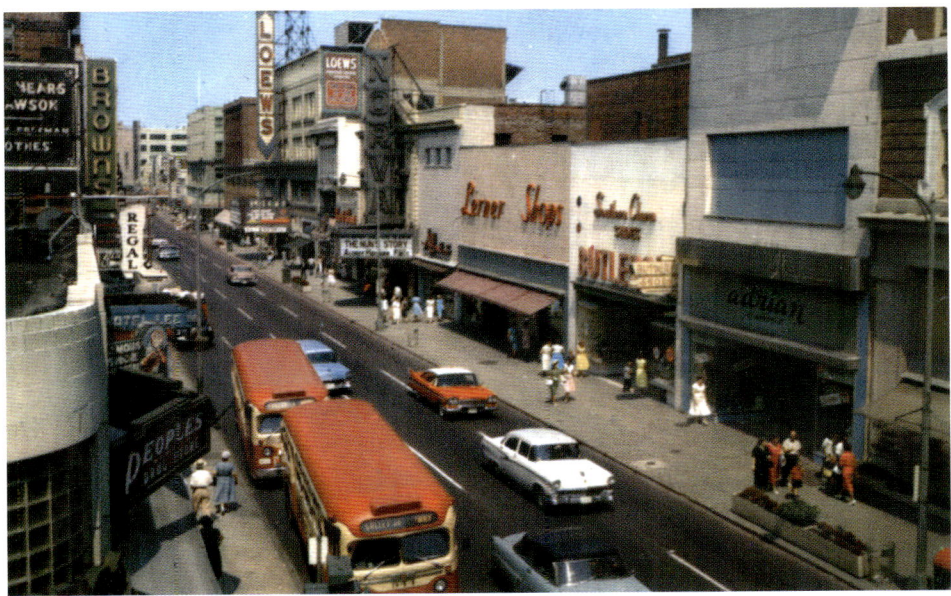

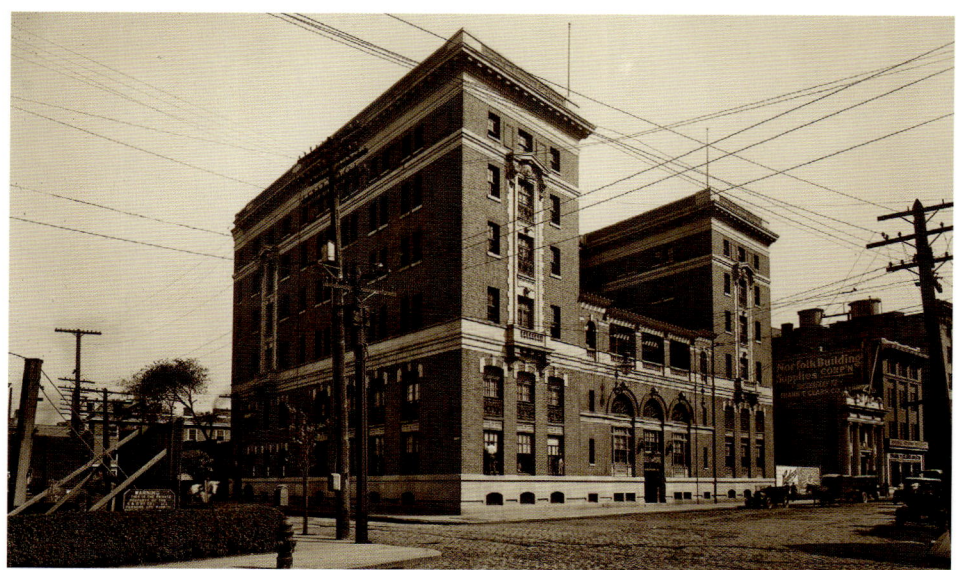

NAVY YMCA: The Navy YMCA at Brooke Avenue and Boush Street remains one of downtown Norfolk's most important early twentieth century buildings. On June 18, 1906, it was announced that American industrialist John D. Rockefeller had given $250,000 to build a Navy YMCA in Norfolk (shown here, top, in 1910 at 130 Brooke Avenue at the corner of Boush Street, *Detroit Publishing Company, Library of Congress*). Formally dedicated on March 17, 1909, with William Sloane, of New York and Norfolk presiding, it was intended to be among the finest YMCAs in the country with the most modern equipment available. The Navy YMCA movement began at the end of the Spanish-American War. The first Navy YMCA in the country opened in 1902 at the Brooklyn Navy Yard. In the same year, a Navy YMCA was also established on Norfolk's Church Street. The Navy YMCA building, shown on this 1956 Kodachrome postcard (bottom), was used by the United States Navy until 1972, and subsequently sold to the Union Mission for use as a homeless shelter. The Union Mission sold the building in 2013 to Marathon Development, which announced plans to transform it into luxury apartments and build a five-story building on an adjacent parking lot.

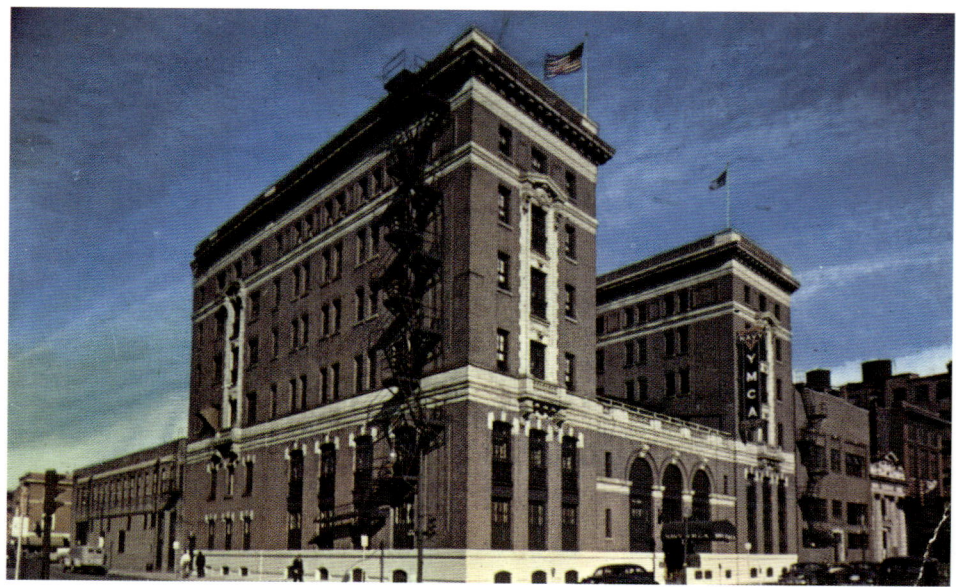

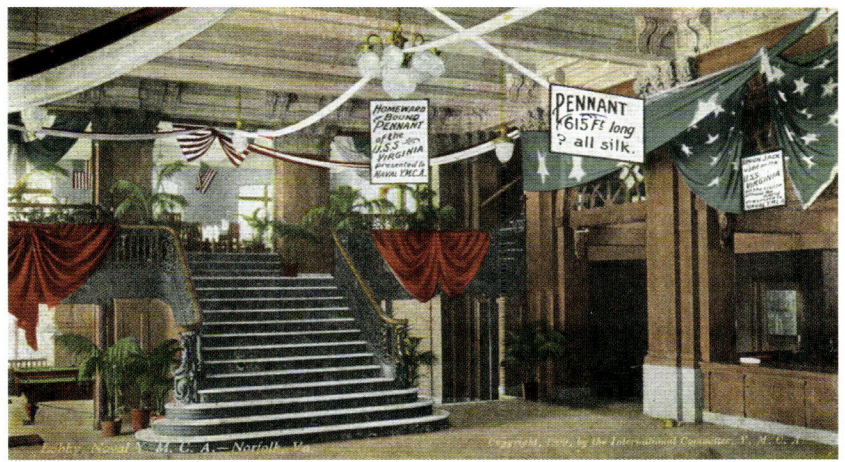

GREAT WHITE FLEET DONATION: Dedication of the Navy YMCA on Brooke Avenue occurred less than a month after the return of the battleship USS *Virginia* (BB-13) from its round-the-world voyage as part of the Great White Fleet, which departed Hampton Roads December 17, 1907 and returned February 22, 1909. The *Virginia*'s crew presented the Navy YMCA with the 615-foot silk homeward bound pennant, which ship's officers had made-to-order in China for $605, in honor of its opening. *Virginia*'s officers and enlisted sailors also presented the Navy YMCA with $1,000 cash raised on the trip home, as well as another $450 from the battleship USS *Kentucky* (BB-6), to furnish the building.

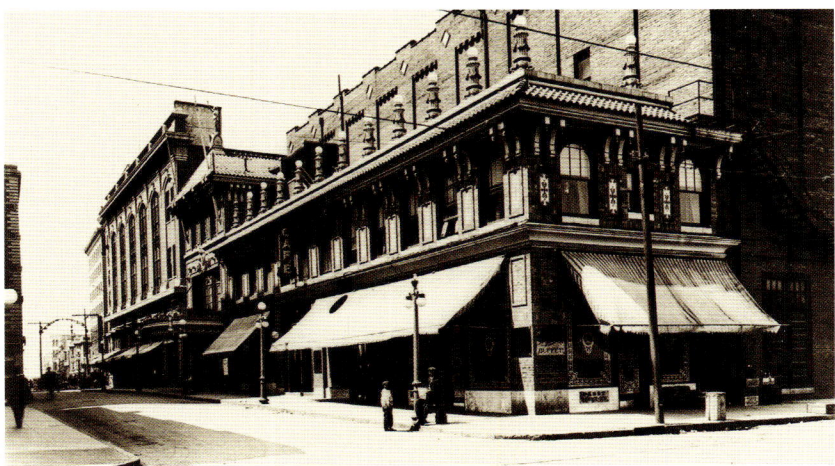

WELLS THEATRE: The theatre on Tazewell Street was photographed by Harry Mann in 1917 looking west from Monticello Avenue. The Wells was the creation of Jake Wells, who chose Norfolk as the first city (beyond the theatre he owned in Richmond, Virginia) to open a new theatre. Otto Wells, Jake's younger half-brother, arrived from Pensacola, Florida, to open the Granby Theatre in 1901. Ten years later the brothers operated the largest theatre circuit outside New York, and by the early 1920s Jake Wells was known as "The Father of Vaudeville in the Southeast." The brothers eventually operated 42 theatres in nine states. In Norfolk, Wells operated The Granby, Academy, Colonial, Norva, Strand, Wells and the American Theatre. Otto managed the brothers' entire theatrical enterprise from Norfolk with multiple ticker-tape machines that allowed him to calculate each theatre's box office earnings. Jake's namesake Wells Theatre opened on August 27, 1913, with the musical comedy *The Merry Countess*.

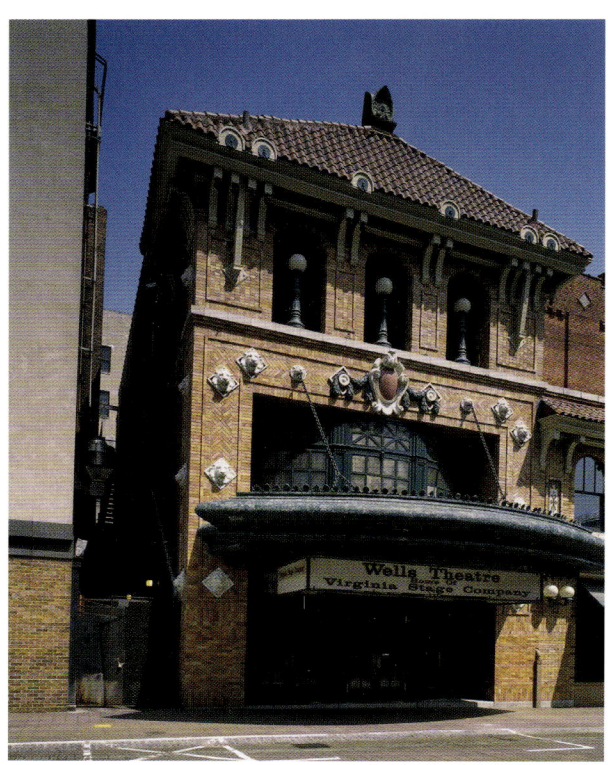

BEAUX ARTS MASTERPIECE: The Wells' ornate decoration made the theatre the flagship of Wells Amusement Enterprises, and continues today as a well preserved example of Beaux-Arts Classicism and a National Historic Landmark. According to the theatre's history, the first year it was open, Maude Adams flew across the stage as Peter Pan and Wells presented Ben-Hur complete with teams of horses on treadmills. Fred and Adele Astaire, Will Rogers, Billie Burke, John Drew, John Philip Sousa and Dorothy Gish all appeared on the Wells stage. Carol Highsmith took this contemporary photograph of the Wells Theatre. *Carol M. Highsmith Archive, Library of Congress.*

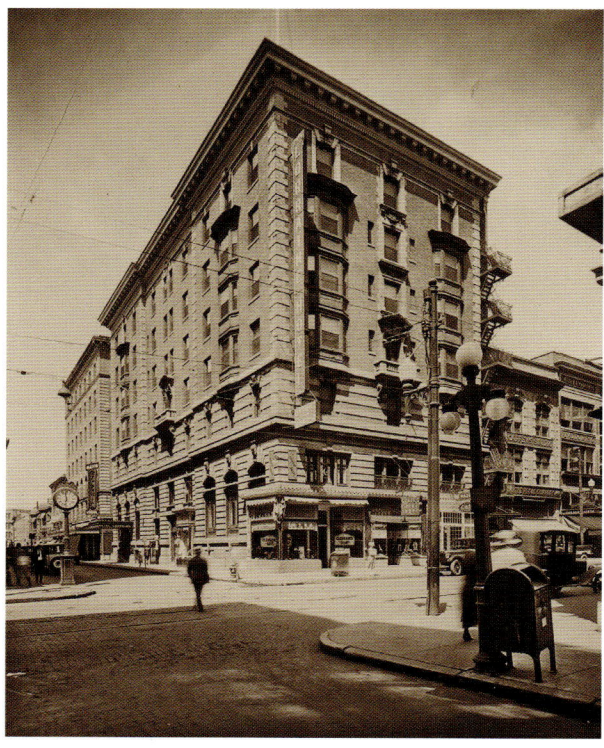

LORRAINE HOTEL: The hotel, located at the corner of Granby and Tazewell Streets, is pictured as it looked about 1920. The building was completed to accommodate guests for the upcoming Jamestown Exposition in 1907. Ferguson and Calrow were the architects of this once beautifully appointed seven-story hotel. While not large, the Lorraine was believed to be among the most elegant and prominent hotels of its day, boasting a fine café for ladies and gentlemen, and a stag grill room known as The Lorraine Hotel Rathskeller. The charm and gentility of the old Lorraine Hotel have long since faded from Granby Street.

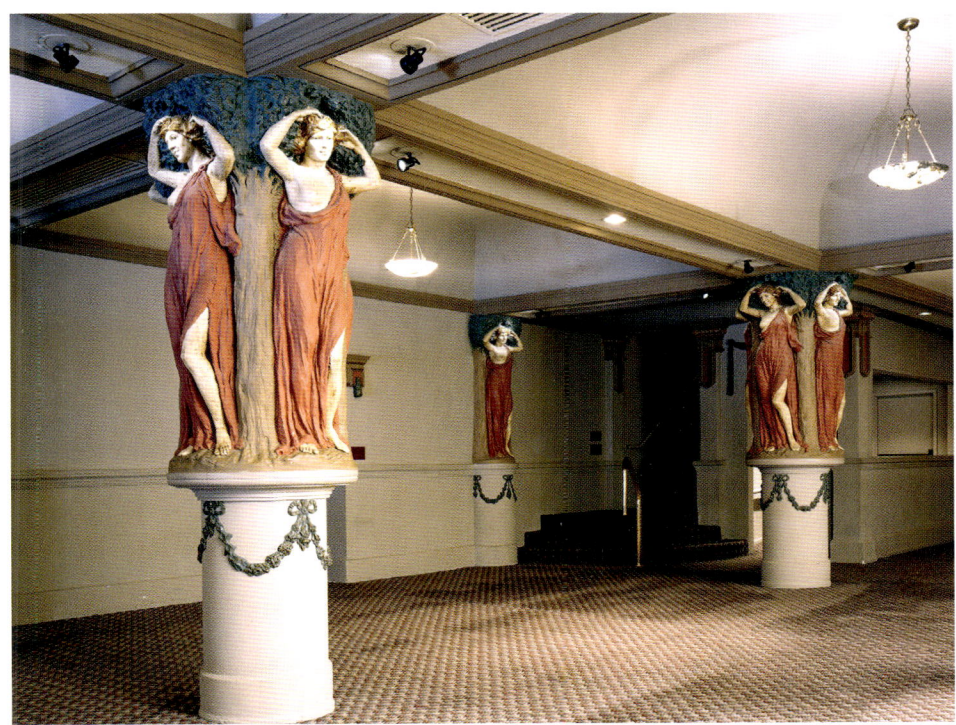

HIGH ART: Exotic figures (top) adorn the lobby of the Wells Theatre. Carol M. Highsmith, a distinguished and richly-published American photographer, has donated her work to the Library of Congress since 1992 and is often called "America's photographer." She took the contemporary photographs of the Wells Theatre included here. The theatre (bottom) originally had 1,650 seats with 12 boxes and three balconies. The top balcony served as a segregated balcony "For Negro Audiences Only," and had its own entrance and box office. A system of stairs made inside access easy, allowing waiters from Wong Ping's Chinese Restaurant to serve theatre patrons on the second floor roof garden before and after performances. The downstairs Trustees Lobby facing Tazewell Street housed Doumar's first location in Norfolk. The Virginia Stage Company has occupied the theatre since 1979. The Wells was restored in 1986 to its former grandeur. *Carol M. Highsmith Archive, Library of Congress.*

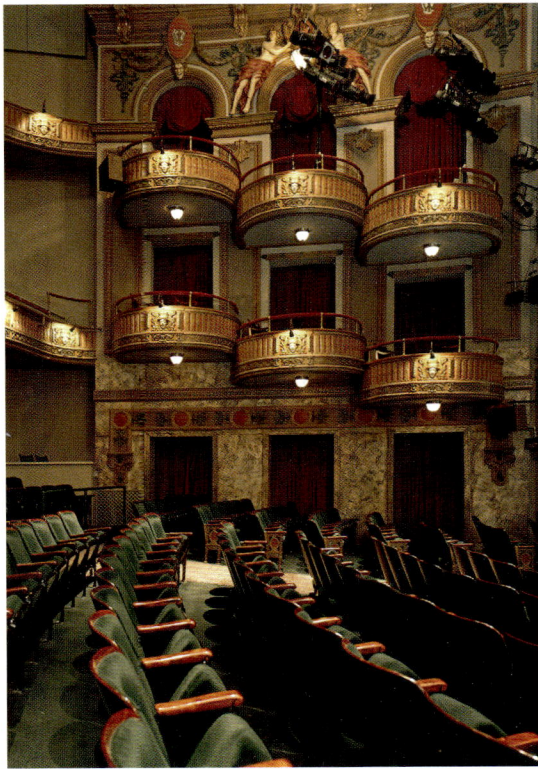

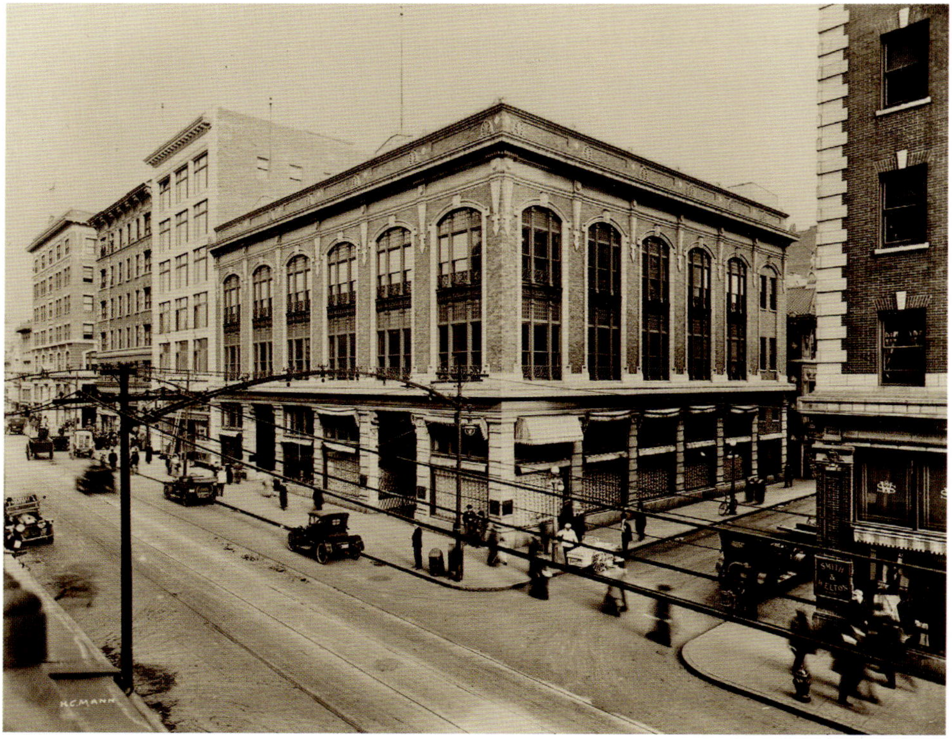

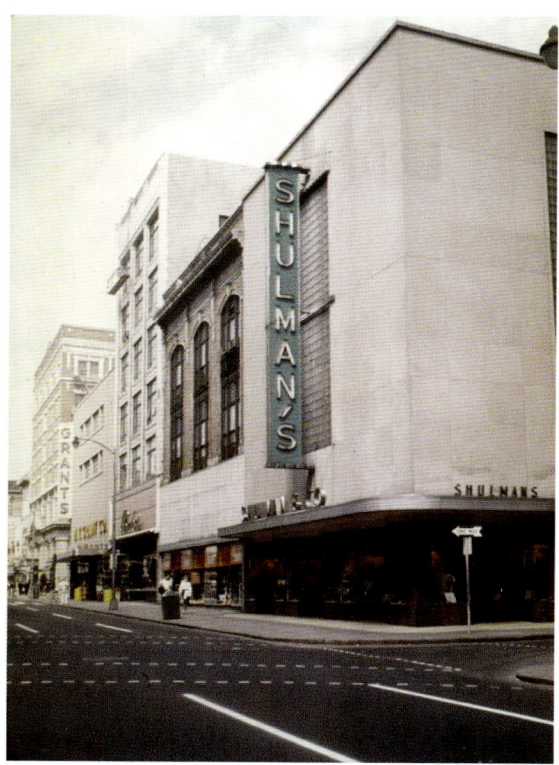

SPRATLEY BUILDING: Harry Mann took this picture (top) of Granby Street between Tazewell (foreground) and Wolfe (later Market) streets in 1914, just after Schreier & Son, a millinery, ladies, misses and children's ready to wear clothing store that opened in 1912, went bankrupt; the retail space on the first floor of the Spratley Building are covered and there is a "For Rent" sign in the window facing Tazewell Street. Smith & Welton department store (right foreground) is on the southeast corner of Granby and Tazewell streets. James Murdaugh took this picture (bottom, *Sargeant Memorial Room, Norfolk Public Library*) of Granby and Tazewell streets in April 1961. The Spratley Building was given a new façade, including extensive use of glass block that was popular among retailers post Second World War. Shulman's men's store occupied the retail space on the corner of Granby and Tazewell streets for many years.

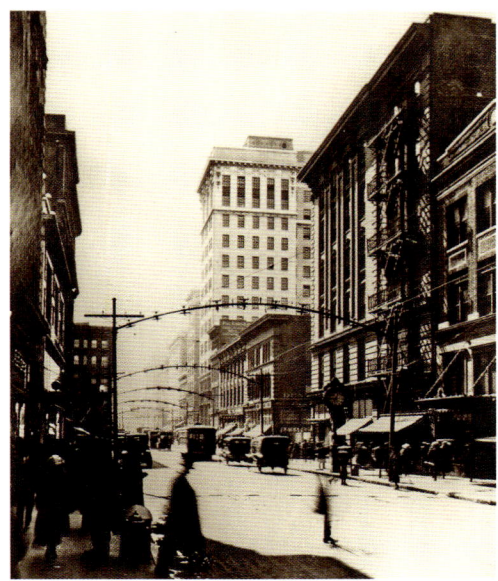

GOOD TIMES: An unknown photographer took this picture of Granby Street looking south toward the F. S. Royster Building in the winter of 1923. The building right foreground with the fire escape is the Tazewell Building, situated at the corner of Granby Street and Brooke Avenue; this office and retail building first appeared in the 1901 city directory. The Tazewell Building was an important part of early twentieth century of commercial and retail enterprise that moved down Granby Street into what had up to that time been a residential section.

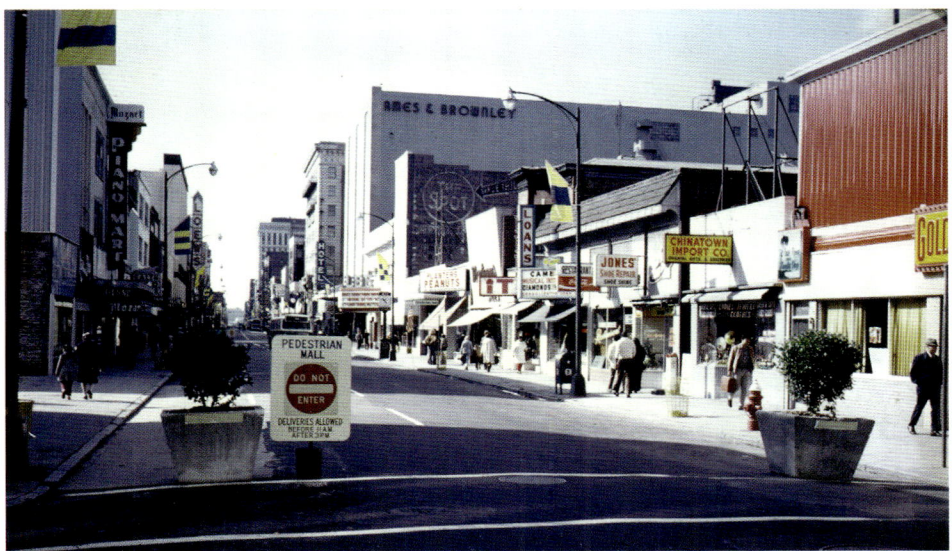

DOWNTOWN DECLINE: What a difference 50 years makes. Like many traditional commercial corridors that had thrived in the salad days of the city, Norfolk's downtown went into decline in the mid-twentieth century, partially due to new enclosed shopping centers on the city's suburban edge and partially due to misguided urban renewal policies. Granby Street businesses were failing in the early 1970s (shown here looking south in 1976, the year a pedestrian mall closed off six blocks of Granby's retail corridor). The opening of Pembroke Mall in Virginia Beach, the region's first climate controlled shopping mall, and JANAF Shopping Center in Norfolk's Military Circle area, helped foment Granby Street's spiral into commercial obsolescence. With amenities such as ample free parking at the door of a favorite store, and in the case of Pembroke Mall, climate control, the businesses of downtown's Granby Street found it harder and harder to compete. To compete with the suburban shopping destinations, Norfolk city leaders tried to create the same mall experience on Granby Street that customers might experience at JANAF Shopping Center. The city rebranded its commercial core the "Granby Mall."

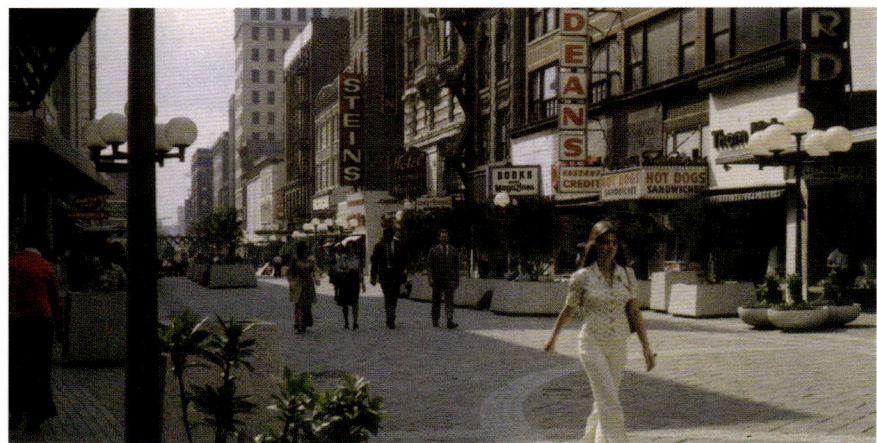

PEDESTRIAN MALL: Granby Street was closed to automobile through-traffic, repaved, landscaped and new street furniture and fixtures were installed (shown here looking south, same perspective as the 1923 photograph, in 1978). Granby Mall was developed with the best of intentions, but it actually ended up speeding the demise of Granby Street as a viable commercial destination. The closing of Granby Street to automobile traffic actually made the district more inconvenient for potential customers and reduced the amount of pedestrian traffic that passed by the businesses. The reduced pedestrian and automobile traffic on the street created an atmosphere of abandonment and also contributed to an increase in downtown crime, which further fueled customer fears of downtown that in turn caused additional businesses to close. The pedestrian mall was eliminated in 1988 and the street reopened to two-way vehicular traffic.

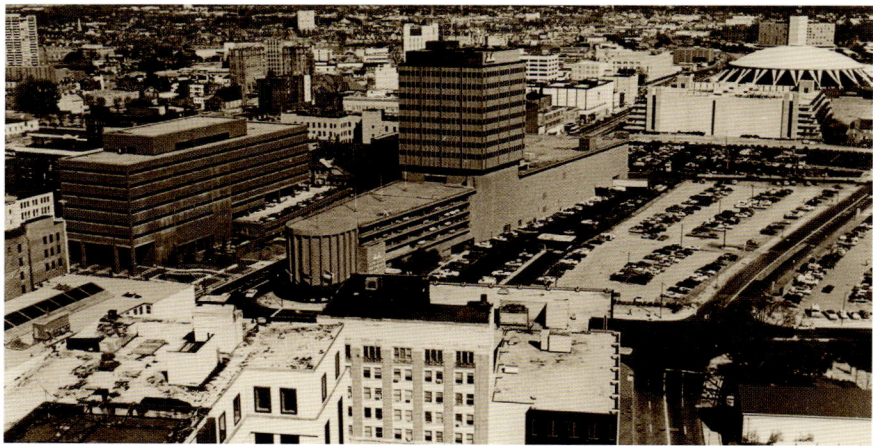

THE CITY CENTER: Carroll H. Walker took this photograph looking north over Norfolk's city center in 1980. The Monticello Hotel and Dickson Building (located directly behind the hotel on Granby Street) were razed to make way for the federal building (far left). The Rennert Building, then home to Dominion National Bank, and Maritime Tower (center) replaced the old city market and armory and the new market that was completed in 1923. In the repetitive cycle of "out with the old, in with the new" in Norfolk, the Rennert Building, Maritime Tower and all of the parking lot area in the center of this photograph were redeveloped into the MacArthur Center shopping mall. Additional redevelopment north of MacArthur Center to the Scope arena complex and east to Saint Paul's Boulevard has produced a welcome mix of residential, retail and entertainment opportunities in downtown Norfolk.

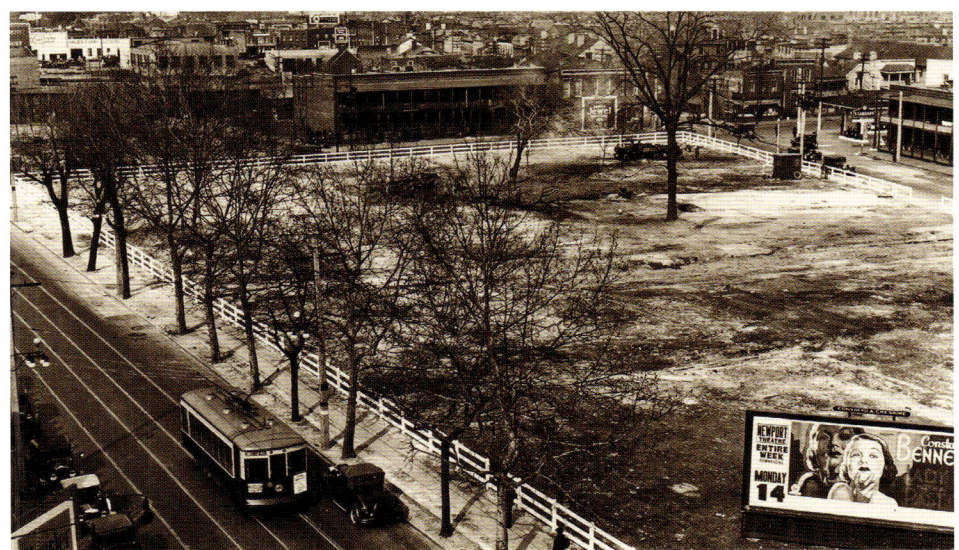

Walter E. Hoffman United States Courthouse: The future site of Norfolk's federal courthouse and post office (top, *Sargeant Memorial Room, Norfolk Public Library*) at the 600-block of Granby Street looking north toward Queen Street (later Brambleton Avenue) was photographed by Charles S. Borjes on March 14, 1932. The large tank structures in the background are the gas works up on Monticello Avenue adjacent to Cedar Grove Cemetery. The cornerstone of the city's federal courthouse and post office (shown here on a 1950s period postcard) was laid on September 7, 1933. Norfolk architects Benjamin F. Mitchell and the firm of Rudolph, Cooke, and VanLeeuwen were jointly responsible for the building's remarkable Art Deco design in the Art Moderne style of the 1930s and 1940s. Limestone is the primary exterior material, with a contrasting dark granite base and decorated aluminum spandrels between aluminum-framed windows. On the interior, the design and use of slick materials, such as granite, marble, aluminum, are presented in a simply composed geometric design with a high level of refinement. All of the cast aluminum designs are the work of a young local artist named Wyatt Hibbs. The building, renamed the Walter E. Hoffman United States Courthouse, seat of the United States District Court for the Eastern District of Virginia, was placed on the National Register of Historic Places in October 1984.

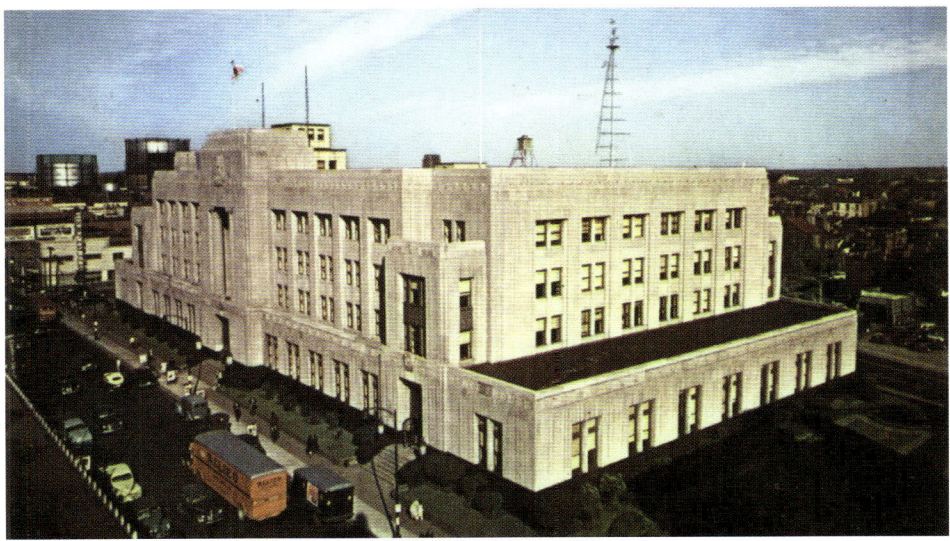

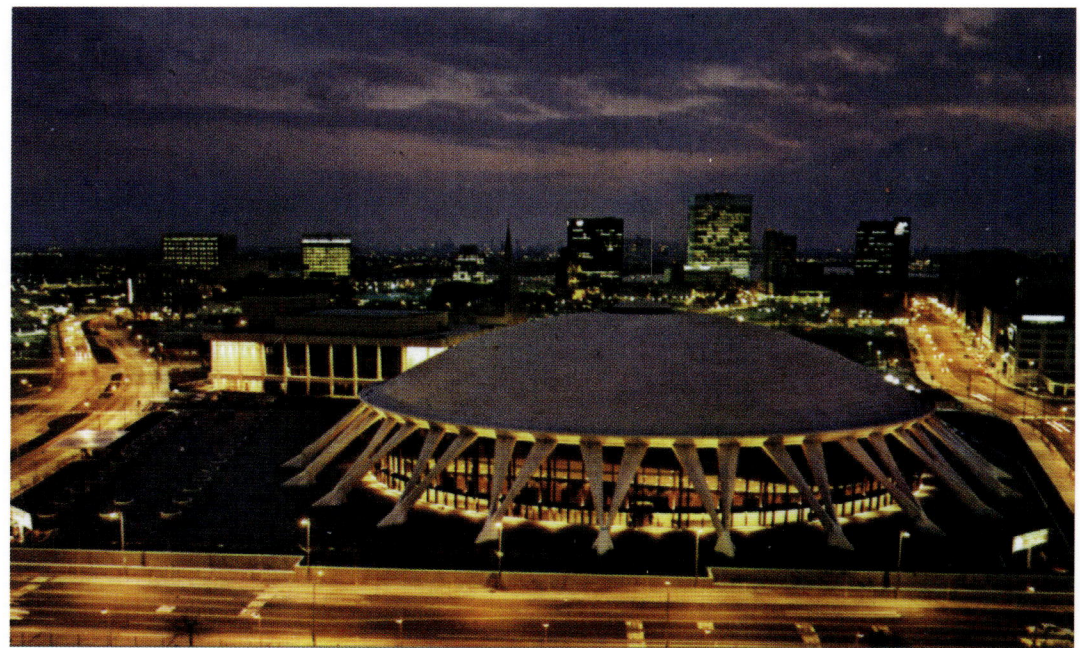

SCOPE ARENA: The arena, bordered by Brambleton (bottom of picture) and Monticello (right) avenues, Saint Paul's Boulevard (left) and Charlotte Street, was designed by Italian architect and engineer Pier Luigi Nervi in conjunction with the Norfolk architectural firm Williams and Tazewell, which designed the entire complex, to include Chrysler Hall (left of Scope in this photograph). Construction of Scope began on June 6, 1968, on land cleared as part of the city's extensive urban renewal effort; it was completed in 1971 at a cost of $35 million. Federal funds covered $23 million of the cost, and when it opened formally on November 12, 1971, the structure was the second largest public complex in Virginia; only the Pentagon was larger at that time. Scope features the world's largest reinforced thin shell concrete dome. The name "Scope" is a contraction of Kaleidoscope, the name originally chosen for the complex. Scope is shown here as it looked in September 1974.

OPPOSITE PAGE:

TOWN BACK CREEK: The last of Town Back Creek, which at one time extended nearly all the way to Church Street, today known as Saint Paul's Boulevard, was first platted in 1680. By 1880 the name City Hall Avenue was given to land that had been filled-in marsh land. The last of the creek in this photograph extended from just east of today's Granby Street (to the corner of what is today Monticello Avenue) to modern-day Boush Street. This picture was taken from the Norfolk and Western Railroad trestle visible in the accompanying image of McCullough's Wharf. The last of Town Back Creek was filled in by 1905 and Boush Street extended to Main Street. The buildings in the picture include the Market and Armory Buildings, left, constructed in 1892, the city courthouse, center, built in 1850, and the Haddington Building, right, completed in 1893. The Haddington Building was considered Norfolk's first skyscraper.

MCCULLOUGH'S WHARF: Also called McCullough's Dock, it was located at the terminus of City Hall Avenue and Boush Street. The picture was taken about 1895. The boat slip in the foreground is all that was left of Town Back Creek. To the left was the building supply company of Gammage and Waller and lower right McCullough Lumber Company. The trestle bridge connected Boush Street to Newton Street, later Boush Street extended. Railway docks and warehouses are also visible in this photograph.

On the River

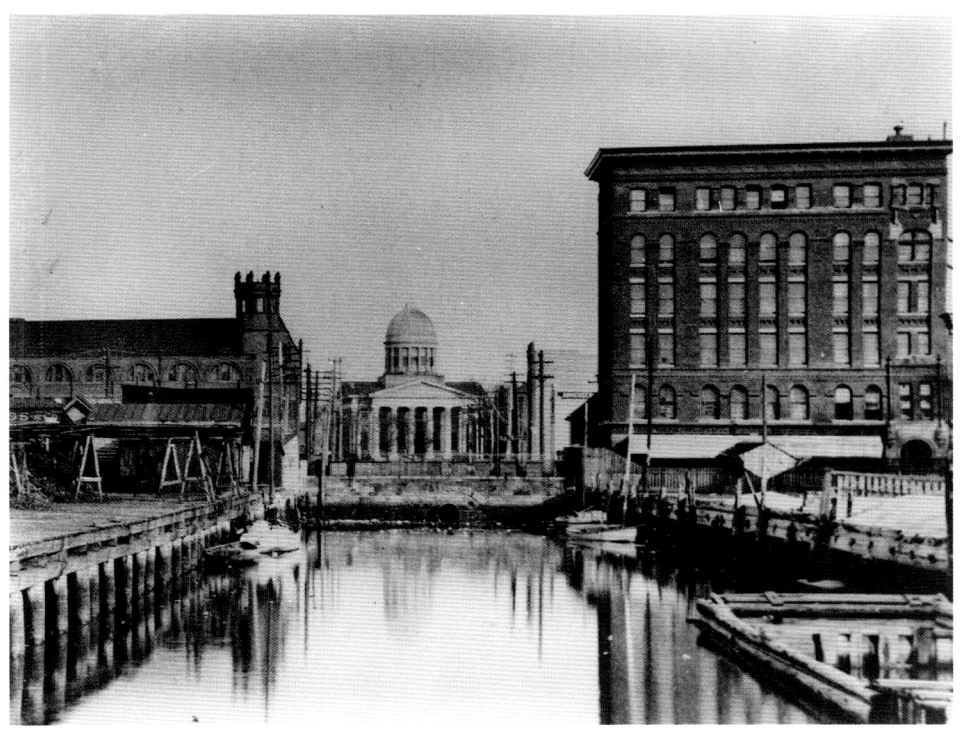

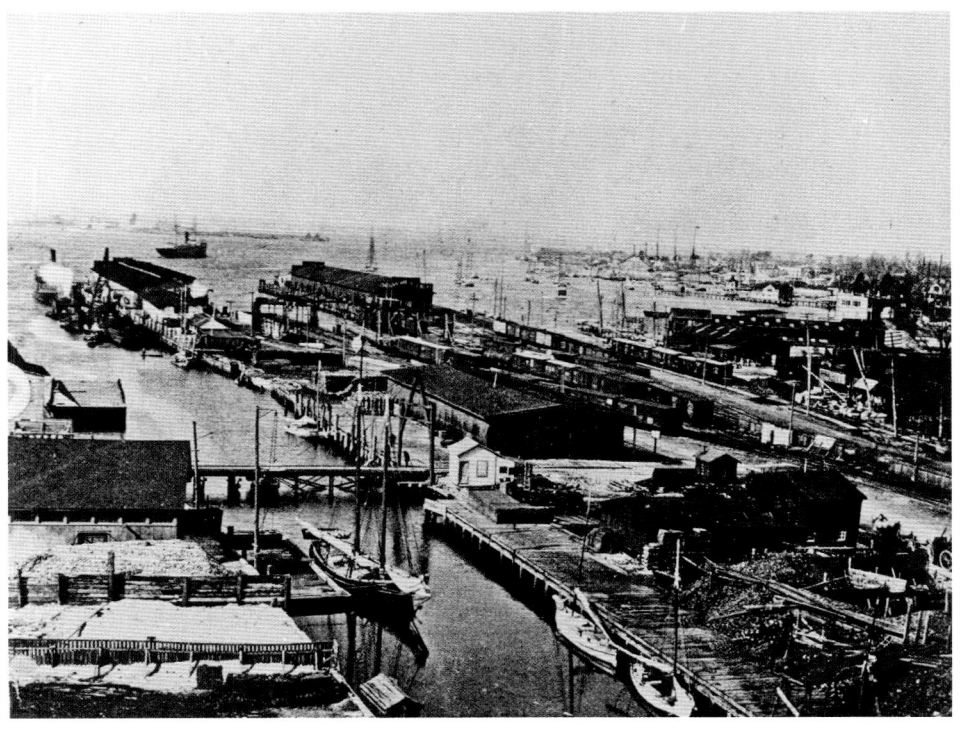

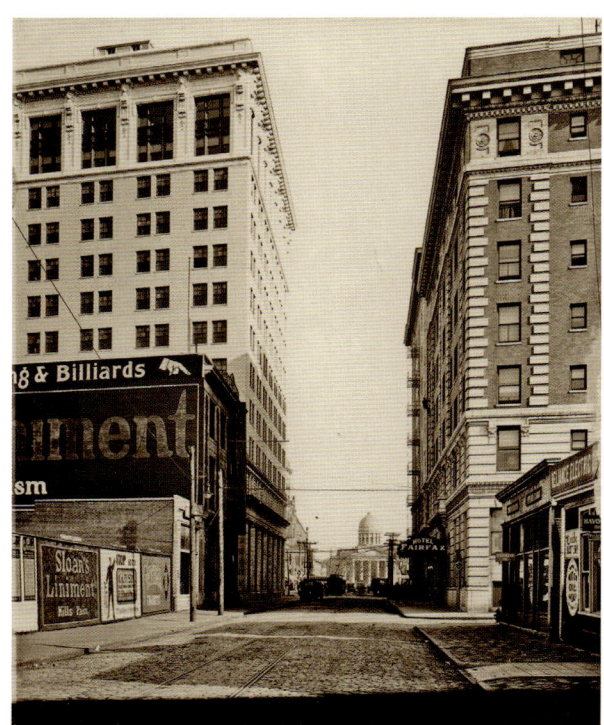

TOWN BACK CREEK NO MORE: Harry Mann stood looking east from Boush Street down City Hall Avenue to demonstrate the dramatic development that had taken place in less than a decade of an area that had been water and wharves. Three of the city's most distinctive buildings are in his picture: the F. S. Royster Building (left), completed in 1912 on the site of the former Builders' Exchange; the 1850 City Hall (center); and the Fairfax Hotel (right). Mann took this picture in 1915.

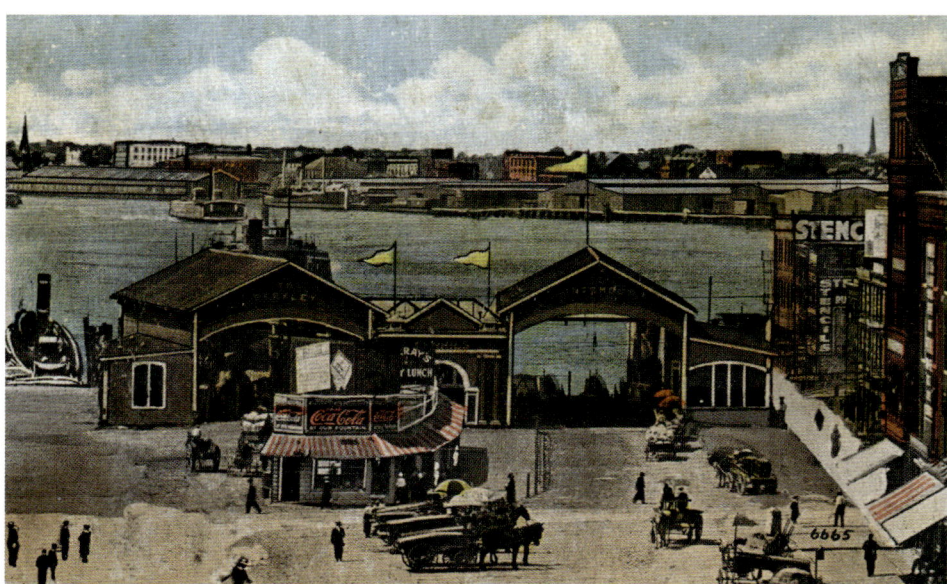

FERRY SERVICE: Established in 1636, the ferry service between Norfolk and Portsmouth and, later, Norfolk's Berkley ward, represented the oldest corporate utility in the United States before service was first suspended on August 25, 1955, the date the *City of Portsmouth* took its last passenger and car across the Elizabeth River, eclipsed by the opening three years earlier of the first tunnel between the two cities on May 23, 1952. Passenger ferry service was reestablished in 1983. The ferry service's Berkley and Portsmouth terminal is shown here as it looked in 1905 (top).

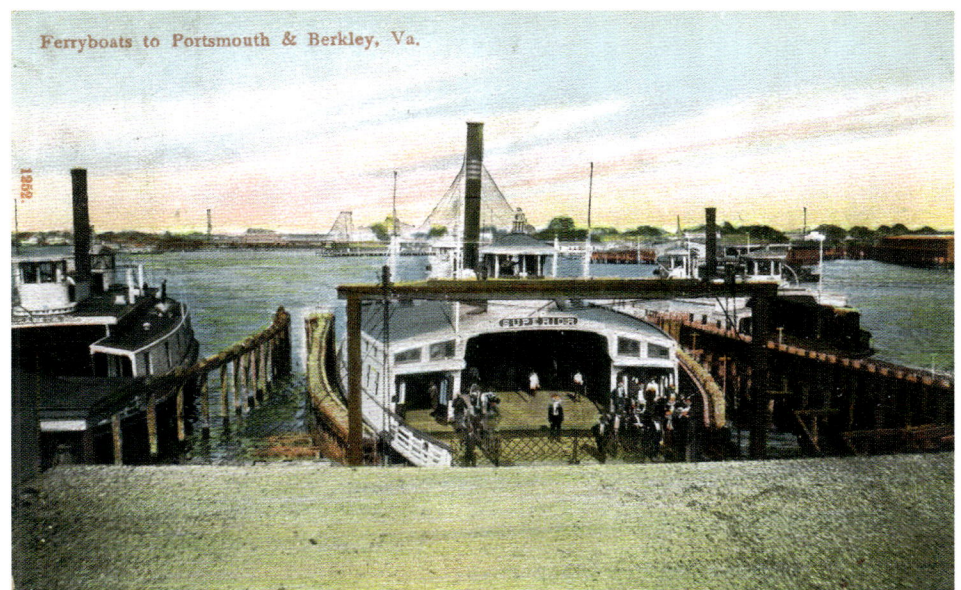

FROM NORFOLK TO PORTSMOUTH: The ferryboats *Elizabeth* (left) and *Superior* (foreground) took foot traffic and larger horse-drawn carts and wagons from Norfolk to Portsmouth and Berkley. The scene, captured on a postcard dated April 3, 1912, tells the story of steam-powered ferries that once moved thousands of people and tons of goods across the Norfolk harbor in the absence of a bridge-tunnel system that would not be built for another 40 years. Of note, the ferryboat *Columbia*, large enough to transport 200 people and 40 vehicles, did not come into service until 1918.

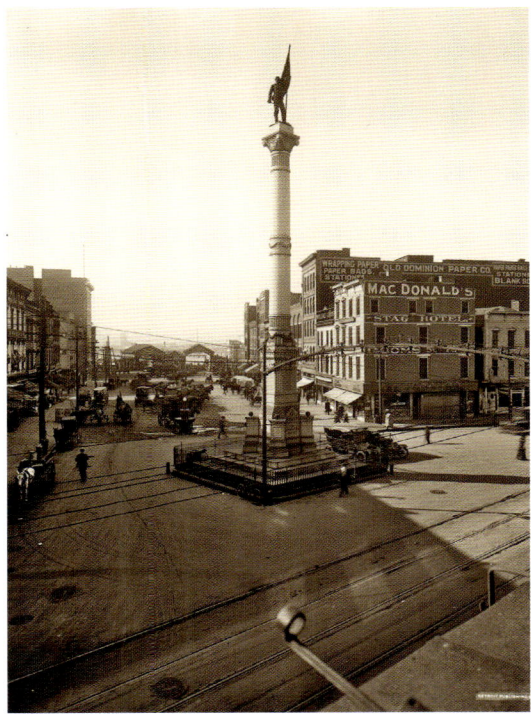

COMMERCIAL PLACE: In the fall of 1681, Lower Norfolk County surveyor John Ferebee mapped a main street for Norfolk, but also "the street that leadeth down to the waterside," later known by other names—"The Parade," Market Square and Commercial Place. The latter name came about in 1894 when Market Square and Commercial Row were enjoined and renamed Commercial Place. At the intersection of Commercial Place and Main Street the Confederate Monument (shown here) was erected; this view is looking past the monument toward the Norfolk ferry terminal as it looked in 1915. *Detroit Publishing Company, Library of Congress.*

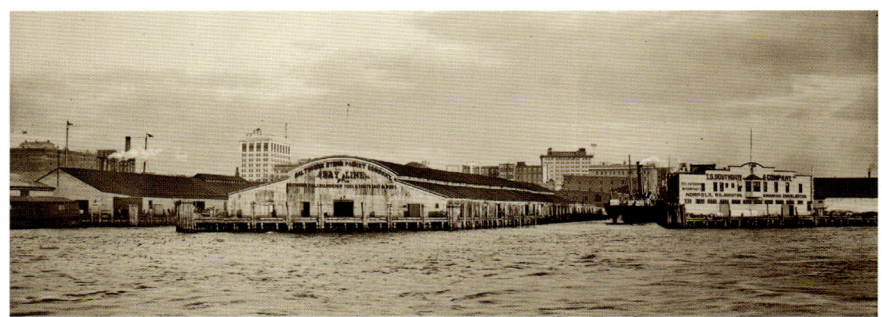

MR. SOUTHGATE'S ENTERPRISE: The export, import and shipping business of T. S. Southgate & Company was established in October 1892, by Thomas Somerville Southgate, a Richmond native, who developed it from a very small enterprise to one of the most important business establishments in Norfolk. At its inception the business was simply a brokerage enterprise, afterward merging into an agency and distribution business, and later added a shipping business, with a considerable amount of export and import operations. The goods handled were principally food products, procured directly from producers and manufacturers. Through this company, Southgate owned and operated the Southgate Terminal Corporation, equipped with modern fireproof warehouse construction (148 Water Street, shown here, 1913) of more than half-million square feet, and also having an ocean pier 700 feet long, with 30 feet of water. The Baltimore Steam Packet Company Bay Line (or "Old Bay Line"), left, was at the west end of Main Street. The steamship line operated from 1840 to 1962, providing overnight steamboat service on the Chesapeake Bay, primarily between Baltimore, Maryland, and Norfolk. When it closed in 1962, it was the last surviving overnight steamship passenger service in the United States. *Detroit Publishing Company, Library of Congress.*

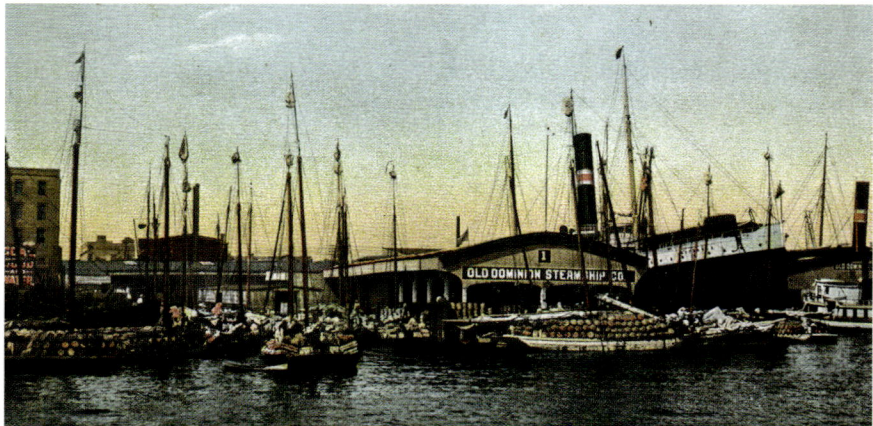

OLD DOMINION STEAMSHIP COMPANY: The company's docks and warehouses at the foot of Norfolk's Church and East Main Streets, photographed in 1910, attracted small work boats loaded with produce and assorted goods from nearby farms along the rivers and waterways in the area—some from as far away as northeastern North Carolina—that came to Old Dominion Line's docks to load steamers bound for New York City. The turnaround time for fresh produce delivery from Norfolk to New York was one day. The steamship company maintained daily service to New York except Sunday. The docks were destroyed by fire on June 7, 1931, and never rebuilt. The service was continued from the old extension of Boissevain Avenue in West Ghent, where Old Dominion Steamship Company had built new piers and warehouses. The company's ships were taken over by the United States government during the Second World War; some were sunk. The line never resumed service when the war ended. This picture was taken in 1910.

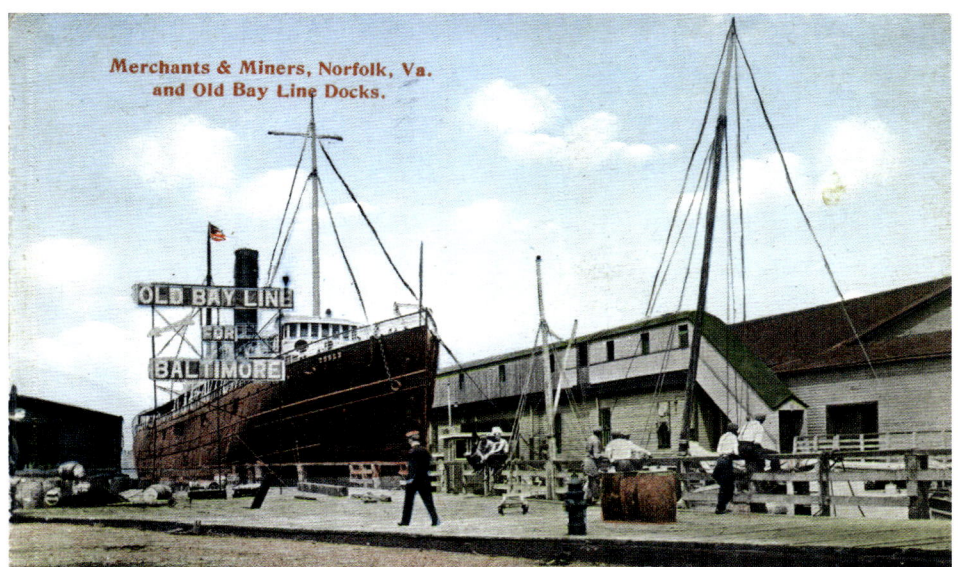

MERCHANTS & MINERS TRANSPORTATION COMPANY: The company was incorporated at Baltimore, Maryland, on April 24, 1852, and served several East Coast port cities, including Norfolk. Shown here (top), is the company's operation on the west end of Norfolk's Main Street in an area called "Boston Wharf." Merchants & Miners was in Norfolk in 1880. The company began the process of dissolution and liquidation on March 17, 1948, and was out of business completely in 1952. Next door to Merchants & Miners is the Old Bay Line dock. The picture dates to 1913. In the second photograph taken in 1914 (bottom, *Detroit Publishing Company, Library of Congress*) the Merchants & Miners wharf is to the right. The buildings in the center are the F. S. Royster Building and the Fairfax Hotel with City Hall Avenue not yet filled in and extended to what is today Boush Street. To the far left is the Anheuser-Busch Brewing Company and cold storage plant (later the Boush Ice and Cold Storage Company). Anheuser-Busch came to Norfolk in 1887–88 and since it was located so close to the water's edge, its address was originally approximated as "City Hall near Granby." The Boush Cold Storage building, absent its additions, was later adaptively reused as a Harbour Place condominium building.

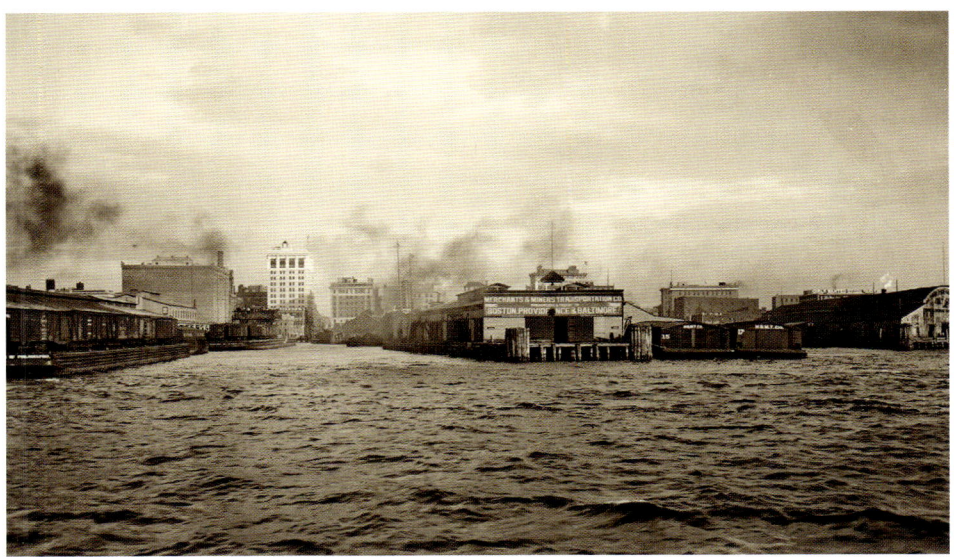

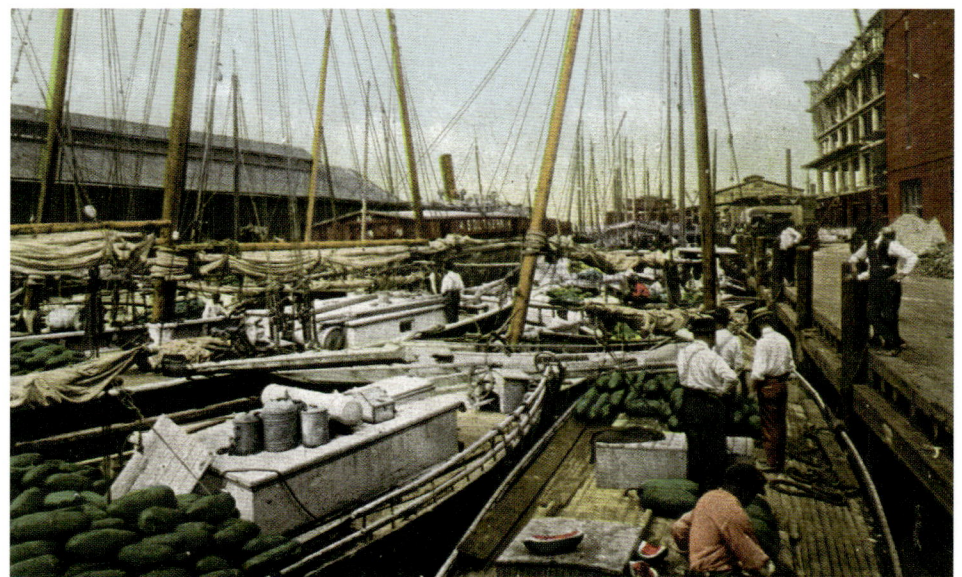

WATERMELON SEASON: During the summer, boats laden with the succulent, fleshy fruit, appeared up and down the Norfolk waterfront, from the foot of City Hall Avenue between T. S. Southgate & Company and Anheuser-Busch Brewing Company's cold storage (visible on the right) to Roanoke Dock. The picture shown here (top) was made into a Detroit Publishing Company postcard that dates to 1910. The second scene (bottom) from Roanoke Dock at Roanoke Avenue and Water Street, also taken during watermelon season, on June 1, 1916, paints a colorful picture of what Norfolk's waterfront once was, the rich fabric of sail makers, ship chandlers, fish and oyster houses, produce, butter and cheese dealers lining the dock on either side. On the left is T. C. Hurst & Son (Thomas C. and Floyd C.), ship chandlers, who prospered at 9–11 Roanoke Avenue. To the right, at 18 Roanoke Avenue, is Odell Brothers (Albert J.), a large oyster and produce house. At the top of Roanoke Dock, at 237 East Water Street, is R. W. Hudgins & Son (R. Wesley and A. Herman), ship chandlers.

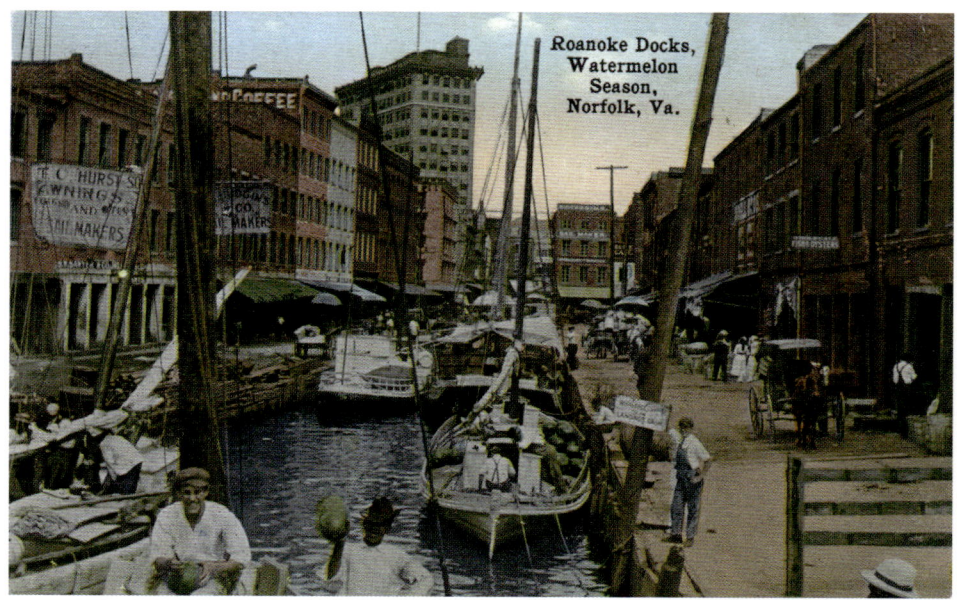

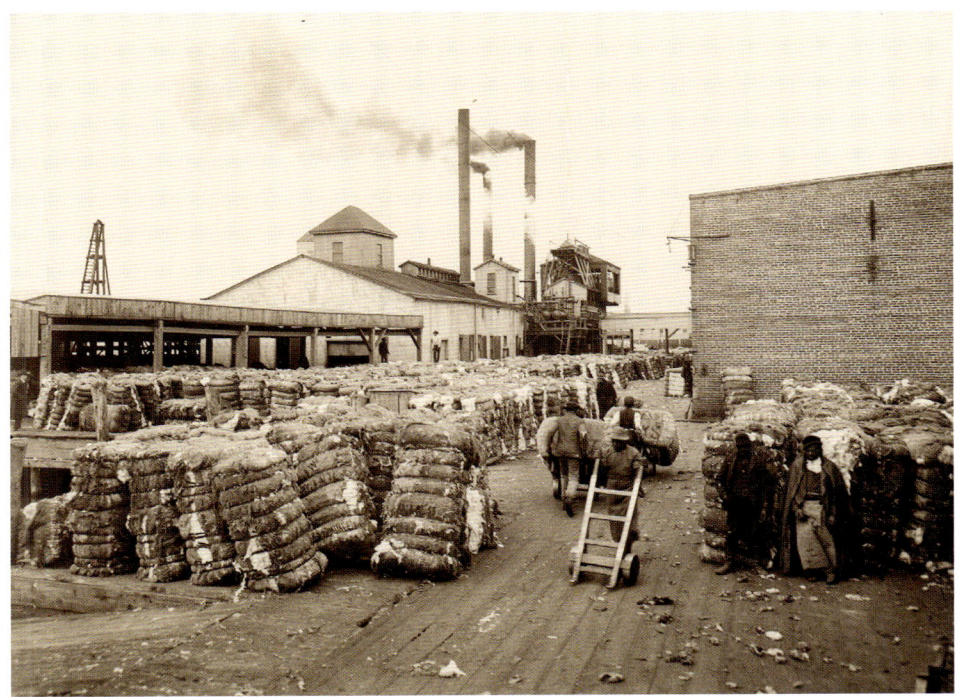

COTTON PORT: By 1900 most of Norfolk's cotton merchants had relocated from the downtown area to the Atlantic City waterfront along Front Street. In 1905, when this picture (top, *Detroit Publishing Company, Library of Congress*) was taken of the International Cotton Compress Company's operation at 135 Front Street, bales of compressed cotton, awaited shipment. In the second picture, taken by Harry Mann in 1910 (bottom), compressed cotton was loaded onto steam barges at the Atlantic City dock. At that time, Norfolk was the fourth largest cotton port in the United States and the city's cotton buyers, brokers and exporters occupied most of Front Street in the city's Atlantic City section.

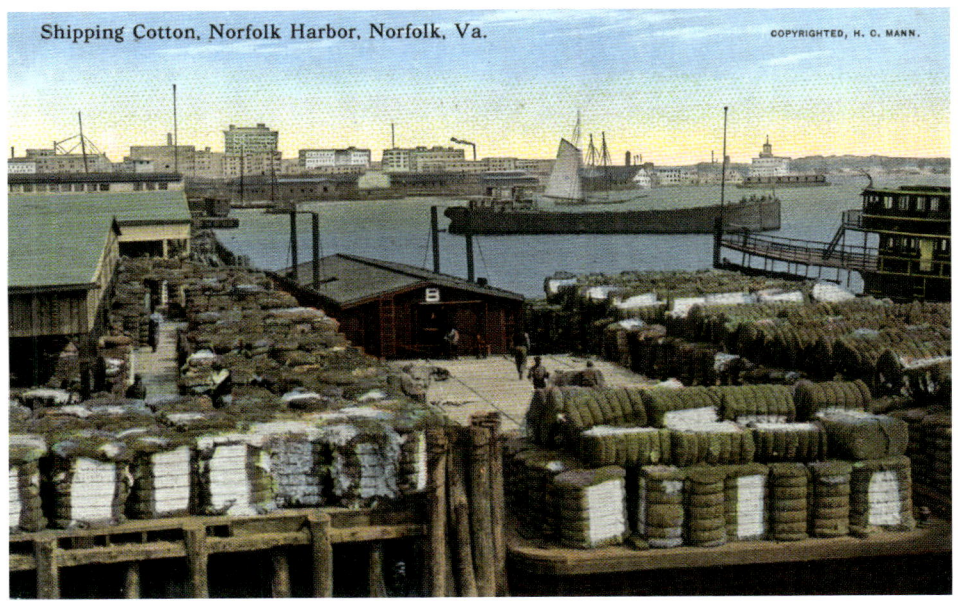

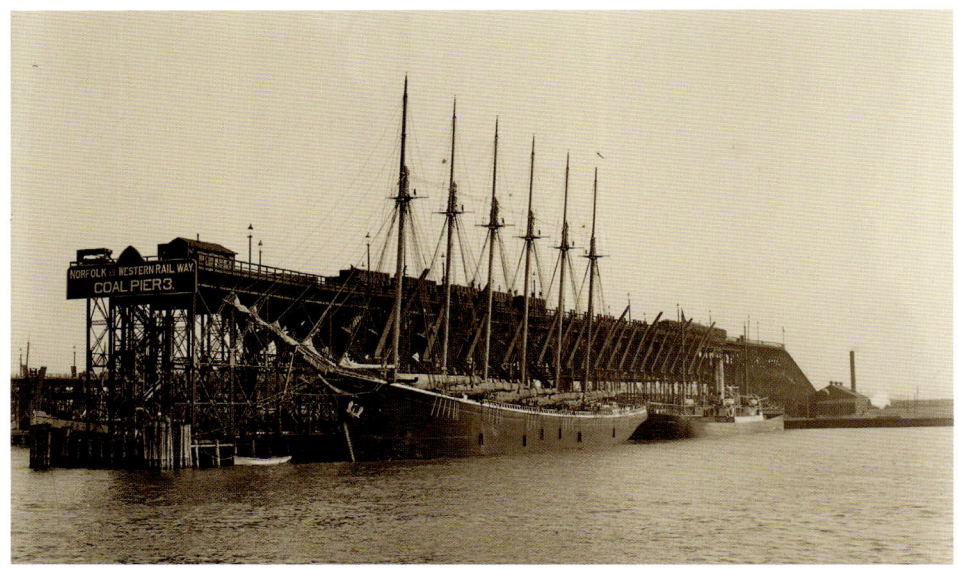

THE ELEANOR A. PERCY: Norfolk & Western Railway Coal Pier Number 3 at Lambert's Point, photographed in 1905, had already begun to ship coal by steam colliers than sailing vessels but the use of coal schooners persisted, evidenced by the six-masted schooner *Eleanor A. Percy* at the dock. During the 1870s, it is recognized that coal shipped from the Delaware River and the Hampton Roads area of the Chesapeake Bay encouraged the building of increasingly larger schooners. By the late 1890s, the first five-masted schooners were introduced and, in 1900, the first of ten six-masted coal schooners, the *George W. Wells*, was launched on August 14, 1900, at Camden, Maine, soon followed two months later by the *Eleanor A. Percy* on October 10, 1900, built by Percy & Small of Bath, Maine. *Detroit Publishing Company, Library of Congress.*

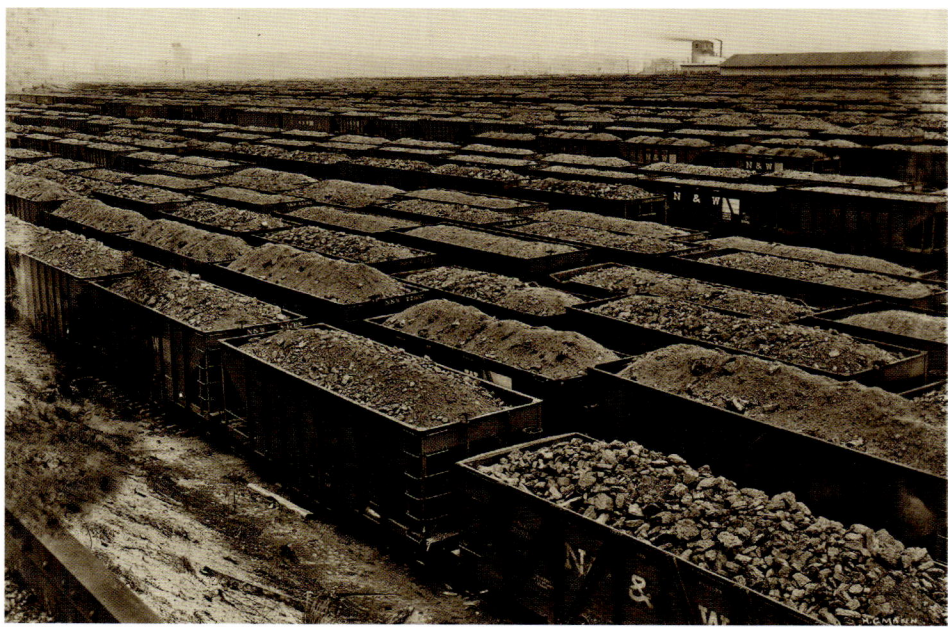

LAMBERT'S POINT: Harry C. Mann photographed Norfolk & Western Railway coal cars at Lambert's Point in 1920.

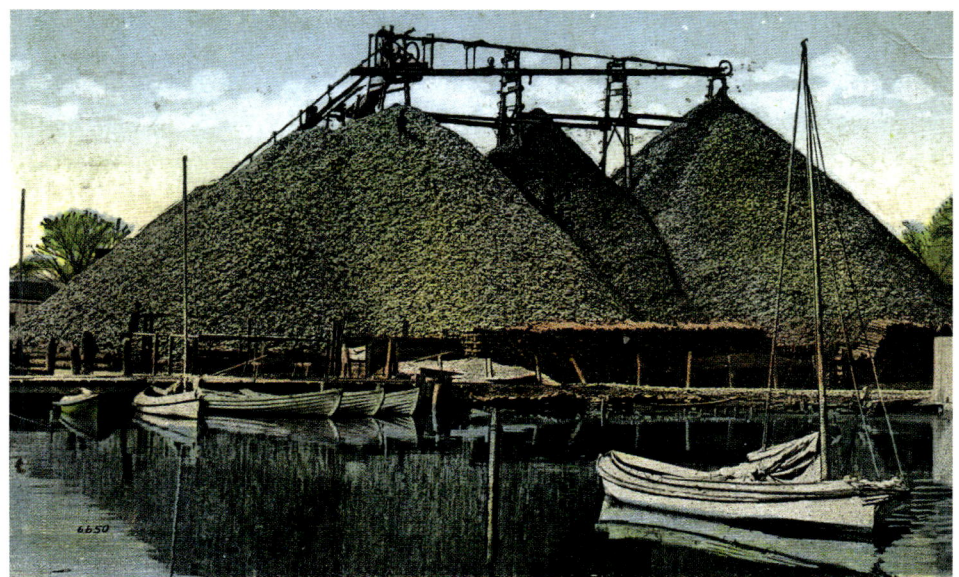

WHEN THE OYSTER WAS KING: This postcard, dating to 1920, touted 200,000 bushels of oyster shells piled high in Norfolk. Norfolk was the oyster packing mecca on Hampton Roads' southside. Establishments like Bay Fish & Oyster Company on First Street near Front Street and Harry K. Swann on Front Street and Colley Avenue in the city's Atlantic City section; Hopkins Oyster Company at 426 York Street; R. R. Higgins Company of Virginia and J. T. White & Company at Groner's Wharf, and Norfolk Oyster Company at 114 Boush Street all flourished in this golden age when the oyster was their cash king.

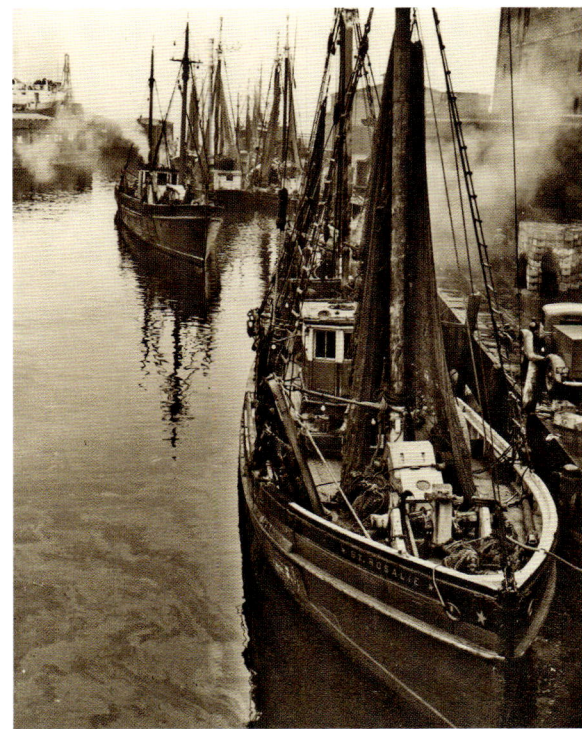

REMEMBERING THE "SUNRISE CITY BY THE SEA": *Norfolk Ledger-Dispatch* photographer Harden David "H. D." Vollmer took this photograph of fishing boats at the foot of City Hall Avenue at Boush Cold Storage in 1935. There was time when this scene was repeated up and down the Norfolk waterfront.

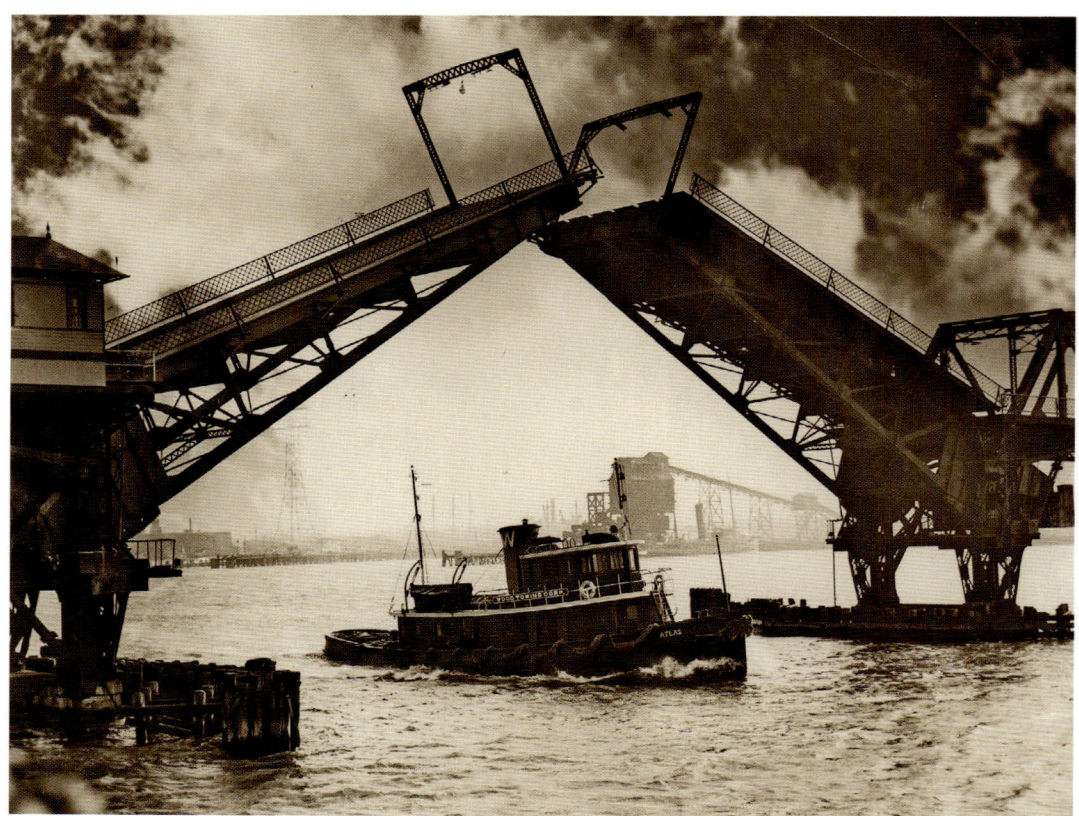

Wood Towing Company: The towing company's tug *Atlas* was photographed by H. D. Vollmer in 1935 as it passed under the old Berkley Bridge. Wood Towing was in business from 1920 to 1951. A number of historic tugs remained in service into the mid-1950s. Several of these tugs participated in some of the most exciting events in history, among them the *Salvor*, which eventually met her fate at the bottom of Smith's Creek—today, The Hague—in the 1930s. The *Salvor* had laid a transatlantic cable for the Western Union Telegraph Company in the first part of her career, and later was used for treasure salvage off Cape Henry. The *Dauntless* was a blockade-runner during the Spanish-American War, and was aptly nicknamed the "Phantom Ship" due to her quickness. The *Dauntless*, renamed the *Restless*, worked the Elizabeth River for many years, not a terrible end for the vessel that carried the first news of Theodore Roosevelt's capture of San Juan Hill back to the United States. Wood Towing Company had the distinction of owning the oldest tug in service on the Elizabeth, and the fourth oldest in the United States—the *Venture*. The *Venture* had been built in 1863 in Philadelphia and named the *Grace Titus*. Soon after the tug came into service, she was bought by the commonwealth of Virginia and renamed *Virginia*, which she carried through the end of the Civil War. Captain Joseph M. Clark bought the *Virginia* after the war and gave her the name *Venture*. Wood Towing later bought the *Venture* to haul barges between Norfolk and Suffolk.

The Horseless Age

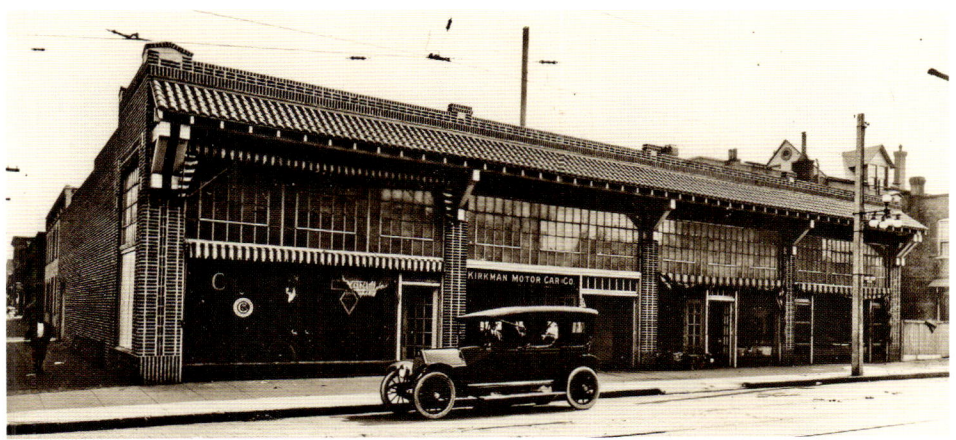

KIRKMAN MOTOR COMPANY: Kirkman, named an official Kissel Kar dealer in the spring of 1914, is shown in this 1915 Harry C. Mann photograph. Located at 614 Granby Street on land that is today part of the footprint of the Walter E. Hoffman United States Courthouse, this Kissel Kar dealership was owned by Zeno T. Kirkman. The business closed at this address the year Mann took the picture and opened very briefly in 1916 at 123 East 18th Street; Kirkman was out of the automobile business by year's end. The Kissel Motor Car Company, founded by Louis Kissel and his sons, George and William, on June 5, 1906, in Hartford, Wisconsin, custom built high-quality automobiles, hearses, fire trucks, taxicabs, and utility vehicles.

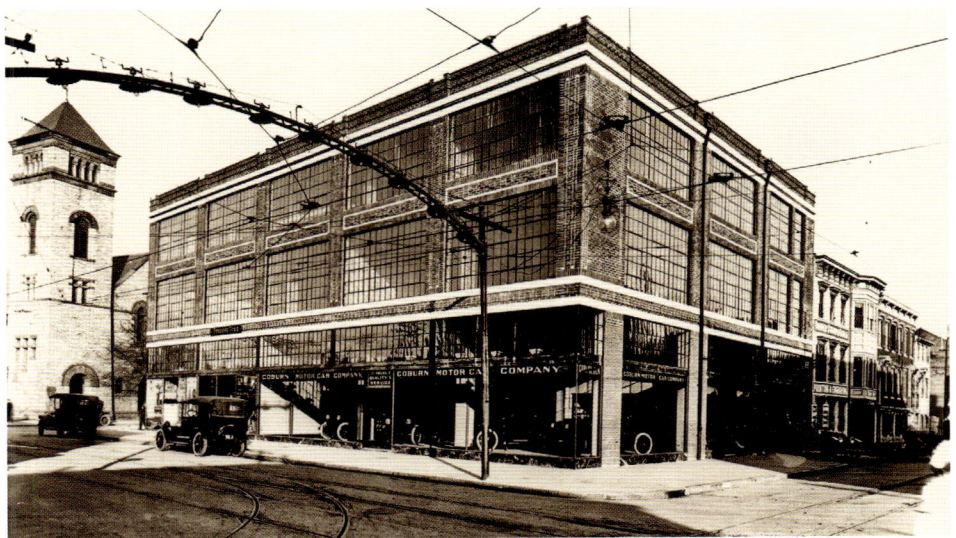

COBURN MOTOR CAR COMPANY: Coburn was located on Granby Street between Charlotte and Bute Streets; Bute is to the left and Charlotte to the right in this Harry Mann photograph, taken in 1914. Owned by Timothy Gray Coburn, the dealership opened in 1910 at this location. He sold Studebakers. Coburn sponsored rising stars on the auto racing circuit as early as the year his dealership opened. Norfolk's Fairgrounds, adjacent to today's Fairmount Park, hosted automobile races as early as December 1–3, 1910, when Coburn and several cars and drivers were suspended for one year by the American Automobile Association (AAA) for holding an unsanctioned meet there. The church (left) is Saint Luke's Episcopal.

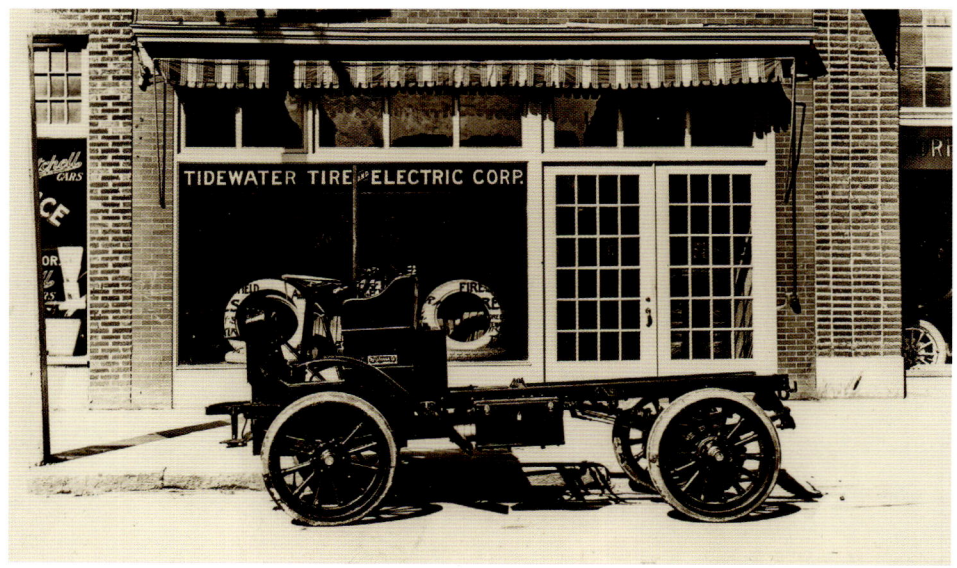

BEFORE AND AFTER: Tidewater Tire and Electric Company was first located at 717 Granby Street, just north of Brambleton Avenue, when Harry C. Mann took this picture (top) in 1919, the year the business opened. Tidewater Tire specialized in automobile tires, batteries and electrical repairs. The company's founding partners were Semmes Chapman, president and treasurer; James H. W. Green, vice president and general manager, and Howard P. Stewart, secretary. The following year the business suspended the tire business and moved down the street to a larger location as Tidewater Electric Corporation. The façade later applied to 717 Granby Street (bottom, *S. L. Nusbaum Realty Company*), constructed in 1912, left it unrecognizable to the period in which it was occupied by Tidewater Tire and Electric Corporation. The building is situated next to Bress Pawn Shop at 719–723 Granby Street, and is in the new Norfolk Arts and Design District. The picture shown here was taken on May 13, 2014.

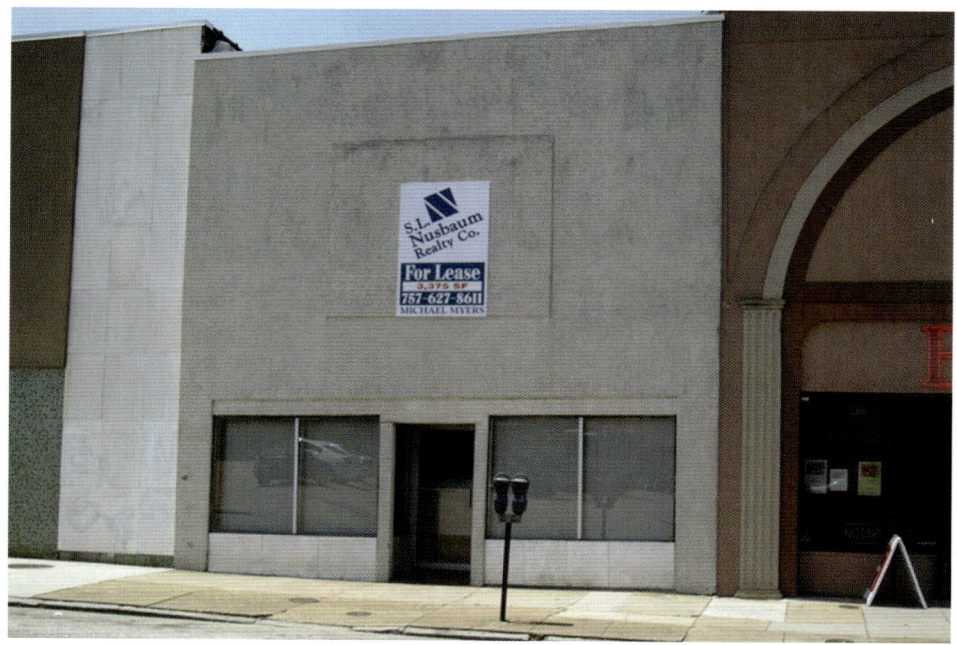

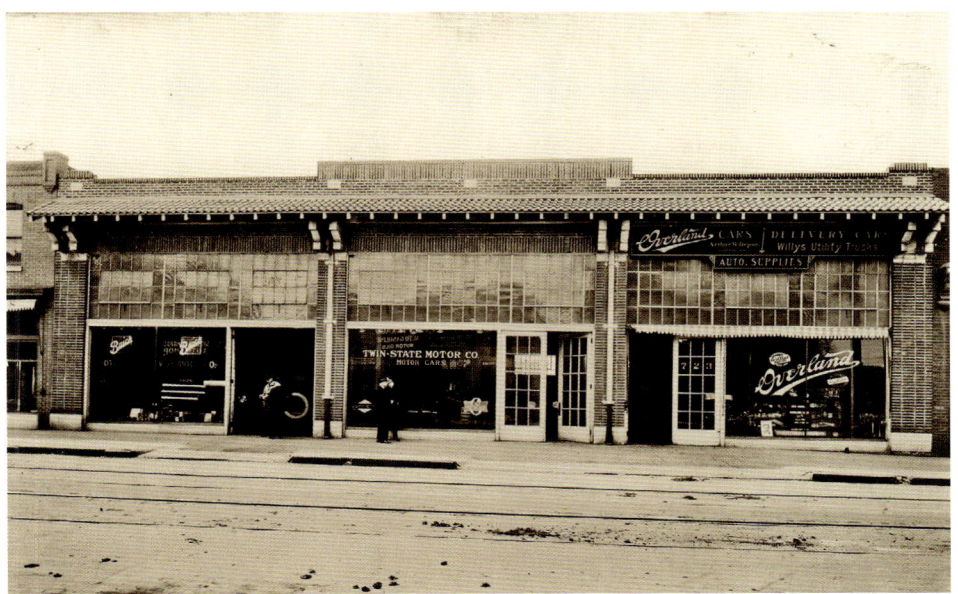

FROM MOTOR TO PAWN SHOP: Frank J. Conway photographed the Twin State Motor and Overland Motor Companies at 719–723 Granby Street in 1917. The building was constructed in 1913, the year property records indicate it was completed and the first businesses opened at this location. Today, this address is occupied by Bress Pawn Shop and bears no resemblance to the Conway picture shown here.

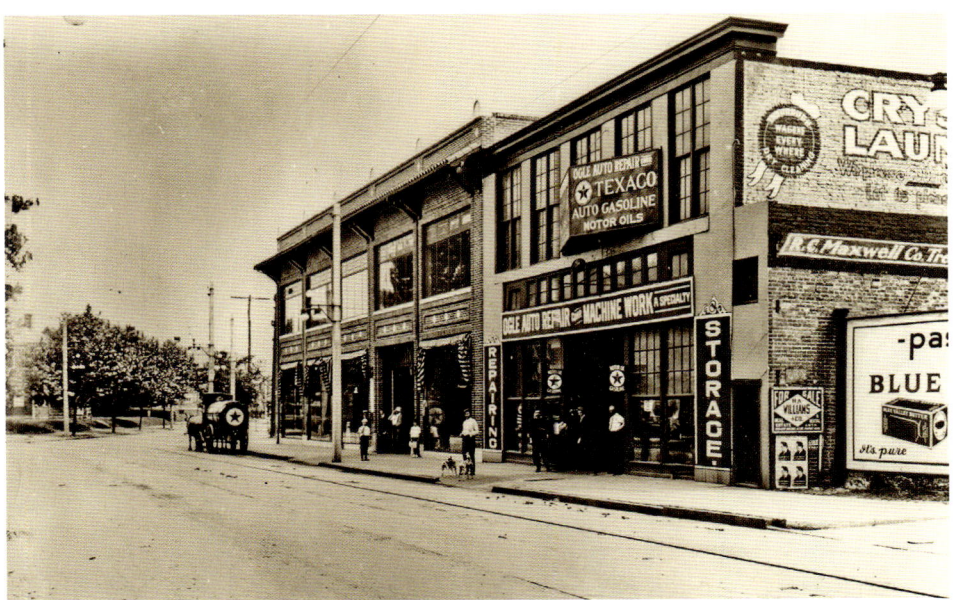

OGLE AUTO REPAIR AND MACHINE WORK COMPANY: Ogle, which sold Texaco gasoline and motor oils, had just opened at 1008 Granby Street in 1916, when Harry Mann took this picture. The shop was owned by William Ogle, a master mechanic. When Ogle chose the location for his first business, he picked the home of the defunct Monarch Laundry Company, a 1907 building that cried for a makeover. Ogle gave the building a new façade, but went out of business the same year he opened. The building, absent Ogle's façade, is still there.

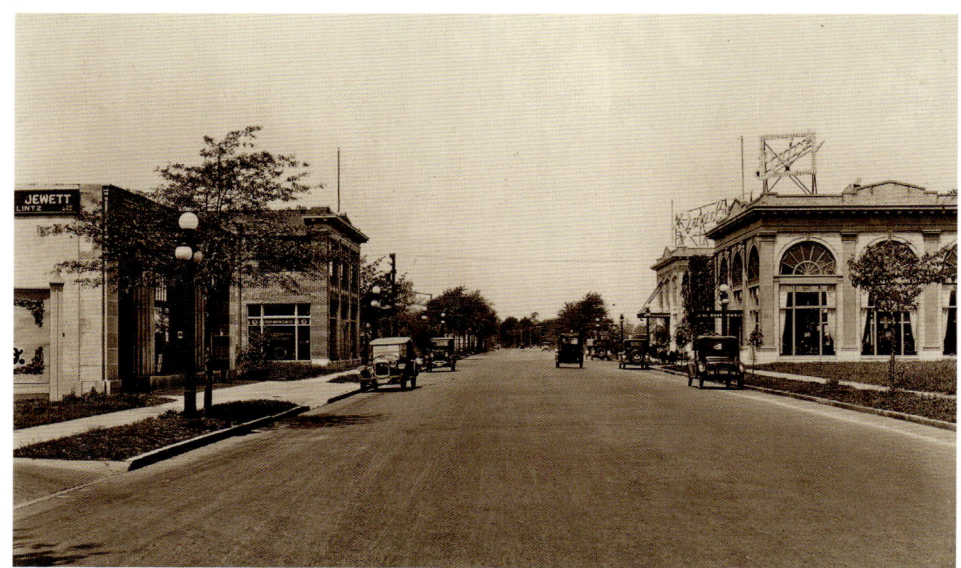

THE "OTHER" AUTO ROW: By the 1920s, Norfolk's Twenty-first Street was an adjunct "Auto Row" to the one that was already flourishing north of Brambleton Avenue. Acme Photo Company founder Henry W. Gillen took this picture of the street in 1925. The Dixie Motor Car Company is the second building on the left, located closest to the intersection of Twenty-first and Manteo streets. Overland Buick occupied the two large buildings on the right. Gillen took the picture looking toward Colley Avenue down the center of the street.

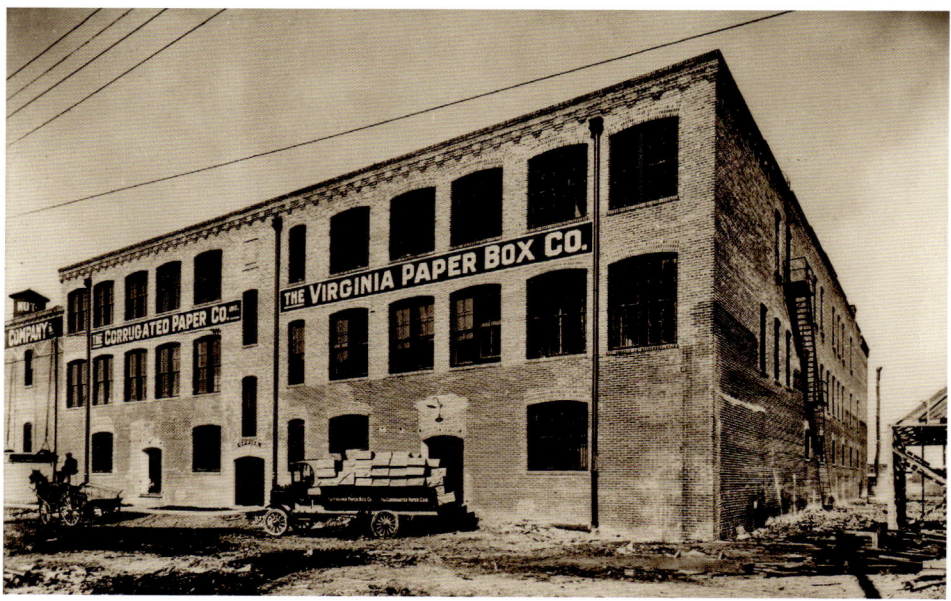

VIRGINIA PAPER BOX COMPANY: The paper box company, located at Granby Street and East Twenty-second Street, was photographed by Harry C. Mann in 1915. The company was owned by William D. Hemingway, president; Jacob S. Heller, vice president; and Samuel Linthicum, secretary. They opened their paper box business at 301 Front Street in 1907 and moved to East Main Street, briefly, before relocating here in 1912.

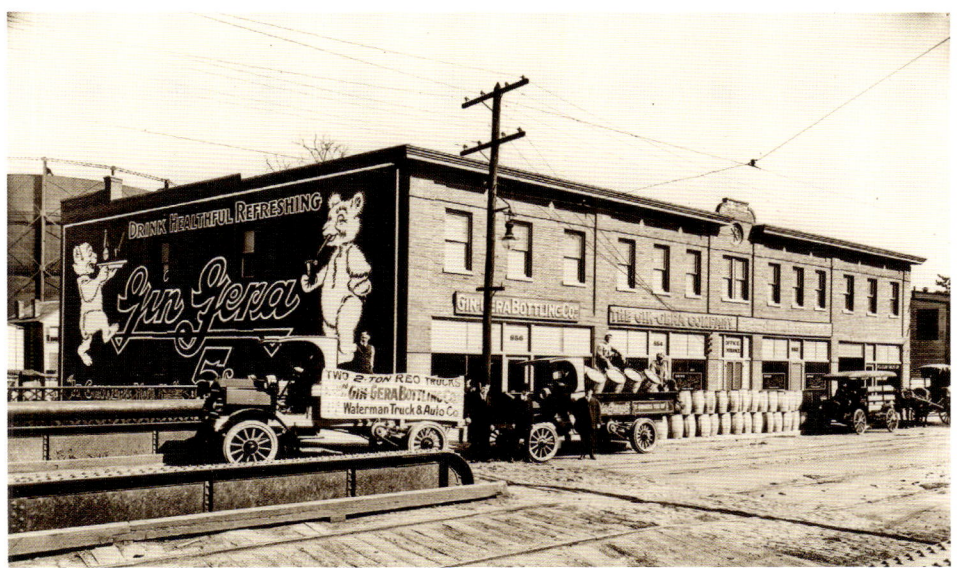

Soda Pop City: Norfolk was home to an often forgotten enterprise of the early twentieth century: the bottling industry. Norfolk could claim one indigenous soft drink company, Gin-Gera Company, which bottled and sold a soda drink similar to ginger ale. Located at 852–856 Granby Street, Gin-Gera Company predated both Coca-Cola and Pepsi Cola, which came to the city in 1902 and 1912, respectively, and remained an innovator in the bottling business until the end of the First World War, when Gin-Gera ceased production of its delectable ginger sweet water. This Harry Mann photograph is dated by the two 1917 Reo J two-ton delivery trucks in the foreground.

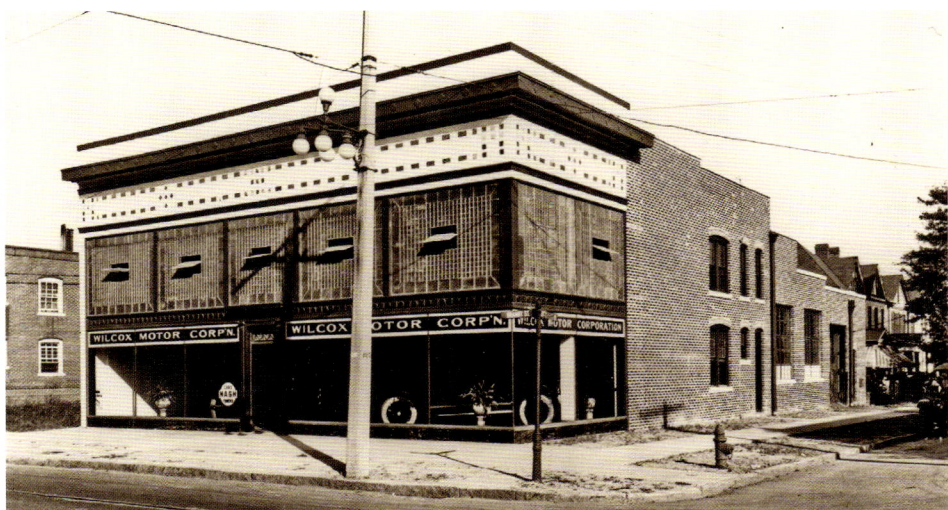

Wilcox Motor Corporation: Wilcox, located at 1500 Granby Street (the corner of Granby and Fifteenth streets), was photographed by Harry C. Mann in 1922. The Alexander at Ghent, an urban apartment community, now occupies this corner. The motor company was owned by Edward W. Wilcox Jr., who moved the business from Olney Road to this location in 1920. In 1925, Wilcox expanded the business and added on to the building shown here. By 1930, in addition to this location, Wilcox opened a used car sales department at 721 Granby Street. Wilcox sold his 1500 Granby Street location to Willard A. Mooers, a Richmond Packard dealer, who opened Mooers Motor Car Company there the following year.

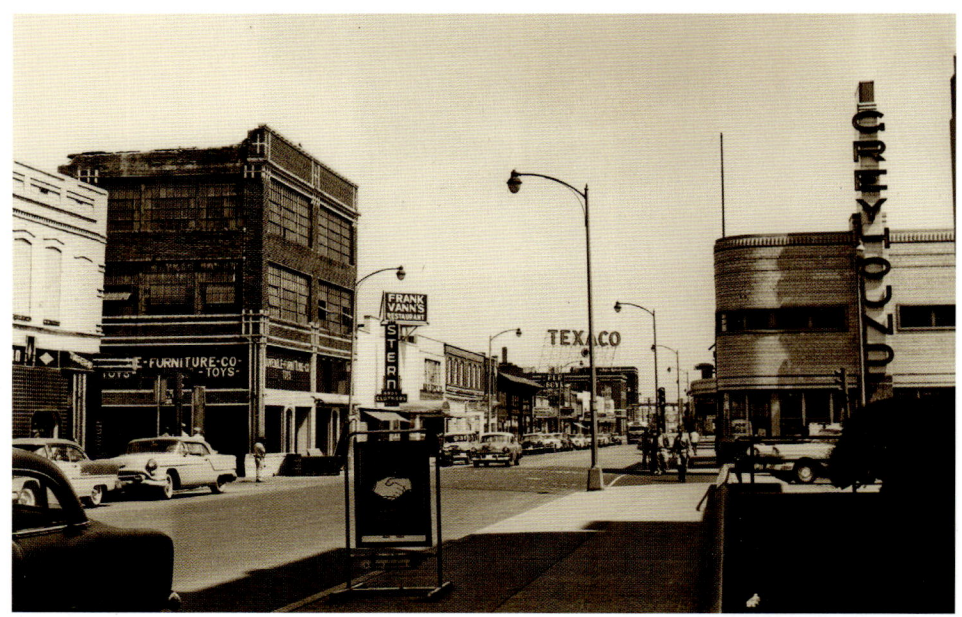

A Scene Long Gone: Carroll H. Walker took this picture of Granby Street looking north from Brambleton Avenue on May 16, 1959.

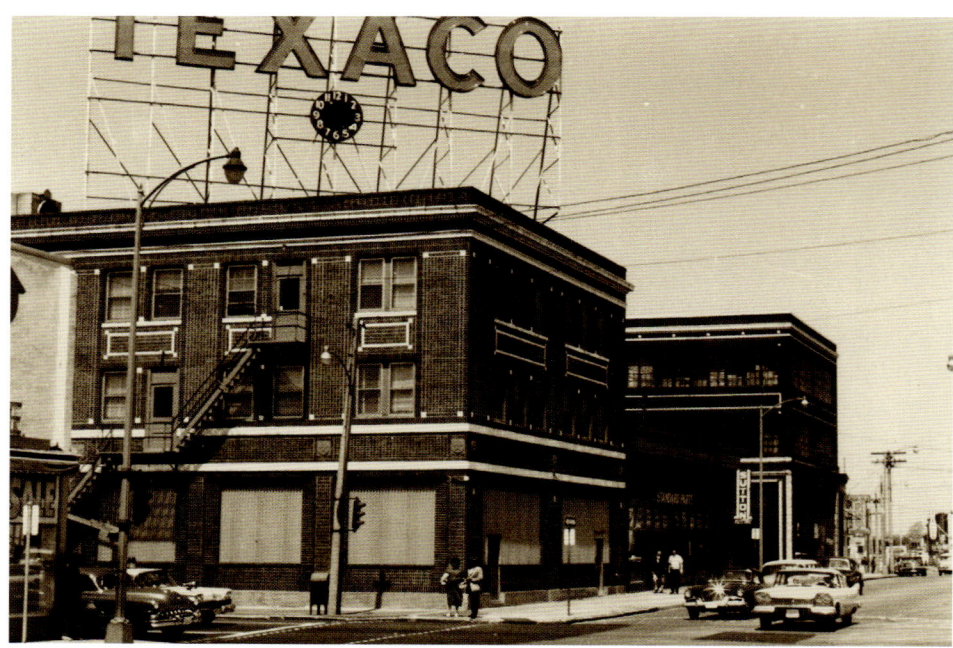

Texaco Building: While this James Murdaugh photograph showcases the Texaco Building as it looked in April 1959, it is also shows us the intersection of Olney Road and Granby Street and beyond. The Texaco Building at 759–761 Granby Street was constructed between 1917 and 1918, early in the building boom along Auto Row. This Colonial Revival structure was designed by the architectural firm of Ferguson, Calrow & Wrenn, and built by Baker & Brinkley, one of the most important contractors in the region at that time. *Sargeant Memorial Room, Norfolk Public Library.*

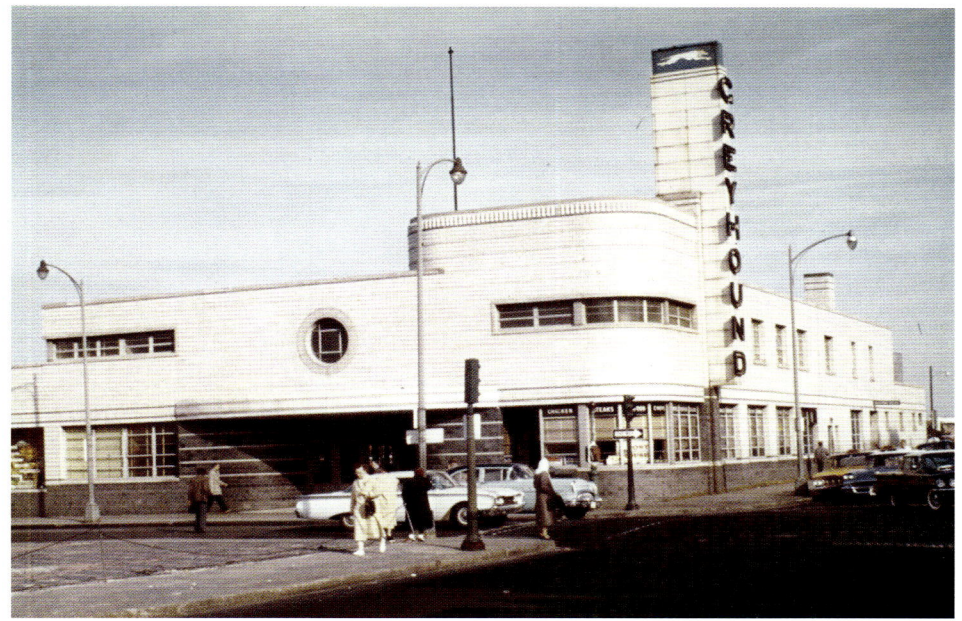

GREYHOUND BUS STATION: James A. Murdaugh took the picture (top, *Sargeant Memorial Room, Norfolk Public Library*) of the city's first Greyhound bus terminal at the corner of Granby Street and Brambleton Avenue in February 1960. This station, with its Art Deco style known as Streamline Moderne, typical of Greyhound's building program from 1937 to 1945 to unify the company's brand identity, was torn down to make way for the expansion and extension of Brambleton Avenue; a new station was built to replace it in 1961. Norfolk's second Greyhound bus terminal, shown shortly after it was completed, is located in the downtown area directly across Monticello Avenue from the former Golden Triangle Motor Hotel but also runs the length of a block of Brambleton Avenue on its southern exposure. The terminal was designed by Clarence W. Meakin. In its early years, the terminal handled between five and six thousand passengers per year.

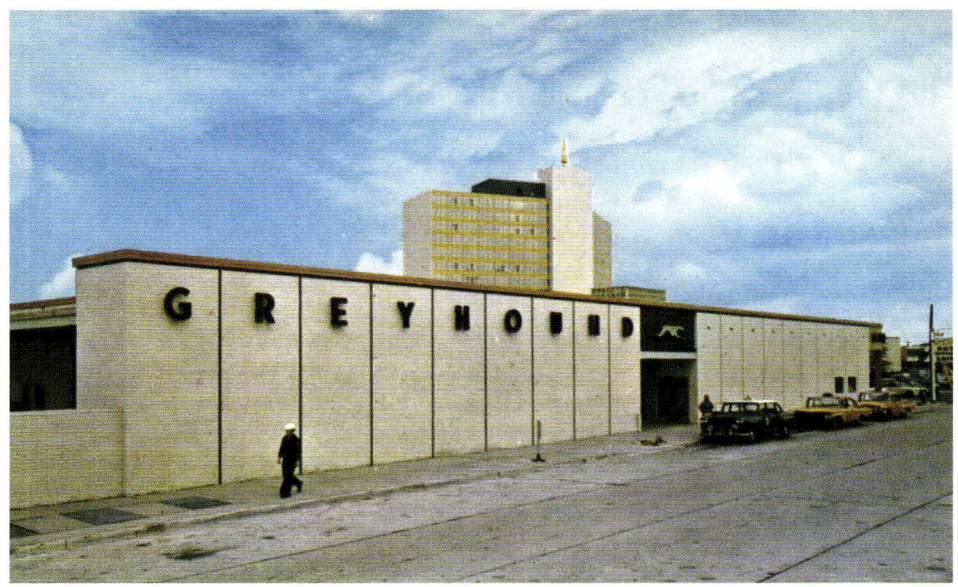

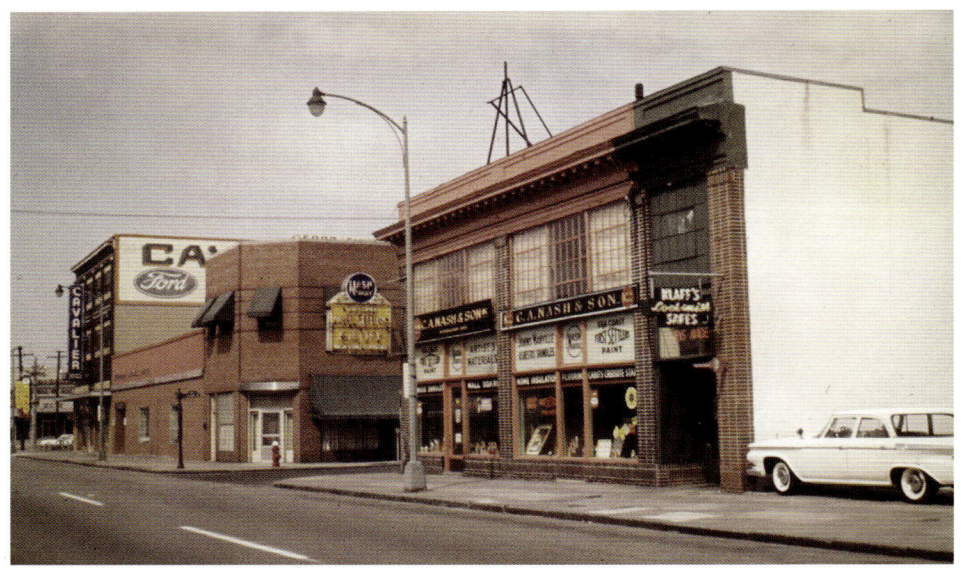

Murdaugh's Only Survivor: The building far left, occupied by Cavalier Ford when James Murdaugh took this picture in April 1961 of Granby Street looking north from Brambleton Avenue, was designed by Peebles & Ferguson, architects, as an automobile showroom for J. Gilbert Grubb Motor Company, a Chevrolet dealer; the building was completed in 1923. Located at 746 Granby Street, it is the only building in Murdaugh's photograph still standing and is presently occupied by Bob's Gun Shop and Sporting Goods. *Sargeant Memorial Room, Norfolk Public Library.*

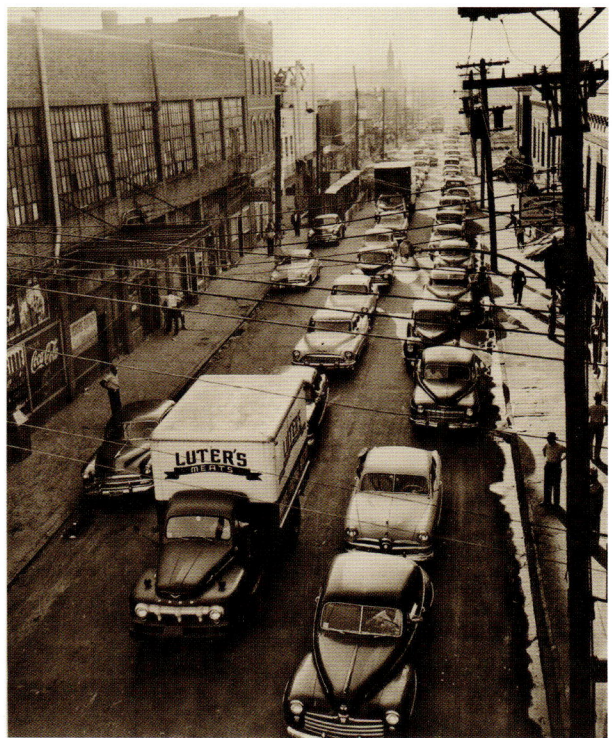

Brambleton Avenue: Photographed in 1955, this picture demonstrates traffic congestion that were the result of the clash between Norfolk's narrow streets and size of the modern automobile.

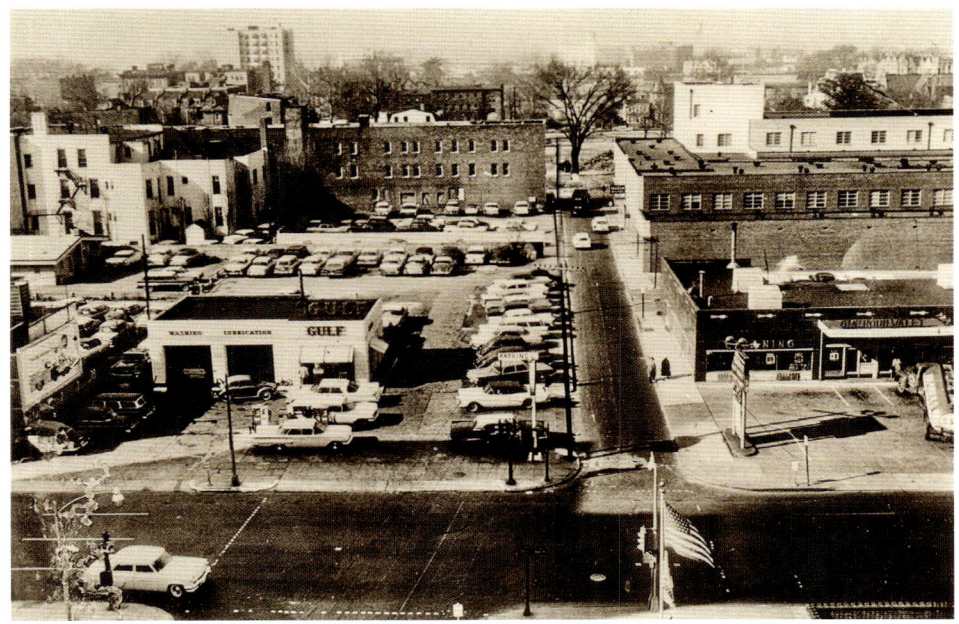

BRAMBLETON TO HAMPTON: The transformation of Brambleton Avenue, formerly Queen Street and today one of Norfolk's most important transportation corridors, had a profound impact on the business and residential communities caught up in the street's expansion and extension to Hampton Boulevard. This is Brambleton Avenue looking west before extension in a photograph (top) taken by Eugene G. Vickhouse on January 27, 1960. The street in the center is Dartmouth Street, which was subsequently eliminated. Brambleton Avenue extended, looking toward The Hague on the right, was photographed (bottom) by George Haycox, of Haycox Photographic, on February 8, 1964.

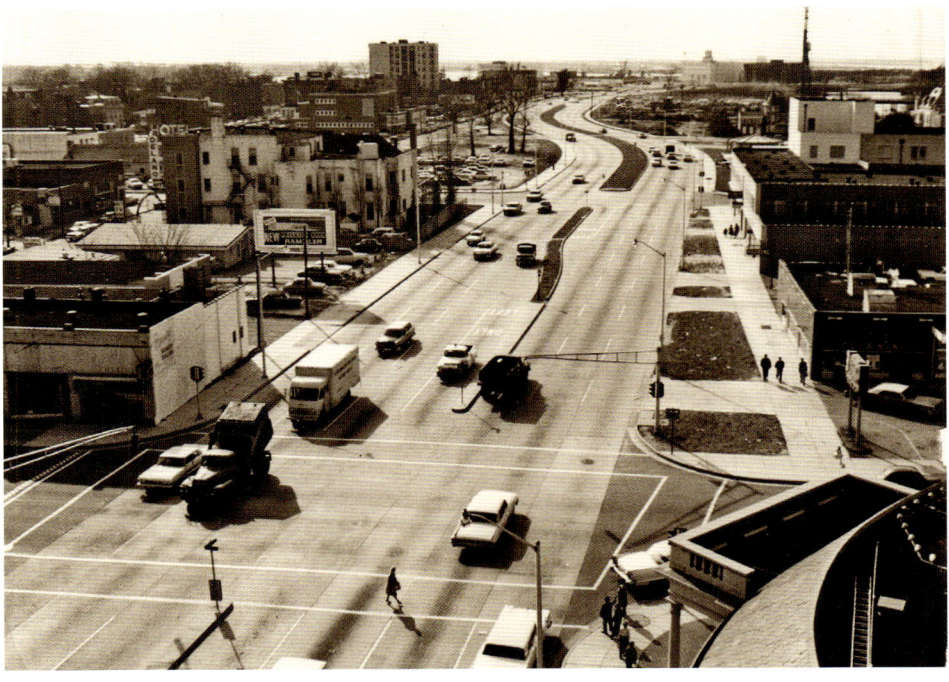

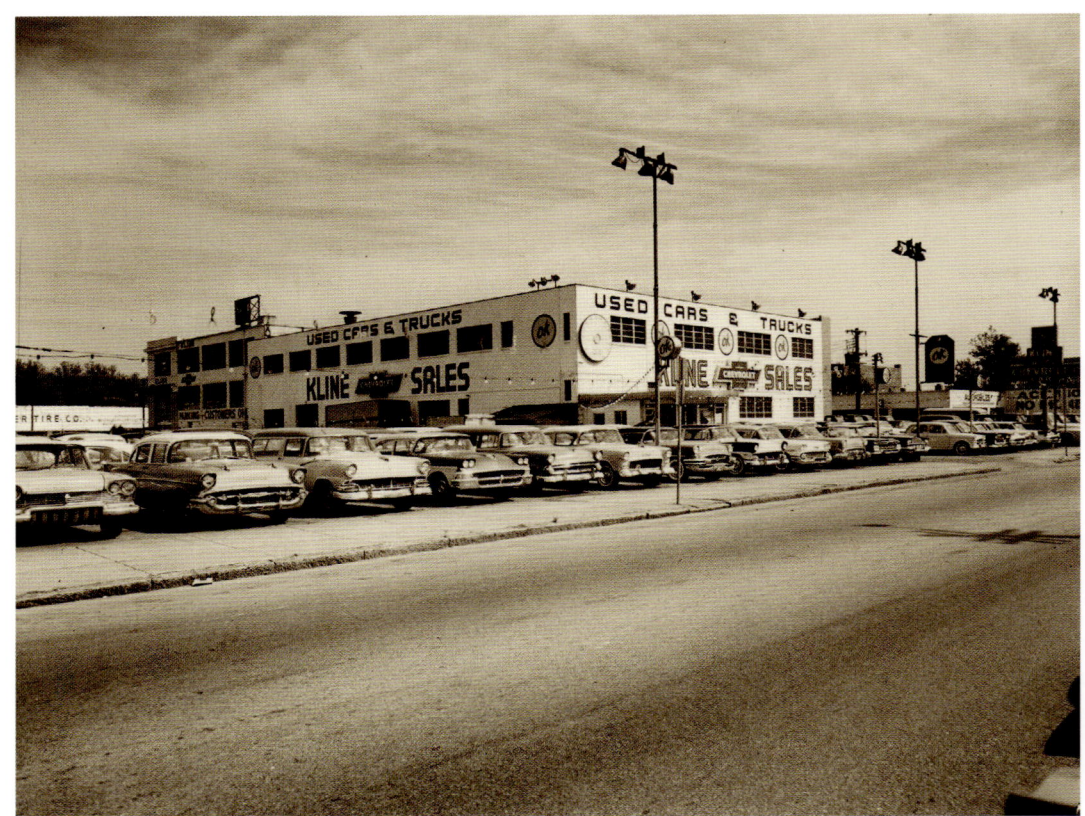

THE BEST OF THE BEST: The building occupied by Kline Chevrolet used car dealership in this 1959 photograph is the best remaining and most impressive former car dealership building in the Auto Row Historic District. The three-story Trant Motor Company building was built in 1924 with a 1950 addition. The 1924 structure was designed by the prolific architectural firm of Neff & Thompson; the façade faces Monticello Avenue. The building at 1301–1303 Monticello Avenue is presently occupied by a U-Haul Moving and Storage dealership.

In the Wards

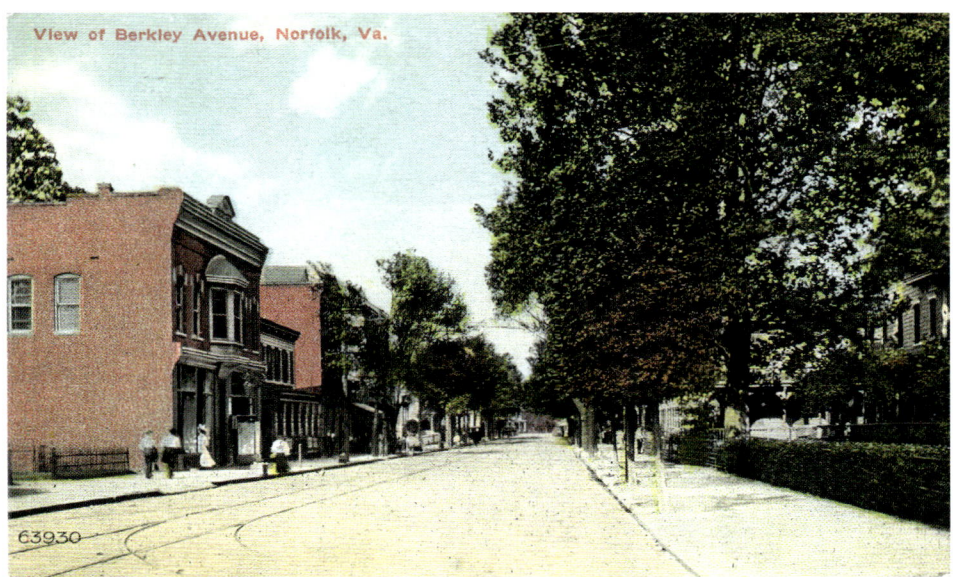

HERBERTSVILLE BECOMES BERKLEY: After the Civil War, Herbertsville was developed by Lycurgus Berkley (1827–1881), who incorporated the town that now bore his name in 1866. The city of Norfolk annexed Berkley in 1906. The oldest and most historic part of Berkley disappeared first with the Norfolk–Portsmouth Bridge–Tunnel, opened on May 23, 1952, and, later, the development of Interstate 464 that cut through the neighborhood in the 1980s. This is a hand-colored postcard showing Berkley Avenue as it looked in 1910.

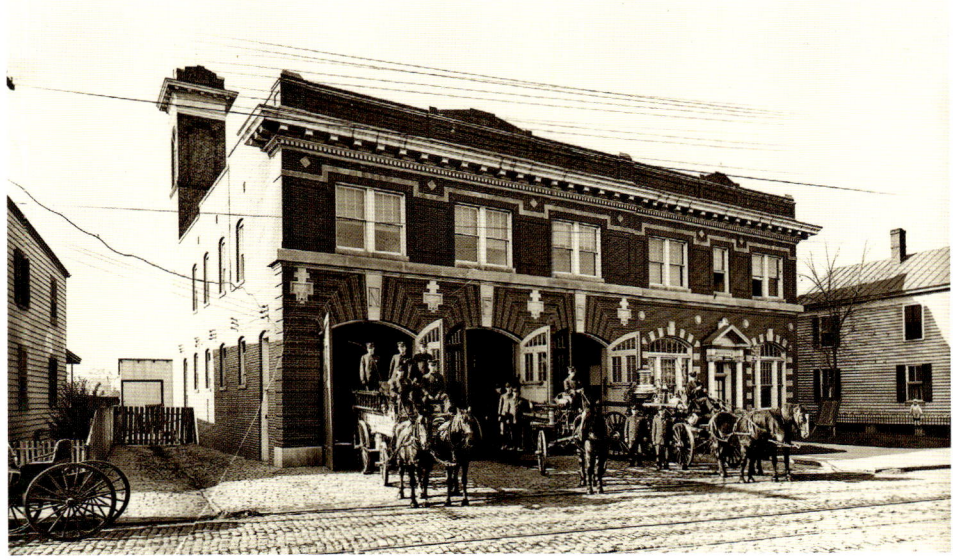

LIBERTY STREET FIRE STATION: Harry Mann took this photograph of the Norfolk Fire Department's Berkley Station No. 8, an engine company, in 1913. The station was located at 311 Liberty Street. The Liberty Street we know today should not be confused with the location of the original street to bear that name.

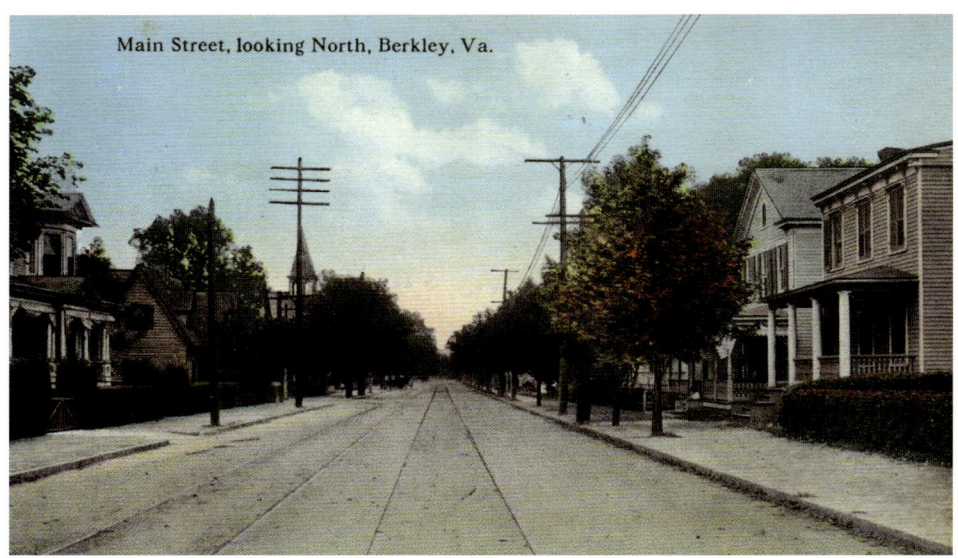

BERKLEY'S MAIN STREET: Norfolk's Berkley section has its own Main Street, shown here on this hand-colored early postcard dating to 1910. Berkley's earliest known name was Powder Point, documented by William Byrd as he passed through the area in 1728. The name came about in 1700 when the little settlement there was chosen to house the first powder magazine outside the town of Norfolk. Between 1790 and 1799, it was called Washington Town, one of the first places in the country to be named for Founding Father George Washington, nine years after his death. Two of the first streets in the section were named Washington and Liberty, the latter for patriotic reasons. Shortly before 1800, the town was called Ferry Point because there was a ferry dock at the foot of Liberty (Chestnut) Street that connected to the county dock on the Norfolk waterfront. Herbertsville, for the Herbert family that owned Riveredge, is also a name associated with Berkley.

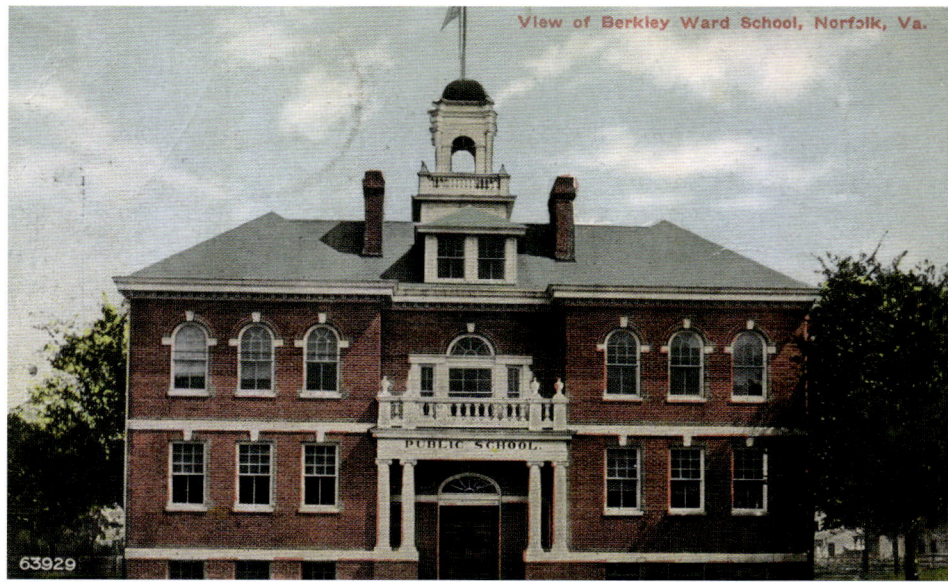

BERKLEY WARD SCHOOL: This school building, shown on this 1910 hand-colored postcard, was located on Walker Avenue between Grayson and Brunswick streets. J. Paul Spence was the principal at that time.

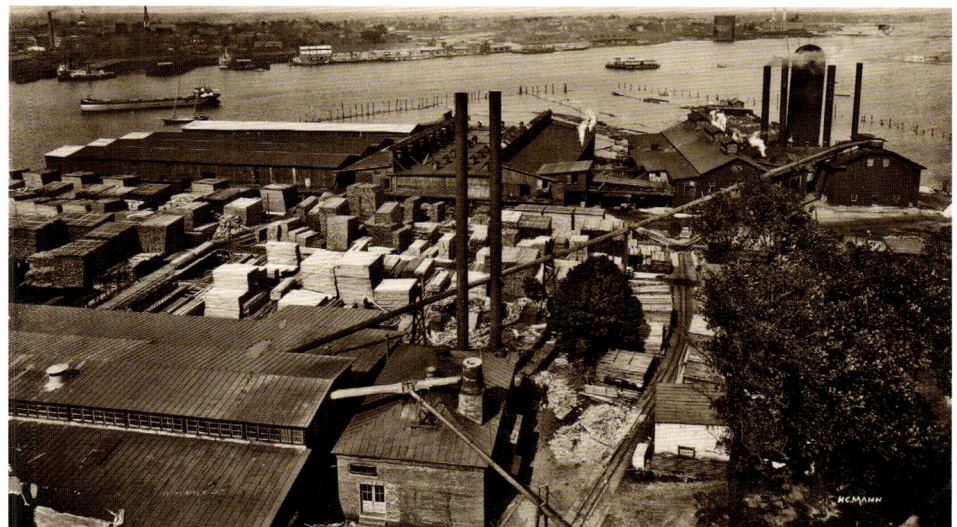

FOSBURGH LUMBER COMPANY: Fosburgh was located on the Berkley waterfront at Walnut Street and Cummers Lane, was photographed by Harry C. Mann shortly after the death of company owner Edgar Charles Fosburgh, who died on trip to Essex, New York, on September 10, 1910. Fosburgh and James F. Barnett founded the company in 1903; it operated from this location until 1919. Fosburgh was an officer of the Cummer Company, another Berkley lumber yard prior, from 1892 until he started his own business.

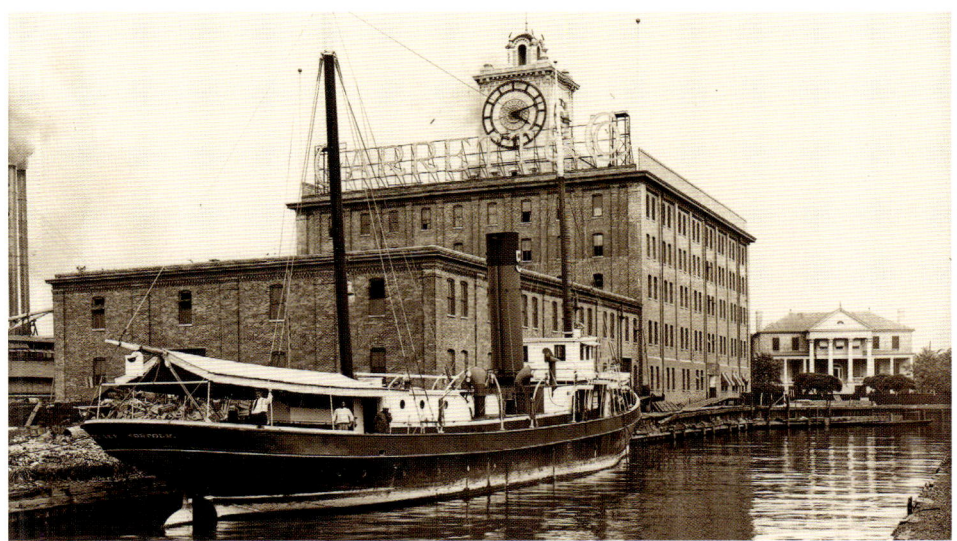

GARRETT AND COMPANY WINERY: The Garrett winery was located at the foot of Berkley's Chestnut Street next to one of the first United States Marine hospitals (the building to the right, by that time the Garrett family's home) and the boat *Relief* at the pier were photographed by Harry C. Mann in 1910. The Garrett winery, begun in late 1903 by Paul Garrett, at peak production, had the capacity for four million gallons and two million bottles of the company's Virginia Dare sparkling wine and boasted the largest clock in the world. The winery closed in November 1916 when Virginia prohibited the sale of alcohol ahead of the ratification of the Eighteenth Amendment. After the winery building was destroyed by fire the Garretts moved out of Berkley. The house was razed decades later for the downtown tunnel connecting Norfolk and Portsmouth.

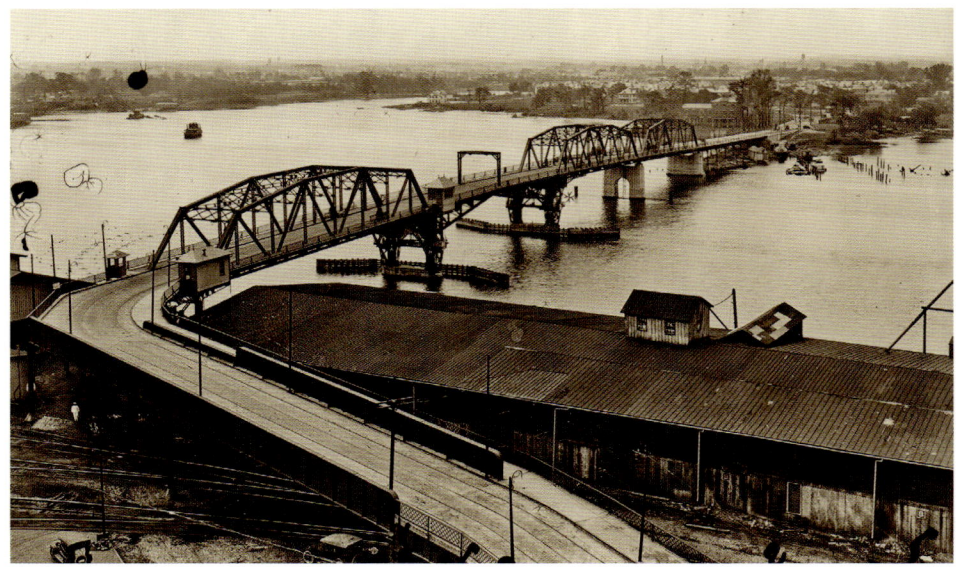

OLD BERKLEY BRIDGE: The old Berkley Bridge extended from the foot of East Main Street to South Main Street in Berkley. Harry C. Mann took this picture from Norfolk looking toward Berkley just after the bridge was completed in August 1916. The bridge was a privately owned toll bridge that cost travelers two cents to cross. The city of Norfolk acquired the bridge in 1946 and took it down in 1952 after constructing a larger structure. At the far end of the bridge (left) is Riveredge, built about 1728 by John Herbert and, later, the home of Mary Pinkney Hardy, mother of General Douglas A. MacArthur.

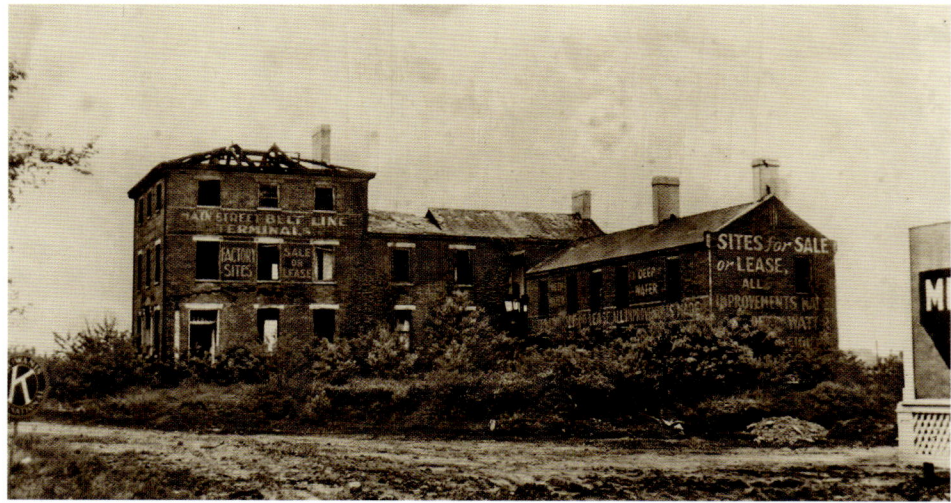

GENERAL MACARTHUR'S BERKLEY CONNECTION: During his visit to Norfolk in June 1951, General Douglas MacArthur made a pilgrimage to the Hardy home, birthplace of his mother, located in the Berkley section of the city at the end of Main Street. Mary Pinkney Hardy's father, Thomas Asbury Hardy, was a prominent local businessman when he purchased the estate in 1847. Built decades before the Revolutionary War and boasting more than 20 rooms, the Georgian Revival house sat unoccupied for more than a decade when this picture was taken on May 4, 1951, having earlier been used as a railroad terminal. Though it was proposed as a national landmark, architects estimated the cost of restoration in excess of $100,000 for initial repairs. Restoration never took place and it was razed.

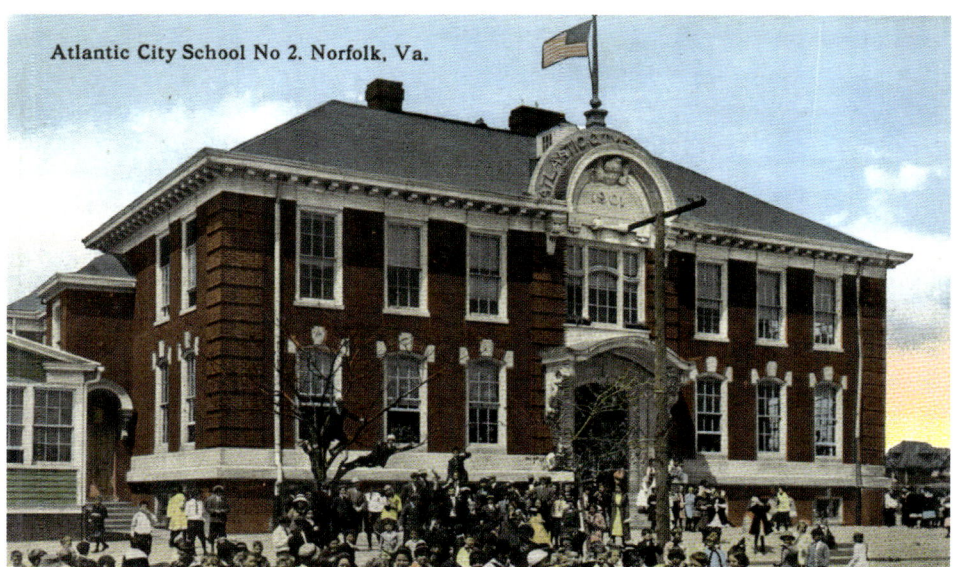

ATLANTIC CITY SCHOOL NUMBER 2: This school, renamed Robert E. Lee School in November 1912, is shown on this hand-colored Harry C. Mann postcard. The building, constructed in 1901 and located at the corner of Graydon and Moran Avenues, was in Norfolk's Atlantic City section. The principal was George L. Fentress when Mann photographed the school. Atlantic City, annexed by the city of Norfolk in 1890, covered a broad swath, including both sides of Colley Avenue southwest of Olney Road and extending from the Norfolk and Western Railroad terminal at Lambert's Point to the railroad tracks at Twenty-third Street all the way to Elmwood Cemetery. The area was so large that three new public schools were built there after 1890: Atlantic City School Number 1, renamed the Patrick Henry School; also Atlantic City School Number 3, renamed John Marshall School, located on Omohundro Avenue, and the school building shown here.

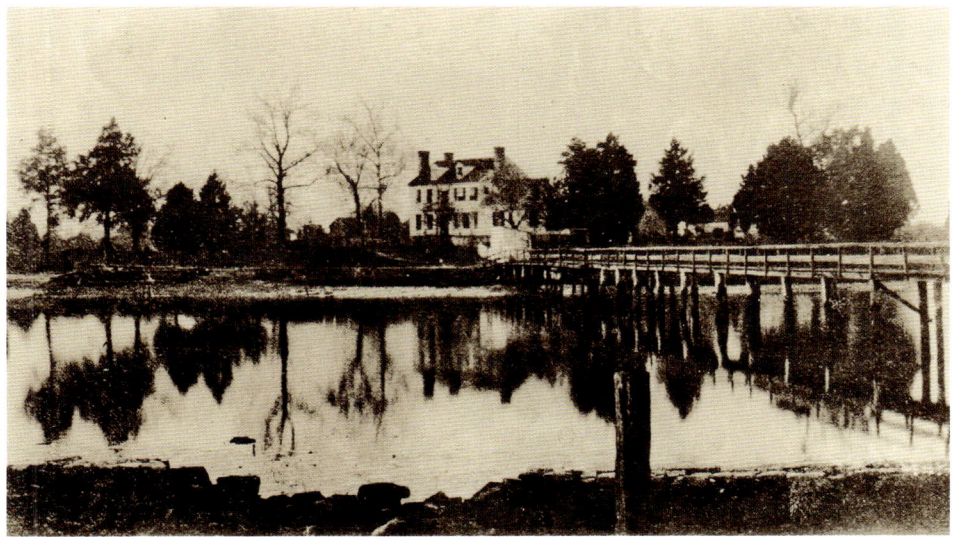

GHENT: This 1885 photograph shows Ghent, then a farm area of roughly ten acres owned by Richard Drummond, whose home is pictured here. The name Ghent was derived from the Belgian city in which the peace treaty ending the War of 1812 was signed. Ghent was laid out in 1890, and the name retained. A new bridge replaced the old Drummond footbridge.

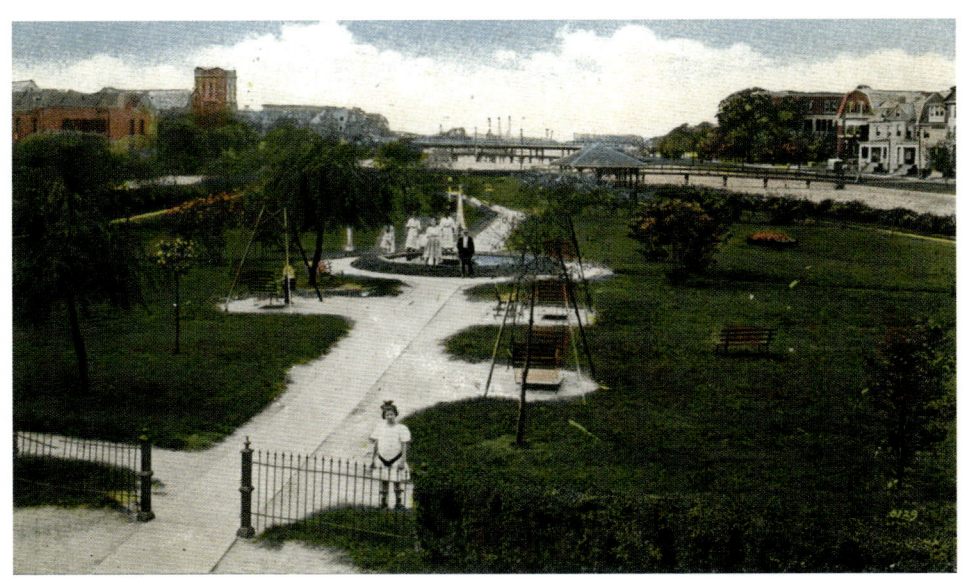

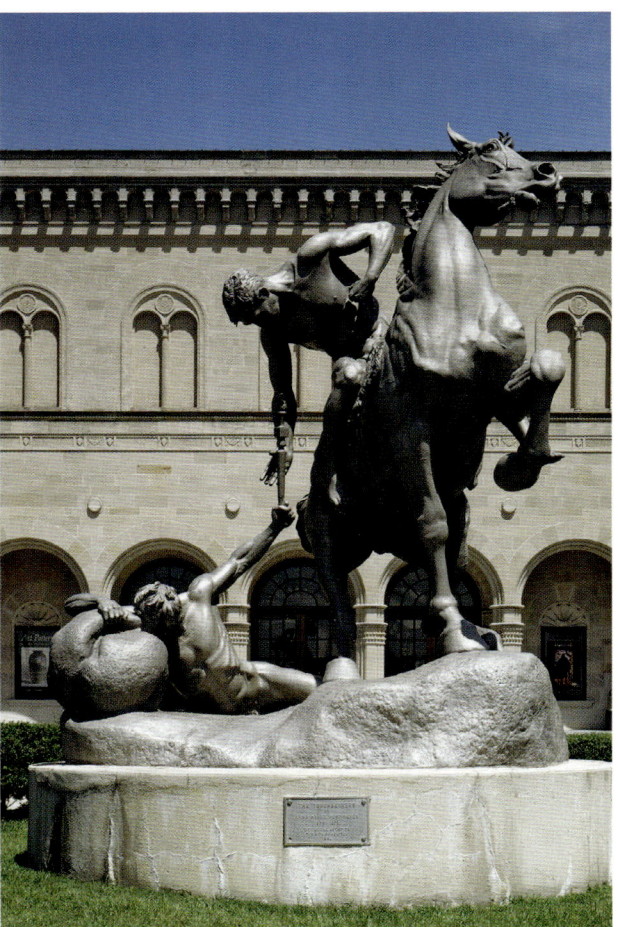

FROM PARK TO MUSEUM: This pre-1910 view (top) of Lee Park shows the three bridges to Ghent in the background, including the Botetourt Street Bridge, a streetcar trestle and a footbridge that connected Yarmouth Street with Fairfax Avenue. The Chrysler Museum of Art now occupies the footprint of what was Lee Park. This view (bottom, *Library of Congress*), taken by Carol M. Highsmith from the front drive of the Chrysler Museum of Art, formerly the Norfolk Museum of Arts and Sciences, shows the museum's iconic sculpture, *The Torchbearers*, by Anna Hyatt Huntington (1876–1973), was gifted to the city by the artist in 1954.

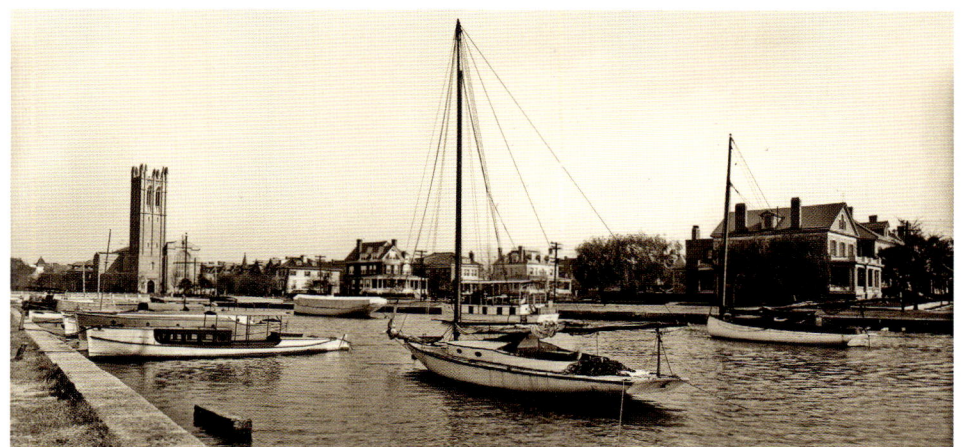

CHRIST & SAINT LUKE'S EPISCOPAL CHURCH: The church's history can be documented back to the Elizabeth River Parish established in the late 1630s by English people in the area now known as Norfolk; the church's banner is dated 1637. The location of the first two borough churches is unknown but the 1739 building is known to have been abandoned in 1800 when the congregation moved across the street to a new house of worship. When it burned in 1825, Christ Church then moved to a building on Freemason Street. From this background a second parish was formed in 1832 and the vestry of Christ Church authorized refurbishment of the old Borough Church, renamed Saint Paul's and still in operation today. In 1872 a third parish, Saint Luke's was created. As Norfolk grew, other Episcopal parishes were formed. In 1909 Christ Church decided to move to the new suburb of Ghent and laid the cornerstone for the current building on October 28, 1909, the feast of Saint Simon & Saint Jude. Opening services were held on Christmas Day, 1910. Harry C. Mann took this stunningly beautiful photograph of yachts and sailboats anchored in Ghent's Smith's Creek, a portion of which was renamed The Hague, about 1915. Christ Episcopal Church is to the left. Fairfax and Pembroke Avenues (left to right) terminate on Mowbray Arch.

THE MERGER: Saint Luke's, shown in other photographs herein, had built a magnificent building on Granby Street on land presently occupied by the Walter E. Hoffman United States Courthouse but it was destroyed by a lightning fire in 1921 and the church moved to Colonial Avenue (adjacent to H. D. Oliver's Funeral Apartments). Given the economic realities in 1935 the Episcopal bishop decided to consolidate Saint Luke's, Saint Andrew's (in West Ghent), and Christ Church at the facilities of Christ Church, naming it Christ & Saint Luke's. Within five years Saint Andrew's resumed its own identity and returned to its facilities on Graydon Avenue. Christ & Saint Luke's is an example of English perpendicular architecture as interpreted by the Gothic Revivalists of the mid- and late-nineteenth century; it is shown here from its Olney Road exposure in 1950.

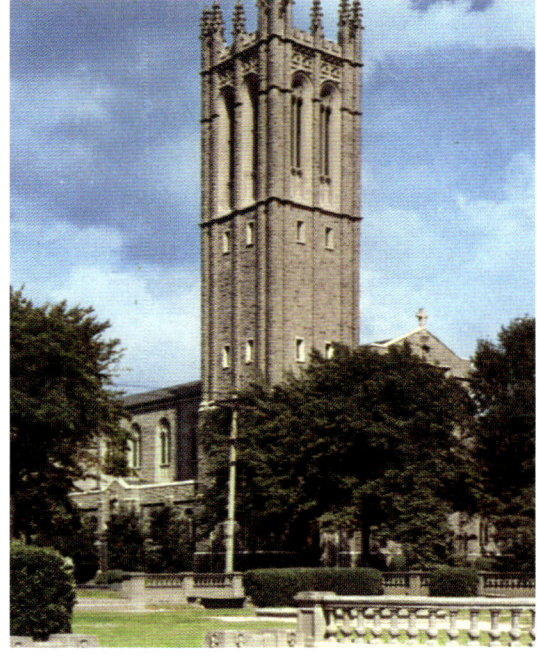

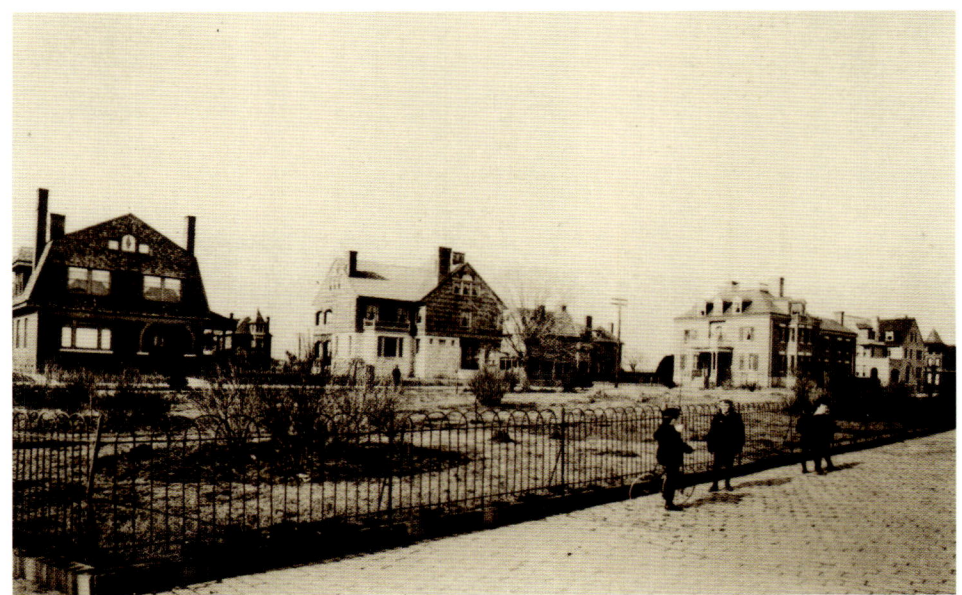

GHENT GROWS: Children pause from playing by the fence around Beechwood Place, a small park between Pembroke Avenue and Warren Crescent, located at the southern end of Colonial Avenue. The photograph was taken in 1895 during Ghent's development. The large house on the right was the residence of John R. Graham Jr. Fergus Reid, a cotton merchant, owned the house in the center. *Sargeant Memorial Room, Norfolk Public Library.*

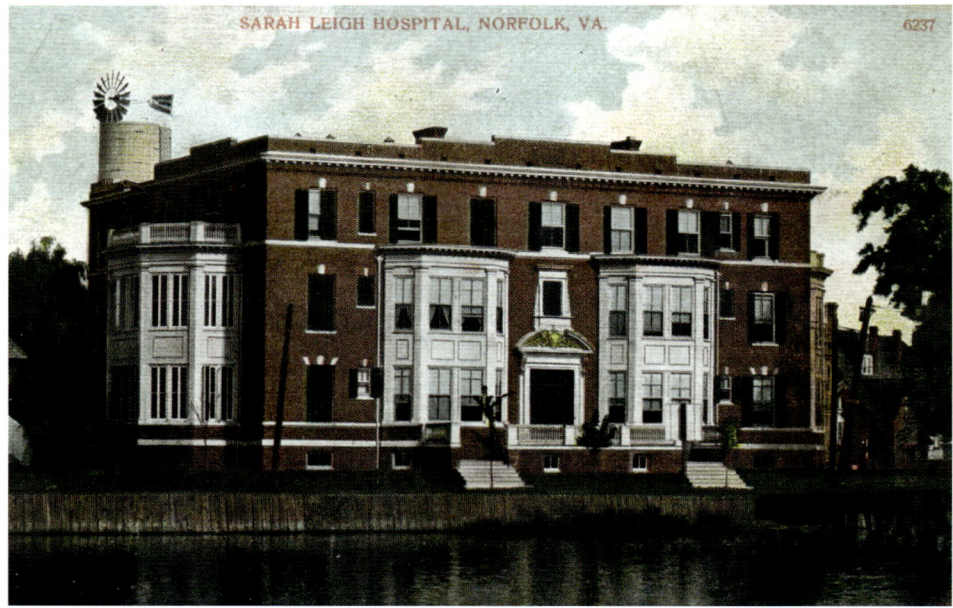

SARAH LEIGH HOSPITAL: This Harry C. Mann hand-colored postcard, from his original photograph, is pre-1910 and shows Sarah Leigh Hospital facing Smith's Creek—The Hague. Note the early bulkheading, and also the footbridge far right. The private hospital, built in the Beaux Arts style in 1902 on Mowbray Arch, was founded by Norfolk physician Dr. Southgate Leigh, who began practicing medicine in the city in 1893.

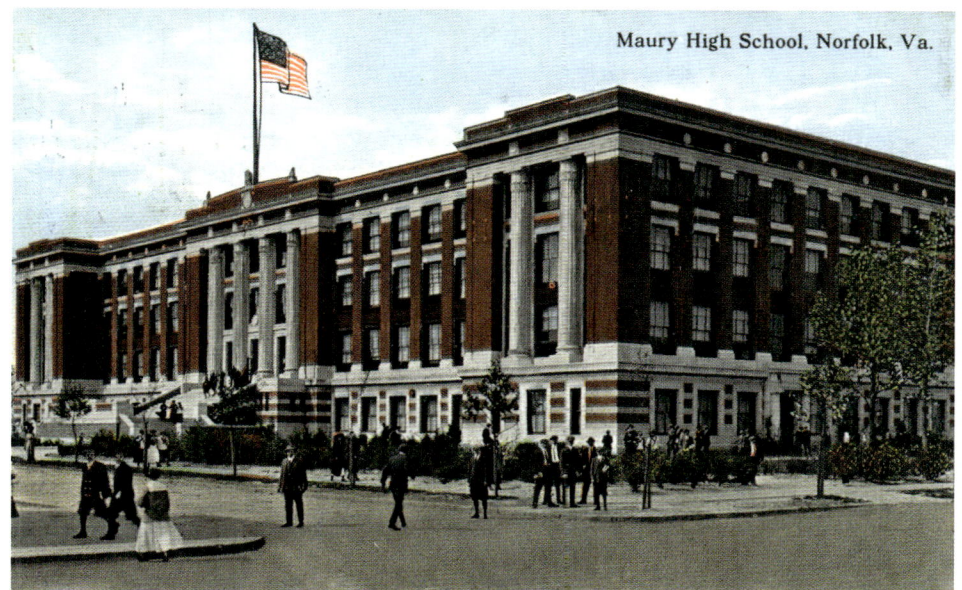

MAURY HIGH SCHOOL: Maury, shown here on a postcard that dates to 1915, was named in honor of Matthew Fontaine Maury, the Pathfinder of the Seas and commodore of the Confederate Navy, and except for General Douglas MacArthur, perhaps the most decorated American in history. The school name was suggested by the second wife of Dr. Frank Anthony Walke, Belle W. Tunstall. Dr. Walke entered the United States Navy as an assistant surgeon after graduating from the Universities of Virginia and Pennsylvania in 1851. Stationed at the United States Naval Hospital at Portsmouth, he went through the yellow fever epidemic there in 1855. He left naval service in 1857, opening a drug store in Norfolk while also practicing medicine. Walke was Maury's contemporary, and both joined the Confederacy within days of Virginia's secession from the Union in April 1861—Walke as a surgeon, Maury as a commander in the navy. Belle Walke's suggestion of Maury as a name was readily accepted.

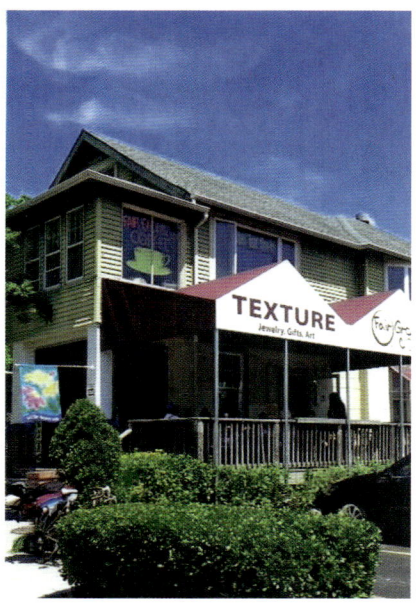

TEXTURE AND ELLIOT'S FAIR GROUNDS: Located at 806 Baldwin Avenue at the corner of Baldwin and Colley Avenues, the two businesses occupy the first and second stories of this renovated Victorian house in the heart of Ghent. Elliot's Fair Grounds, opened in 2001 by Elliot Juren, is the oldest independent coffeehouse in the city. Fair Grounds recently came under the management of new owner Mike Dimirsky. Founded in 1999 by Gail Juren, Texture provides a local source of unique, affordable gifts, jewelry and art. The parking lot installed for Elliot's (now Red Dog Saloon) customers in the spring of 1985 is sited between 806 Baldwin Avenue and Red Dog Saloon. *Elliot and Gail Juren.*

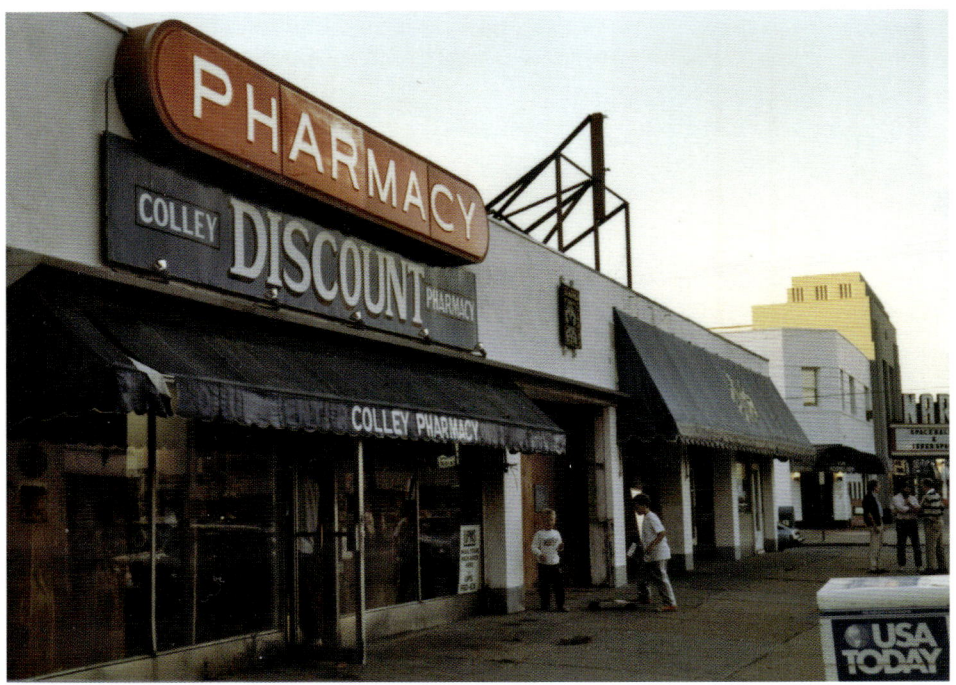

TRANSFORMING COLLEY AVENUE: Elliot Juren opened his Ghent restaurant in 1978 (top), with only 48 seats. This picture, taken in October 1987, shows the beginnings of construction on the pink Art Deco landmark at 1421 Colley Avenue. Down the street, far right in the picture, is the iconic Naro movie theatre. To make way for a Elliot's customer parking, the house shown here (bottom), which had been home to a popular local bookshop, was razed in April 1985. *Elliot and Gail Juren.*

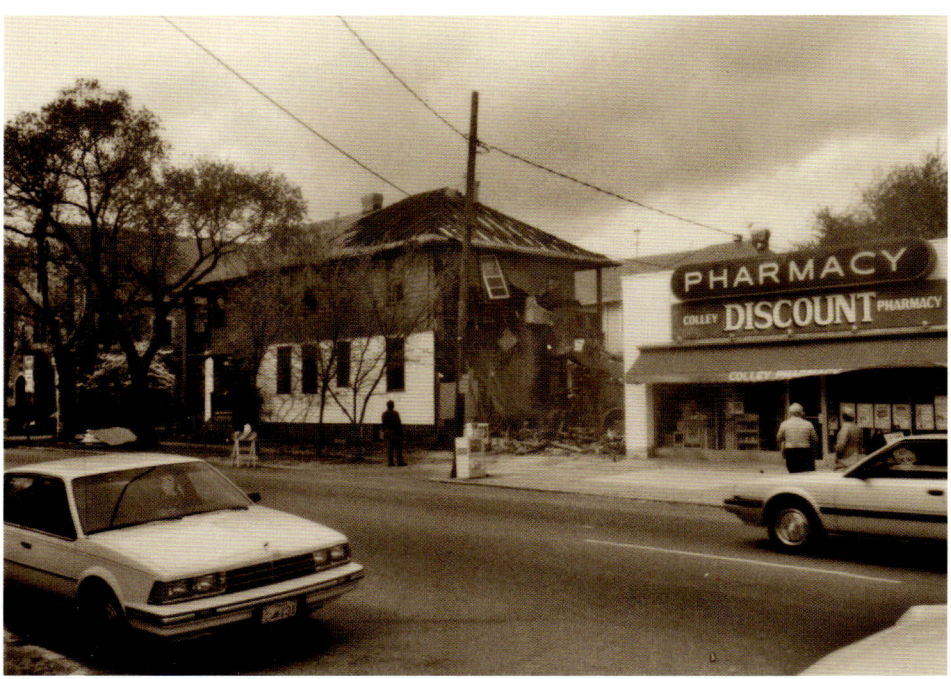

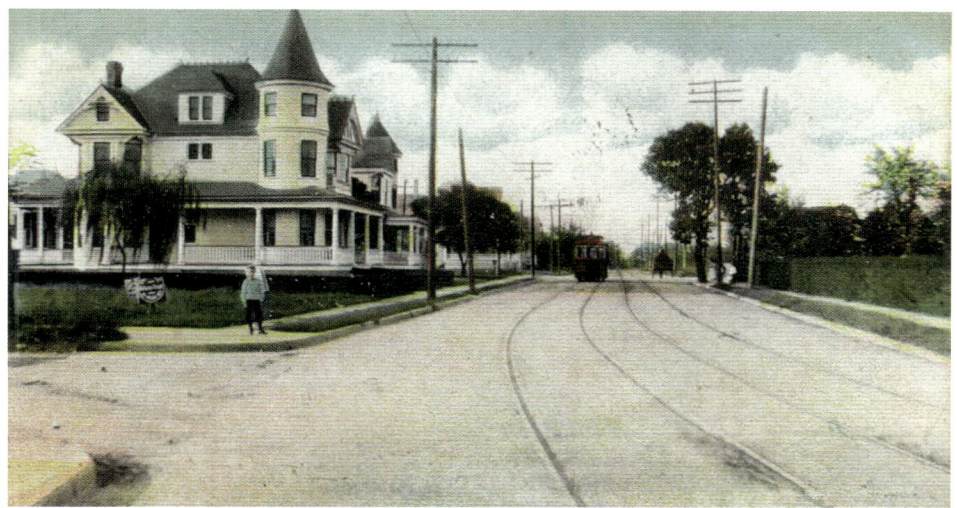

STREETCAR SUBURBS: In 1902, a large swath of land along the Lafayette River and north of Atlantic City was annexed to the city of Norfolk, including North Colonial Avenue, Park Place, Colonial Place, and Riverview. The early development of this land coincided with the 1907 Jamestown Exposition. Large annexations had increased the city's size threefold by 1906 but the outermost suburbs still remained within three miles of downtown. Park Place is an excellent example of the streetcar suburbanization of Norfolk that took place in the late-nineteenth and early twentieth centuries. This scene of early Park Place, on a postcard dated August 21, 1907, shows the original streetcar line situated along Granby and Thirty-fifth Streets. City Park is on the right.

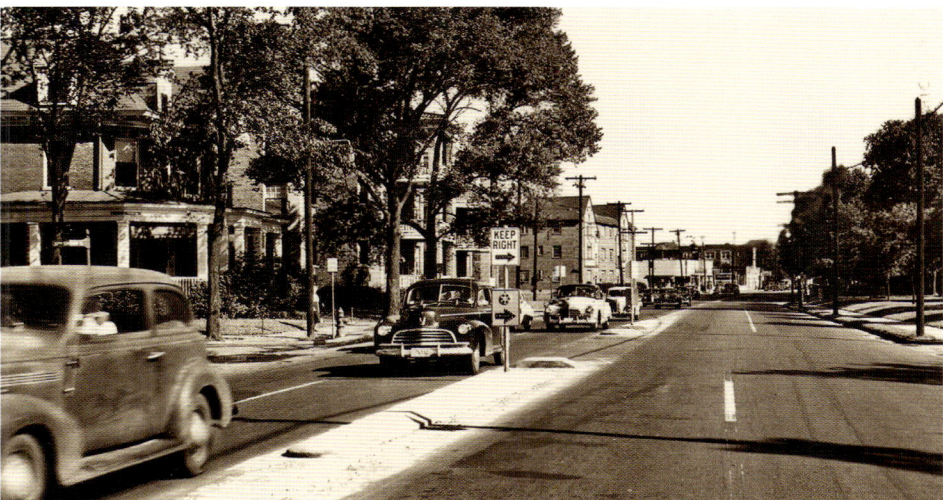

BUS REPLACES STREETCAR: Norfolk started going "all-bus" after the Second World War, a move that necessitated the removal of rail track throughout the city, and the installation of vehicular traffic islands and curbing in its place. Granby Street between Thirty-seventh and Thirty-eighth streets was photographed by Charles S. Borjes after new traffic islands were installed in 1950. The house in the foreground was built in 1909. City Park is on the right. The city's all-bus substitution program was started in September 1947, the first step in Norfolk's public transportation initiative. Norfolk's first public transportation system was owned and operated by the Virginia Transit Company, which also operated the public transportation system in Richmond, Virginia. *Sergeant Memorial Room, Norfolk Public Library.*

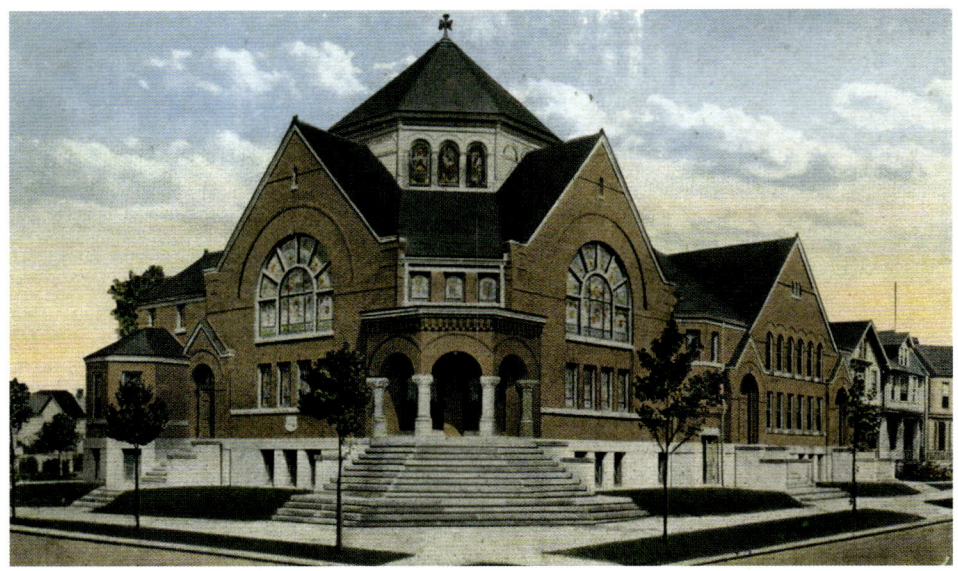

PARK PLACE BAPTIST CHURCH: The church, designed by architect George Washington Kramer, was constructed in 1913 and is shown here on a white border postcard of the period. The church located at 436 West Thirty-first Street features Classical Revival details and stonework. The building's large arched window openings dominate the street fronts on Colonial Avenue and West Thirty-first Street; however, significant alteration to the building, which presumably took place in or around 1958, has rendered it unrecognizable as the sanctuary completed over 100 years ago.

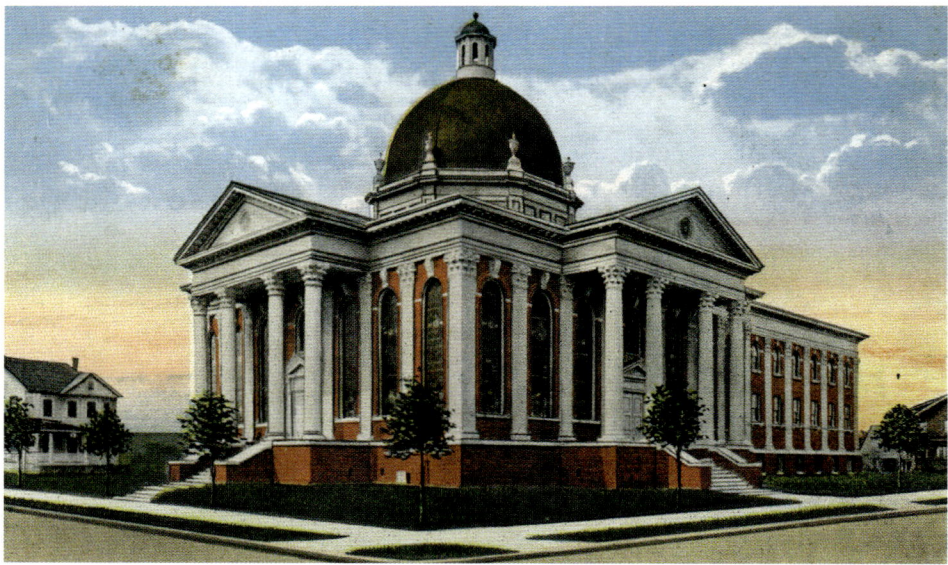

PARK PLACE METHODIST CHURCH: Located at 500 Thirty-fourth Street, it was built in 1920 and is shown here on a postcard of the period. While the building retains many of the features of its original construction, including a monumental portico with stone Corinthian columns supporting a stone pediment and full entablature that marks the south façade, subsequent alteration of the exterior has significantly changed the church's appearance. The large dome and cupola as well as the second set of pilasters and pediment facing Colonial Avenue were removed.

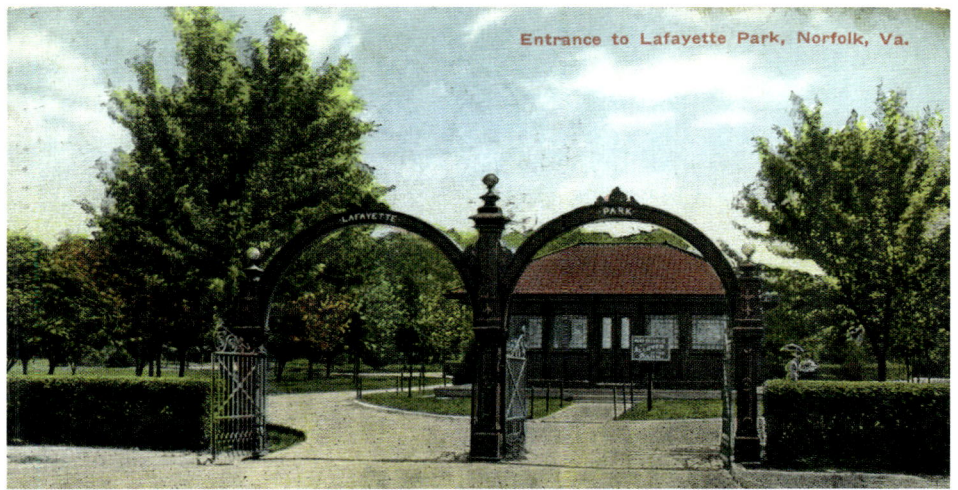

CITY PARK AND ZOO: In 1892, the city of Norfolk purchased 65 acres of land that is currently occupied by Lafayette Park and the Virginia Zoo from six Norfolk residents. This is the Granby Street gate (top) to the park as it appeared on this postcard, dated September 25, 1910, from a photograph originally taken by Harry C. Mann. Though it is hard to see, there is a sign in front of the building that tells visitors "No Dogs Allowed." The house (bottom) in this 1910 picture was located on the grounds of Lafayette Park on the river. The location of the structure was on the point behind the old Conservatory, facing Lafayette Residence Park. At the time, animals were housed in rows of cages nearby, separated by paved rows, which allowed visitors to drive through the park. Also during this period, tennis courts, a playground, and a baseball diamond were added to the park.

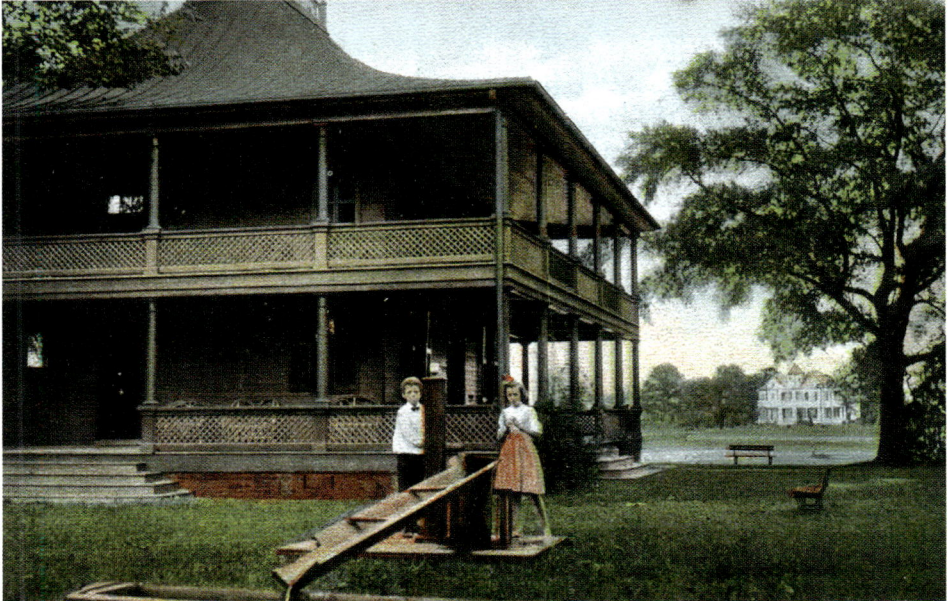

LAFAYETTE PARK: Seven years after the city acquired the land for a public park, in 1899, it was given the name Lafayette Park, and the following year the park began collecting zoological specimens for exhibit. By 1901, the park's collection had over 200 animals, birds and reptiles in it. This is Lafayette Park in 1910. *Detroit Publishing Company, Library of Congress.*

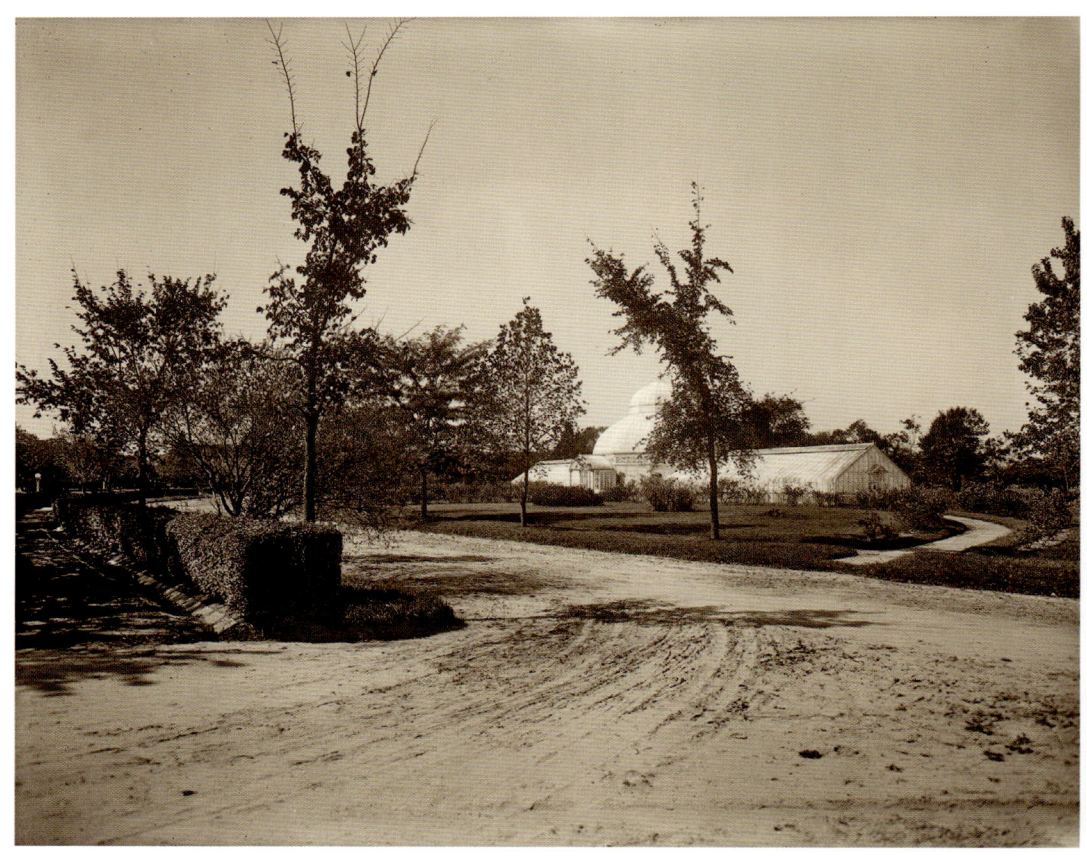

Lafayette Park Conservatory: The conservatory, which cost $10,000 to build, is shown here as it looked in 1910. The Conservatory was acquired in 1907 for the park, and although there is no record as to how the city obtained the structure, it is commonly believed that the Conservatory was donated by the Jamestown Exposition's directors on the condition that the city move it from the Exposition grounds at Sewell's Point to the park. *Detroit Publishing Company, Library of Congress.*

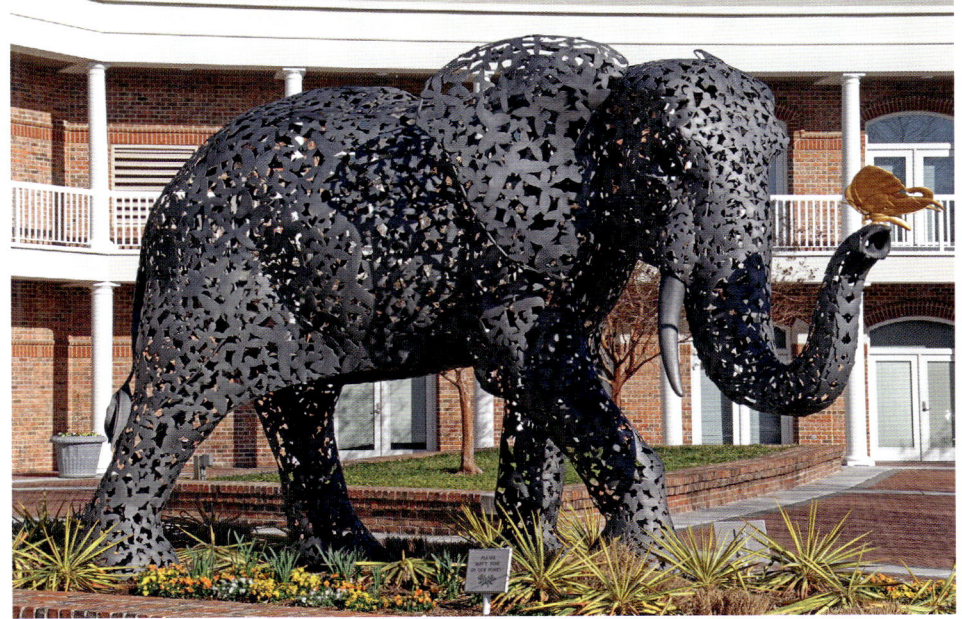

VIRGINIA ZOO: The zoo's elephant sculpture, unveiled on January 16, 2010, at the front entrance to the park, is a life-size aluminum sculpture of an African elephant whose body is composed of more than 10,000 butterfly silhouettes. On the end of the elephant's upturned trunk is a gilded butterfly, whose wings are shaped like elephants. The colossal sculpture stands 10 feet tall, 16 feet long and 7 feet wide. The artist of this iconic work is Matthew Gray Palmer, of Harbor, Washington. Winfield S. Danielson III took the picture shown here (top). The zoo, situated on 53 acres separated in 1974 from Lafayette Park, now houses over 400 animals, birds and reptiles. Here, a child interacts with one of the zoo's tigers through the viewing glass of the tiger pool. The picture (bottom) was taken by David Totten. *Virginia Zoo*.

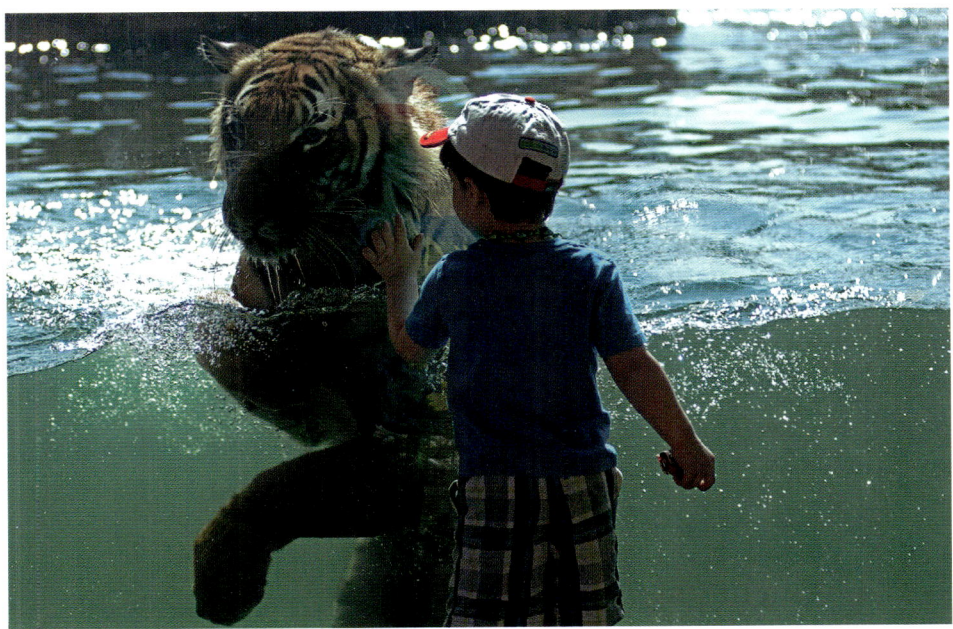

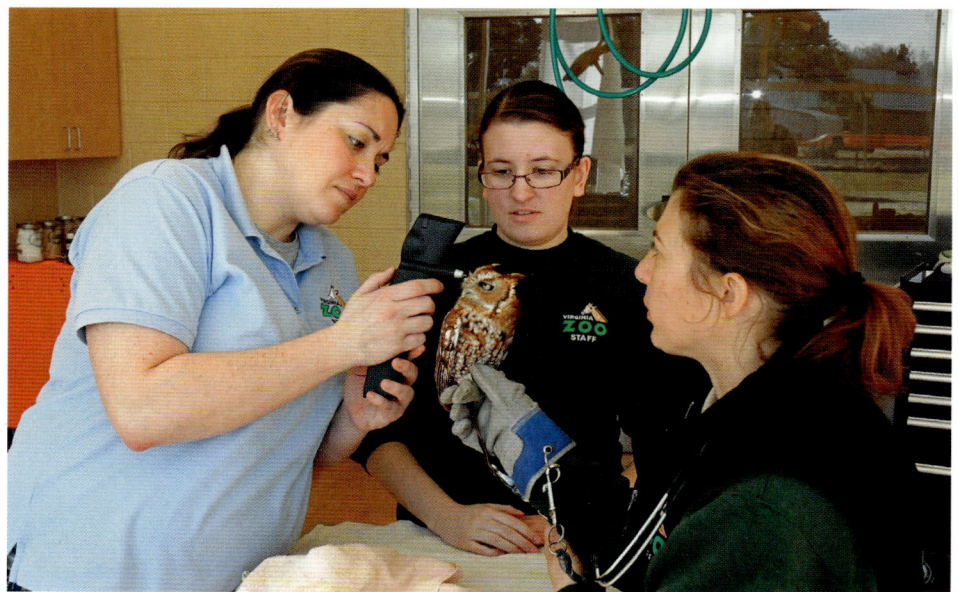

CARING FOR THE ANIMALS, BIRDS AND REPTILES: Alicyn Cross, a Virginia Zoo extern and veterinary student from Virginia Tech's Virginia-Maryland Regional College of Veterinary Medicine, observes Dr. Amanda Guthrie, the zoo's veterinarian, checking for glaucoma in the eyes of Erroll, an eastern screech owl who's been squinting lately, while he perches on veterinary technician Leah Rooker's hand in the new $4 million Animal Wellness Campus' veterinary hospital on February 19, 2014. Guthrie and Rooker have been operating out of the Wellness Campus since January. The photograph was taken by Winfield S. Danielson III. *Virginia Zoo.*

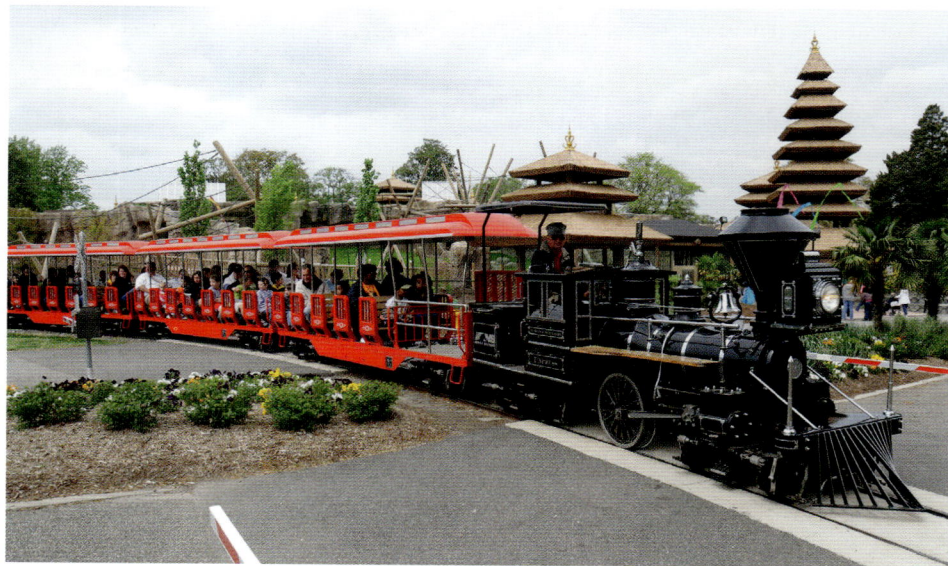

ALL ABOARD: The Virginia Zoo's train, the Norfolk Southern Express, officially opened as a new feature on October 18, 2008; it is shown here, photographed by Winfield S. Danielson III, with the zoo's Trail of the Tiger exhibit as the backdrop. The train is a one-third scale model of a Collis P. Huntington steam engine. The permanent track is three-quarters of a mile long. *Virginia Zoo.*

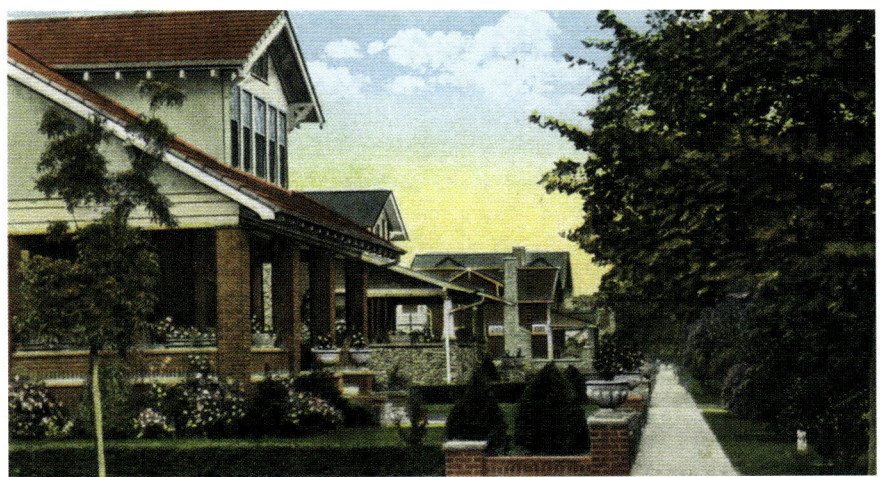

NORFOLK'S WINONA HISTORIC DISTRICT: Winona was listed on the National Register of Historic Places in 2001. The boundaries of the residential neighborhood occupy about 31 of the original 55 acres conceived by the Leicht Real Estate Company in 1909. Winona remains a small, cohesive residential neighborhood just north of Lafayette Residence Park, on the east side of the Lafayette River. The surrounding water, originally known as Tanner's Creek, distinctly forms the north, south and western boundaries of the neighborhood. The borders are further delineated by the streetscape, with Elmere Place forming the eastern edge, Ashland Circle delineating the west and northern boundaries and Holland Avenue and Huntington Crescent constituting the southern edge. According to a 1912 article on Winona, the streets are given a "gentle curve the principle one, Holland Avenue, following the shoreline, making them much more attractive than if they were straight and cut the tract into squares and rectangles." The Holland Avenue homes that appear on this 1920 white border postcard, starting with the house in the foreground and including each homes date of completion, are 1541 (1918), 1535 (1919), 1523 (1919) and 1519 (1916).

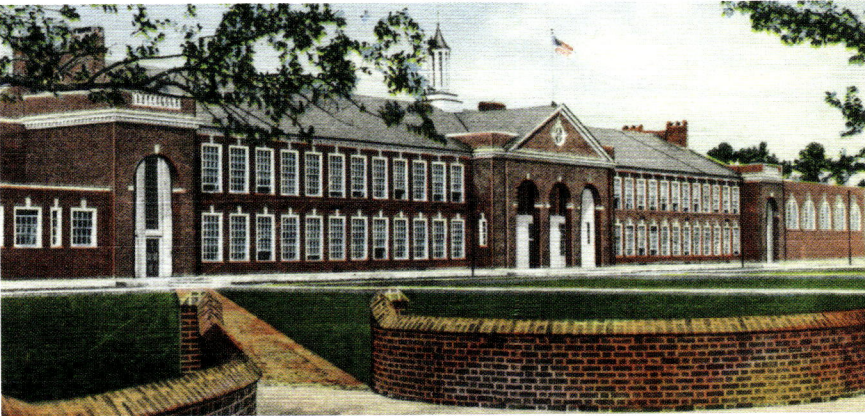

GRANBY HIGH SCHOOL: Opened in 1939, the school was previously known as Granby Street High School, reflecting the street on which it is located. Both the street and the school are named after John Manners, Marquis of Granby, a hero of the Seven Years' War. The twenty-four acre tract on which Granby was built was once part of the Talbot Plantation before the property was donated to the city by preeminent Virginian and lawyer Minton Wright Talbot. The postcard shown here is from the period the school first opened. In 1996, the school system invested $21 million in a construction project in order to expand and renovate the 57-year-old building.

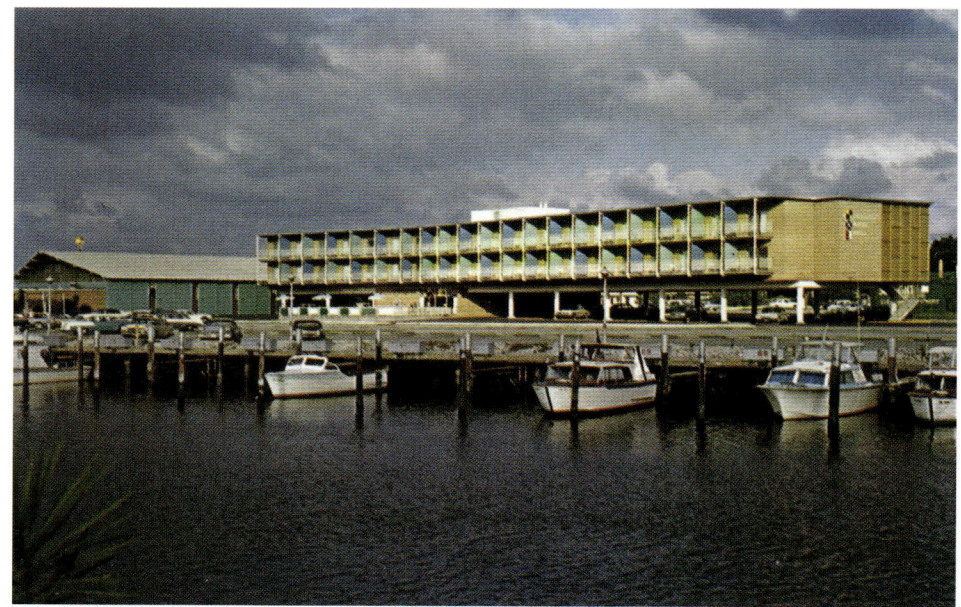

LAFAYETTE TRANSFORMATION: Haven Creek, part of the Lafayette River tributary of the Elizabeth River and part of the 1902 annexation, was eventually developed to accommodate a private country club, marina and motor hotel, the latter hosting many years of Norfolk International Azalea Festival events. The Lafayette Motor Hotel, shown here in 1960 (top), and the yacht club behind it, located at on Granby Street at the foot of the Granby Street Bridge, were constructed largely on a man-made spit of land that sprung from the marshes and soft banks of the creek. The River House apartment complex was developed by the S. L. Nusbaum Realty Company in 2009 on the site of the former Lafayette Motor Hotel and the Lafayette Yacht and Country Club. The picture shown here (bottom, *S. L. Nusbaum Realty Company*) was taken from the Colonial Place side of Haven Creek on September 30, 2009.

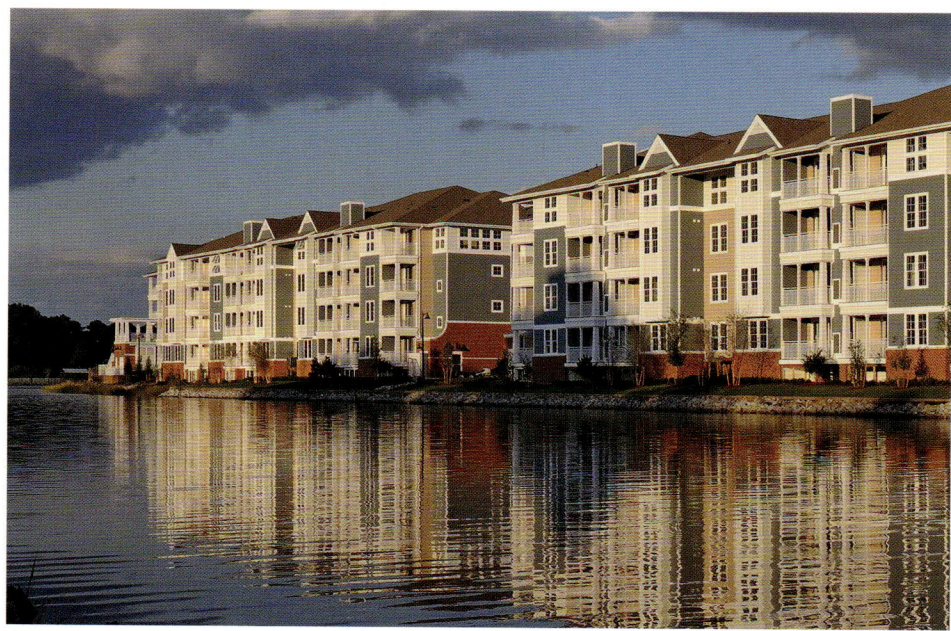

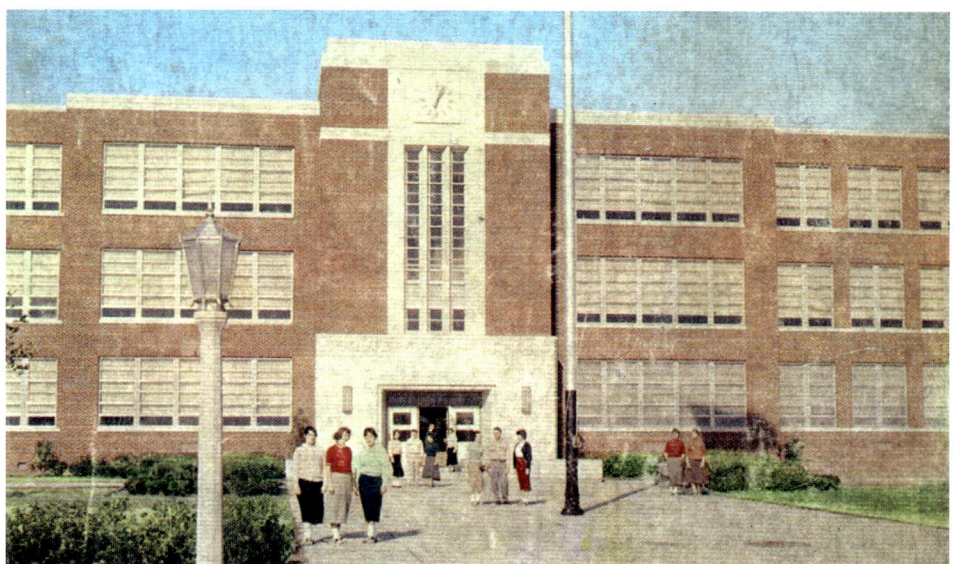

NORVIEW HIGH SCHOOL: In 1921, the first school building to be called "Norview" was a farmhouse, known as the Harlow house. In 1922, Norview students and their first principal, Harvey C. Barnes, moved into a new high school, on the site of what is today Norview Middle School on Sewell's Point Road. Barnes remained Norview's principal for 22 years, when he was replaced by Edwin W. Chittum, who subsequently became superintendent of Norfolk County Schools in 1949 and was a founding father of the city of Chesapeake, Virginia. In June 1952, the cornerstone was placed for the new Norview High School building located on Middleton Place (shown here). The first class to graduate from this building was the class of 1955.

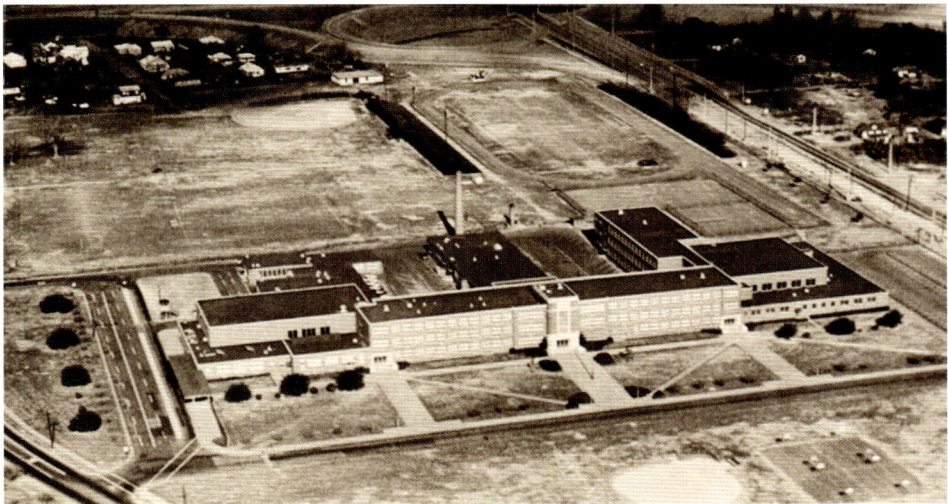

NORVIEW 1952: At the time of its construction, the 1952 Norview High School building, designed by architects J. Binford Walford and O. Pendleton Wright, of Richmond, Virginia, was the largest high school in Virginia. Originally built to accommodate 1,400 students, it opened with 1,800 students and 85 faculty members. The cost of this building was $3 million plus $125,000 to furnish it. In the years to come, other additions were made including a girls' athletic area, guidance complex, and 12 mobile classrooms; air-conditioning was not added until 1999. *Waller, Todd & Sadler Architects.*

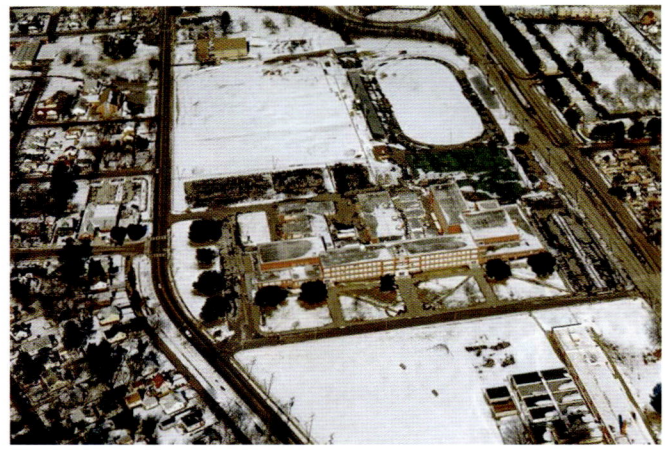

NORVIEW COMMUNITY: Norview High's surrounding community was part of Norfolk County, not the city of Norfolk, when it was completed but that would change with Norview's annexation in 1955. It is for this reason that Norview was the only high school to have its own football stadium, which was built by Norfolk County. This Norview (shown in an aerial photograph taken prior to construction of the new Norview building) had only four principals: Walter E. Campbell, Ph.D., an assistant superintendent of the Norfolk County school system who stepped in to transition Norview from the old high school to the new and remained principal until 1955, when he returned full-time to his duties in the superintendent's office; Charles W. "Bolo" Perdue, who also coached Norview's football team in the late 1940s, who was principal until 1982; Claude Sawyer, principal until 1992, and Marjorie Stealey, Ph.D., the current principal, who was appointed in 1992 and is the first woman to serve as a high school principal in Norfolk. *Waller, Todd & Sadler Architects.*

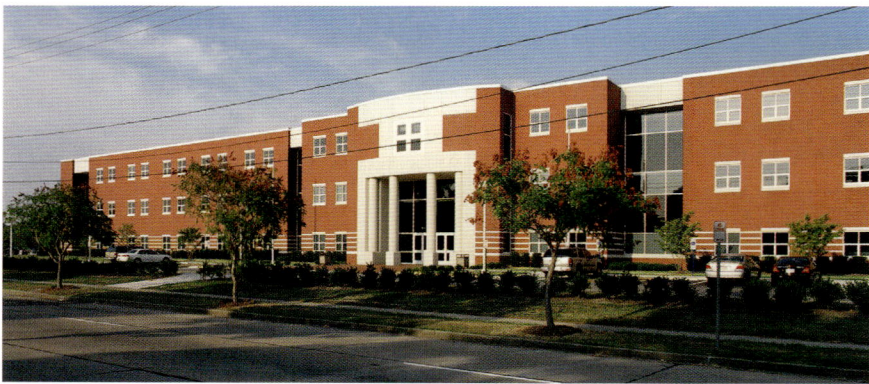

NEW NORVIEW: The deteriorating physical condition of the 1952 Norview High School led to the new building shown here. Due to the community's desire to preserve Norview's long history, Waller, Todd & Sadler Architects, gave the new school building a neo-traditional exterior. At a cost of $31.7 million to build and $4.7 million to furnish, the new Norview, sited to face Chesapeake Boulevard, was completed in 2005. At 295,000 square feet, it is twice the size of the building it replaced and is designed for 1,800 students. The groundbreaking for this building took place in June 2002 in the middle of the old football field where the construction started. The facility, situated on 30.5 acres, is complete, including a new stadium adjacent to Sewell's Point Road. Norview's school mascot—the "Pilot" biplane—has an interesting origin: one of the school's early principals enjoyed amateur flying and often practiced at a field near Norview. Norview Pilots became the accepted mascot. The Pilots' alma mater was written by Arch "Pop" Manning. *Waller, Todd & Sadler Architects.*

To the Bay

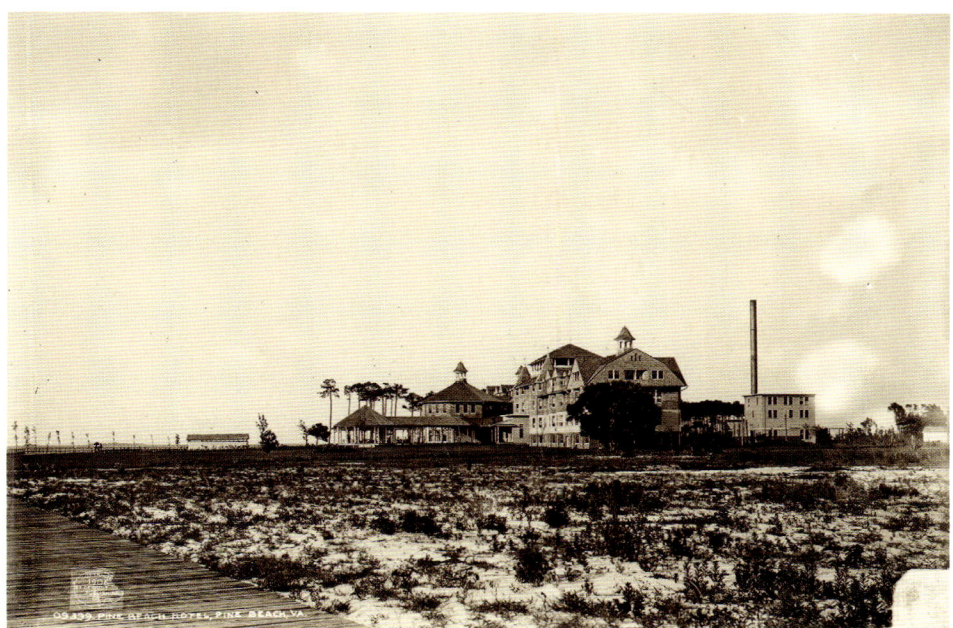

PINE BEACH HOTEL: Located at Sewell's Point adjacent to the Jamestown Exposition grounds, the hotel was a recreational focal point for city and county residents in first decade of the twentieth century. The hotel's boardwalk wrapped around the shoreline and is visible in this 1906 image (top). Here is another view (bottom) of the hotel and boardwalk. Today, this area is the northwest quarter of Virginia Avenue and Gilbert Street on Naval Station Norfolk. *Detroit Publishing Company, Library of Congress.*

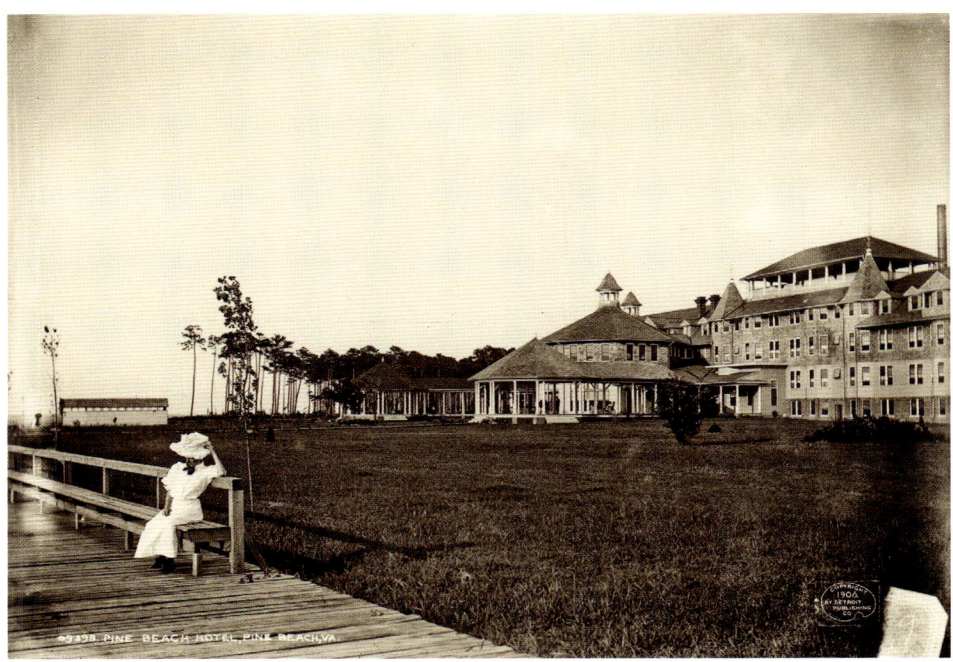

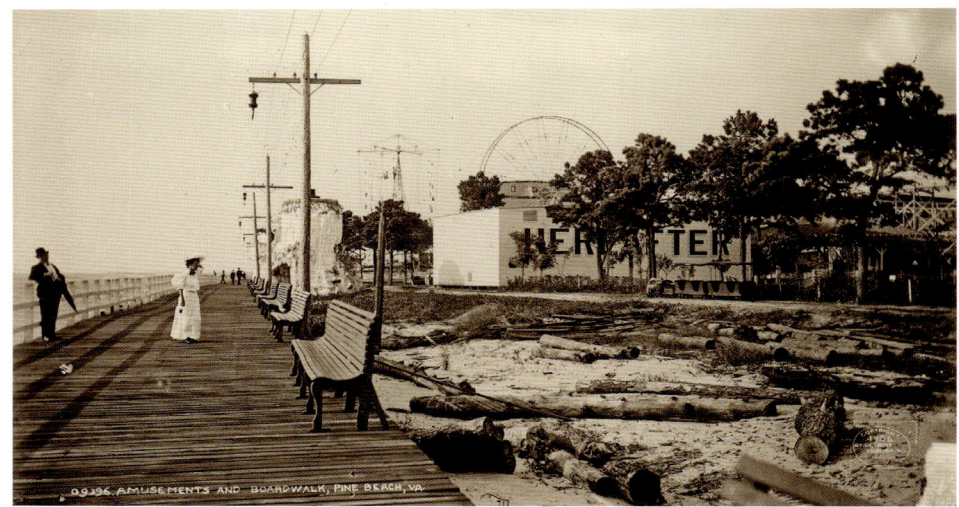

INTERNATIONAL EXPOSITION: The Pine Beach Hotel and surrounding grounds included amusements and a lovely waterside boardwalk, which would be enjoyed by thousands of visitors to the Jamestown Exposition of 1907. The picture was taken in 1906. Along Maryland Avenue (now Hampton Boulevard) ran the Norfolk and Atlantic Terminal Electric Railroad, with a wide turnaround circle at its north end and a spur track to the pier and boat landing at the west end of Ninety-ninth Street (now Taussig Boulevard); this was the ferry landing for Newport News and was still called the Pine Beach Ferry up to the time it was superseded by the Hampton Roads Bridge-Tunnel system. The electric car later became part of the now defunct Virginia Railway and Power Company system and is reported to have terminated at Atlantic Street downtown. *Detroit Publishing Company, Library of Congress.*

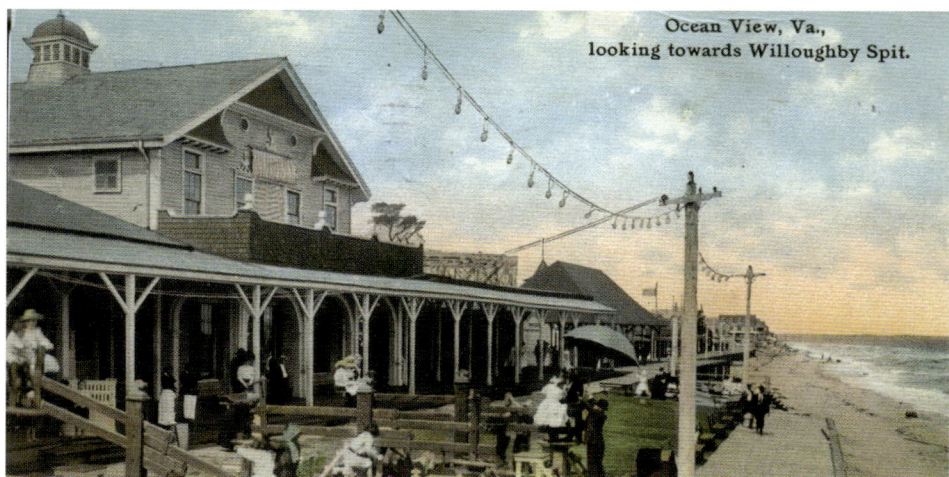

OCEAN VIEW AMUSEMENT PARK: The amusement park and boardwalk, looking toward Willoughby, in 1910 would be transformed in the decades to come. This area had already been remarkably developed by the time this picture was taken and sent out in postcard form. Though Willoughby's history is older, it would be Ocean View that was first developed by the Ocean View Company in 1854 and shortly thereafter advertised and promoted to the public at the beginning of 1855 as a bayside resort. Though Willoughby was largely undeveloped in 1900, the Jamestown Exposition of 1907 led to the construction of additional cottages, the Hampton Roads Yacht Club at the western end of the beach, and a small marina. Willoughby and Ocean View were annexed by the city of Norfolk in 1923.

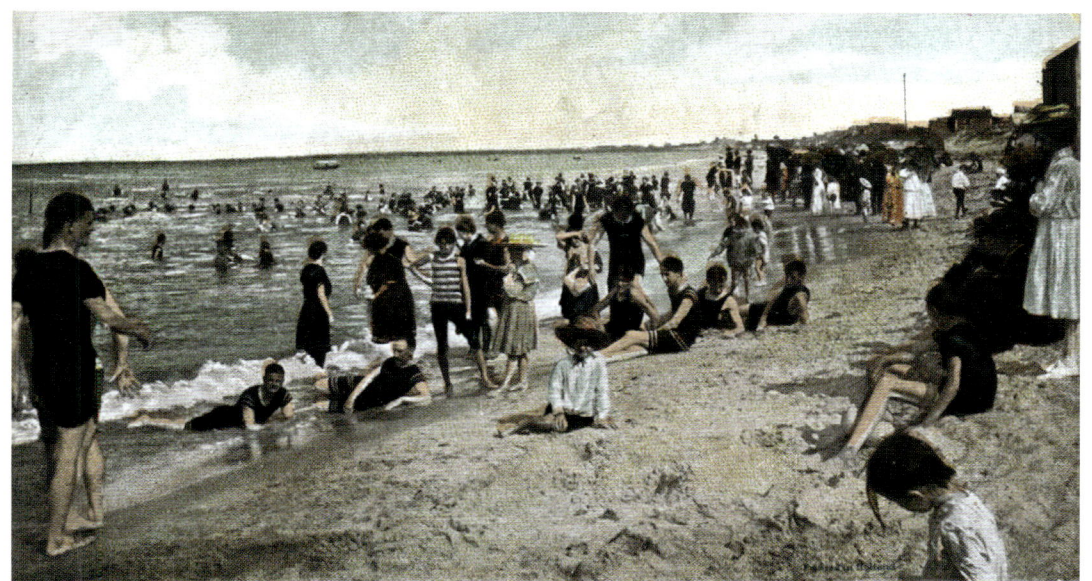

OCEAN VIEW SUMMER: At the peak of summer, likely the Fourth of July, these Ocean View beachgoers enjoyed the warm waters of the Chesapeake Bay in 1905, when the original picture was taken.

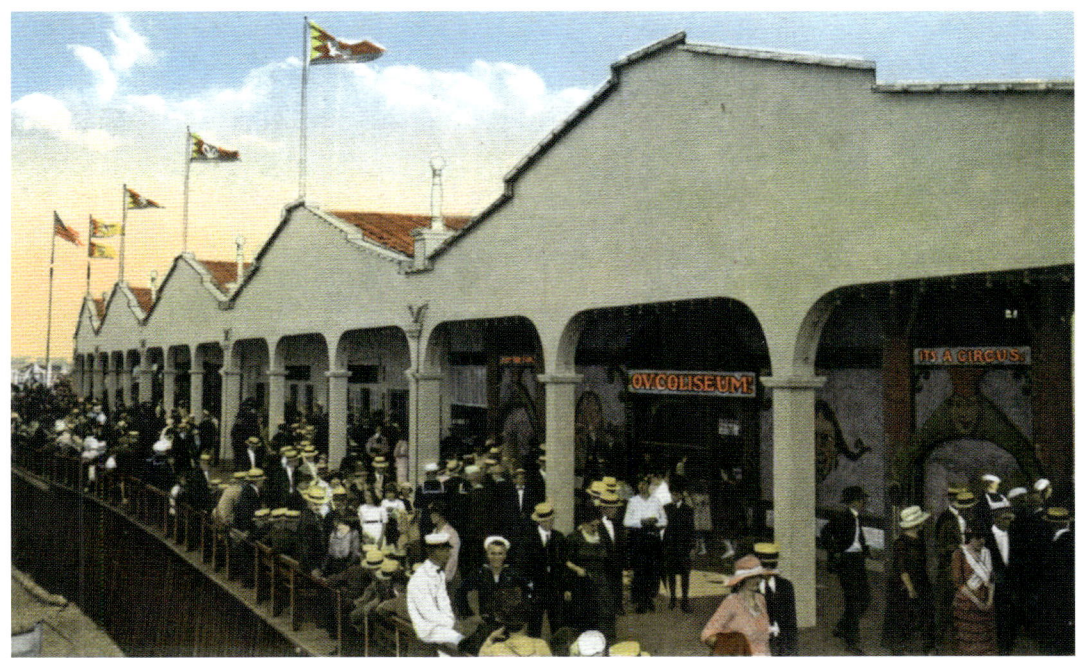

FUN AT THE SHORE: This view of the Ocean View Amusement Park and boardwalk, dating to 1915, shows also the various games of chance and "amusements" that were the order of the day and located north of Leap the Dips on the bay shore.

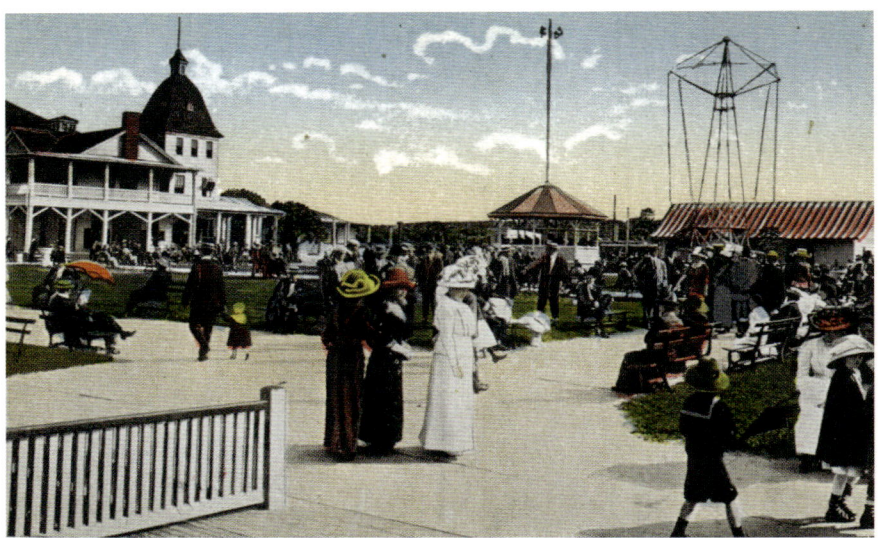

LAWN AND PROMENADE: The extreme east end of the Ocean View Amusement Park was occupied by a row of public bath houses, where the beach going public could shower and change into and out of their swim suits. Around the bath house complex and, later, additional mechanical rides, was an extensive green lawn with walks and benches, where visitors could mingle, socialize, rest on one of the green's many park benches or simply observe the park, other visitors and the beach. This hand-colored postcard of the Ocean View lawn and promenade walks dates to August 20, 1914.

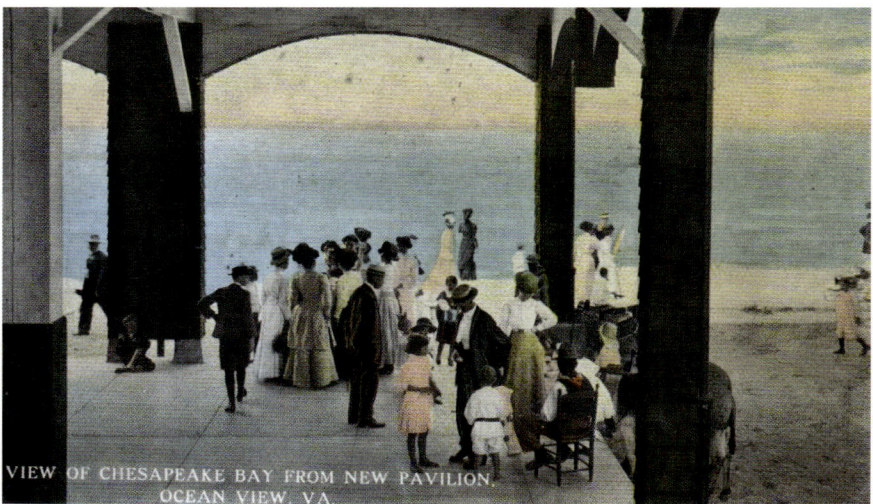

OCEAN VIEW HOTEL: The hotel, pavilion and cottages were built by the Ocean View Railroad and Hotel Company starting in 1880; this was the foundation of the future amusement park. By 1904, an amusement entrepreneur from Richmond, Virginia, named Otto Wells visited Ocean View and quickly observed its moneymaking potential. Wells bought the resort from the railroad and pushed the resort to new heights. As early as 1905, there was a small-scale rollercoaster. The Ocean View pavilion, shown here as it appeared in 1907, offered amusement park visitors an unfettered view of the bay and the diverse and powerful ships of the United States Navy and merchant service that daily passed the shore in front of "the View."

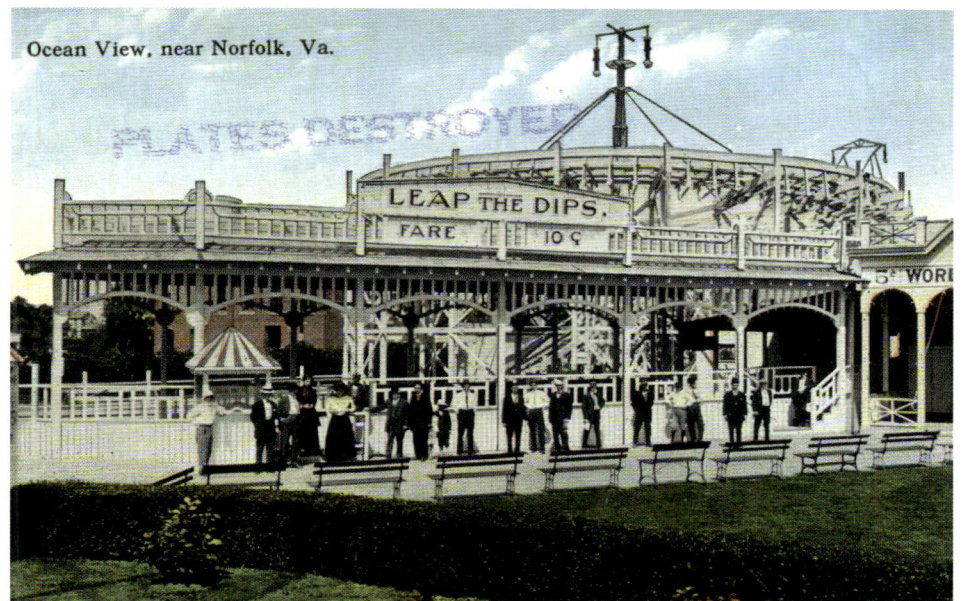

LEAP THE DIPS: A large wooden rollercoaster was always the centerpiece and primary attraction at the Ocean View Amusement Park. Built in the early twentieth century, the original coaster was known as "The Southern Belle," but some time later, the "Figure Eight." This early iteration was serpentine in its design and not high so few were afraid to ride it; those who wanted a real thrill were not impressed. After an extensive redesign, in which the height of ride was increased, it was renamed "Leap The Dips." The entrance to Leap the Dips rollercoaster is shown in this rare 1910 view (top), made from the original postcard plate before the plates were destroyed. In the second view (bottom, also from 1910), of note, the first Leap the Dips was destroyed by fire four years later; it was rebuilt. The new Leap the Dips was fitted with new and improved rollercoaster technology, including safety devices that had been absent from its predecessor.

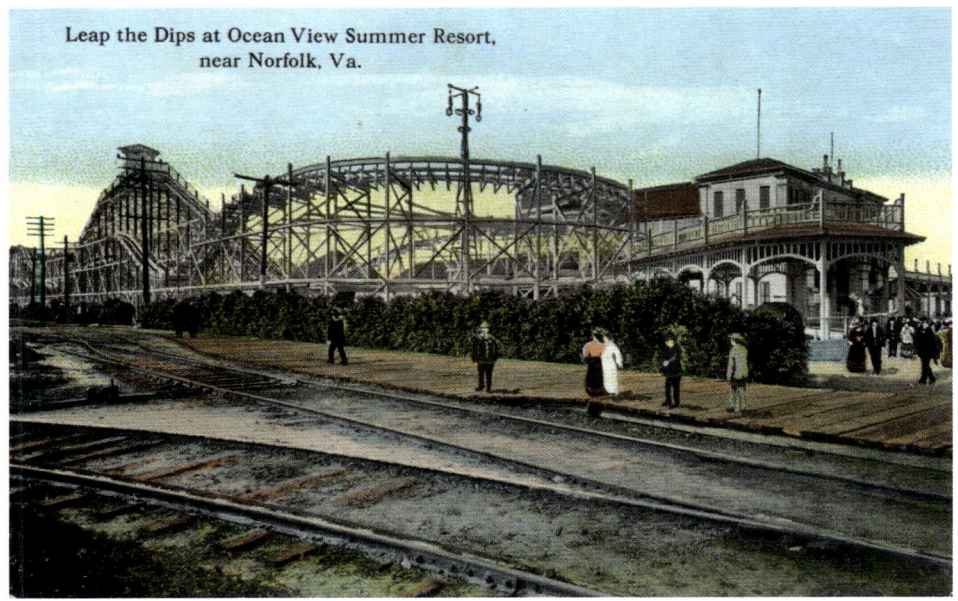

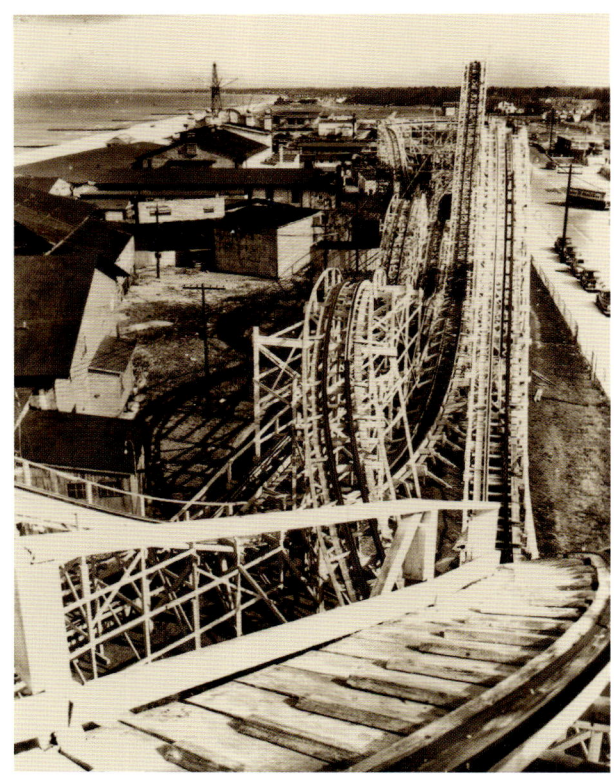

THE ROCKET: Eight years after this picture was taken, in February 1958, a fire destroyed a large portion of the Ocean View Amusement Park's west end and caused extensive damage to "The Rocket." Herbert Paul Schmeck rebuilt the popular rollercoaster. Jim Mays took this picture of "The Rocket" on April 1, 1950, the park's opening day of the summer season. *Sargeant Memorial Room, Norfolk Public Library*.

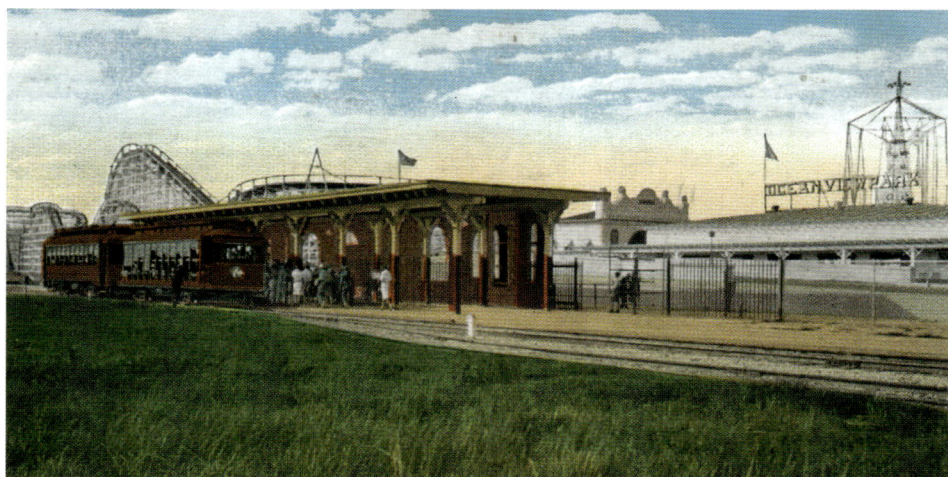

NORFOLK TRACTION COMPANY: laid a narrow gauge railroad to connect Ocean View to the railroad terminus at Church and Henry streets for the Norfolk and Ocean View Railroad and Hotel Company, chartered on February 27, 1878, with track active in September 1879. The company was classified as a seaside pleasure railroad. The cars were drawn by a steam-powered locomotive over a distance of 8.12 miles. The rail was changed to standard gauge in 1894 when the Norfolk streetcar system was electrified. In 1899, the Norfolk Street Railway, Norfolk and Ocean View Railroad, Virginia Electric, and Berkley Electric Light and Power companies were consolidated into the Norfolk Railway and Light Company. A new train station was erected at the park stop (shown here) in the 1915 time frame.

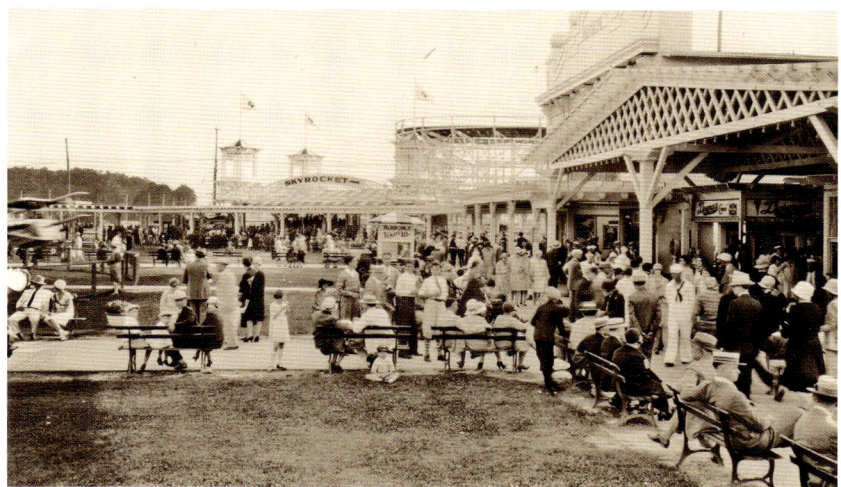

OCEAN VIEW ON THE FOURTH: The Ocean View Casino's Fourth of July crowd in 1928 filled the amusement park to capacity. The newly built "Skyrocket" rollercoaster is visible in the background. The Skyrocket, later truncated to "The Rocket," rollercoaster (shown here) was the star attraction at the Ocean View Amusement Park. Built in 1927 by Edward A. Vettel, the Skyrocket entertained and thrilled park visitors for decades to come. The ride was usually operated with two heavy, iron framed trains fitted with wooden cars run on the track at the same time, and as the trains reached the top drop, riders would plummet 60 to 70 feet at rapid speed before moving over more hills, drops and tight radial turns.

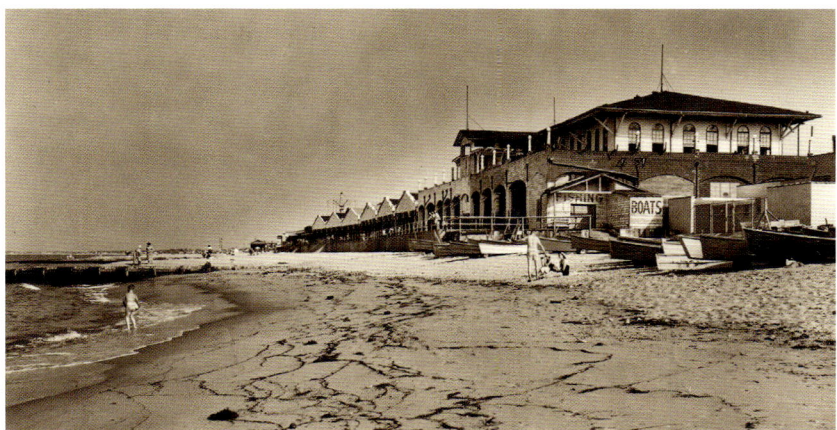

COMMUNITY BOOSTER: Dr. Dudley Cooper, a college-trained optometrist prominent in civic affairs and principal owner of a number of large Virginia manufacturing and retail businesses, and a partner in the ownership of Ocean View Amusement Park from 1942 to 1978, a role for which he was well known in the city, set aside land on park property for use as a United States Army coastal installation; United Service Organizations (USO) programs and entertainment; naval reserve recruitment activities, and various civic groups during the Second World War. Mainly, the navy was interested in using the Ocean View for the recreation of sailors bound for the war overseas, which eventually led to a certain amount of gambling and burlesque to please the soldiers, sailors and airmen who crowded Cooper's park. The Ocean View Amusement Park boardwalk and beach is shown as it looked in 1950—on a calmer day.

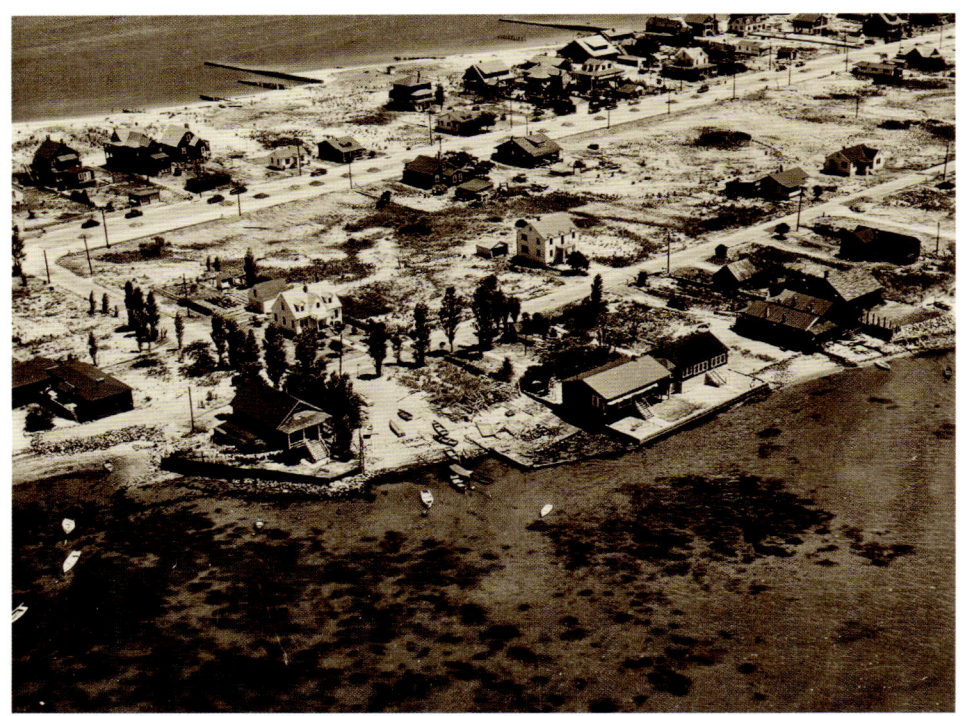

WILLOUGHBY AT FIFTEENTH VIEW: This aerial photograph was taken in 1950. Out of view, lower left, is the ferry service to the Peninsula.

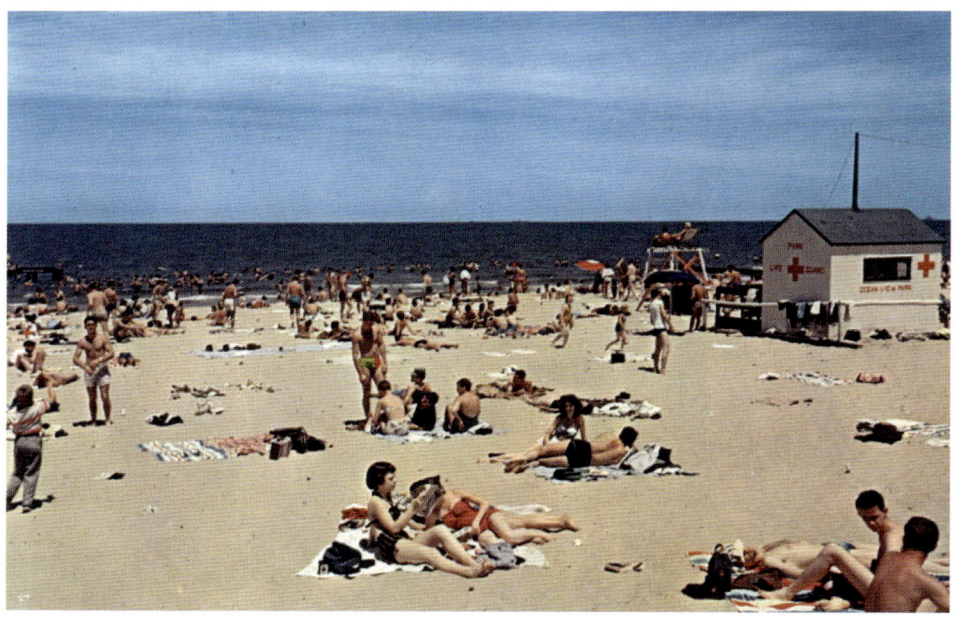

OCEAN VIEW BEACH: Shown here in 1955, this beach was every bit as busy in the summer as nearby Virginia Beach.

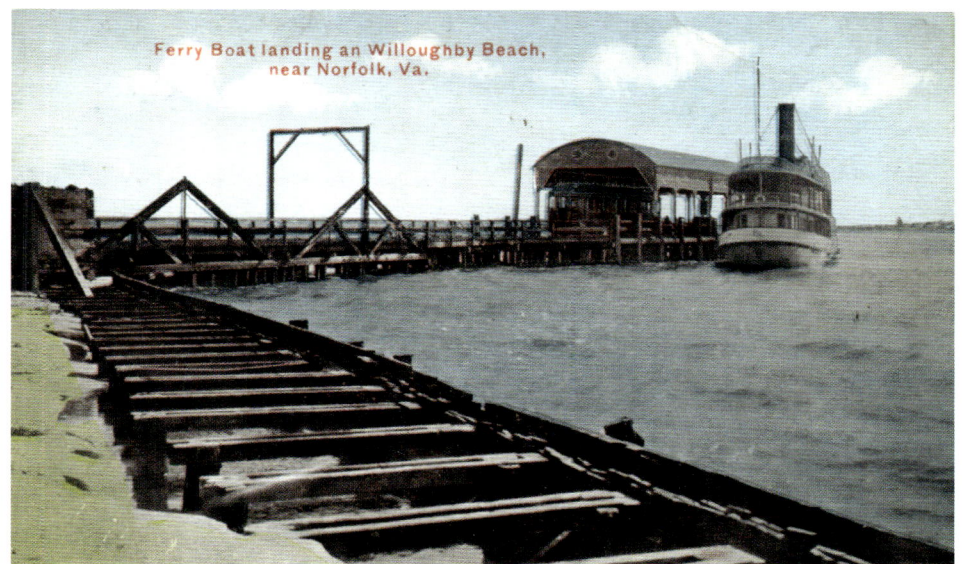

NORFOLK RAILWAY AND LIGHT COMPANY: The railway company and its successors operated the ferryboat service between Willoughby Beach and the Old Point Comfort pier in Hampton, Virginia, from the beginning of the twentieth century until the completion of the Hampton Roads Bridge-Tunnel. The Willoughby Beach ferry landing, shown here in 1910, was the fastest manner for travelers to go between the Virginia Peninsula to Norfolk.

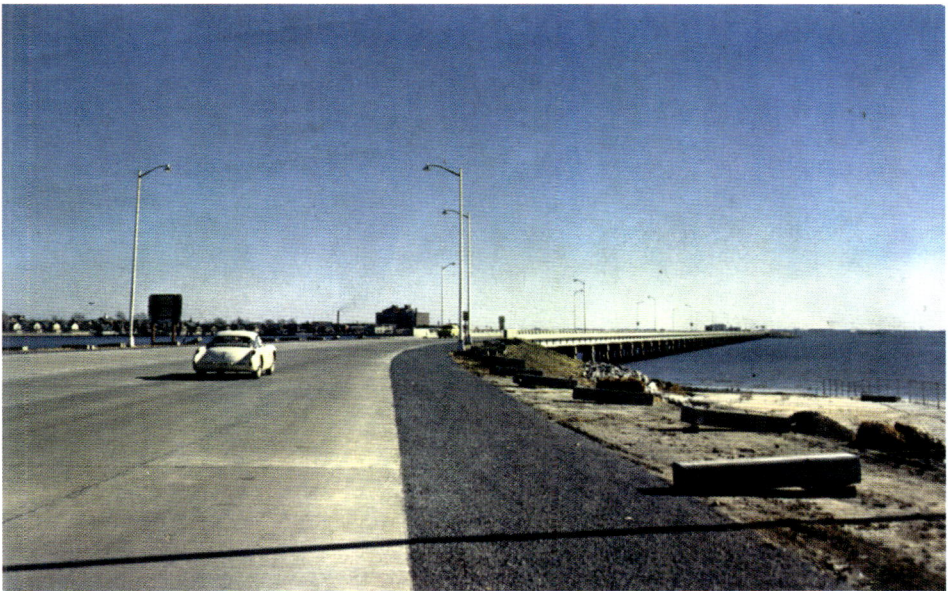

HAMPTON ROADS BRIDGE-TUNNEL: The original two-lane bridge-tunnel (shown here with a 1957 Chevrolet Corvette in polo white making the crossing the following year) replaced the ferry system that had previously connected travelers between Norfolk and Hampton; it opened November 1, 1957, at a cost of $44 million as a toll facility. The bridge–tunnel was originally designated State Route 168 and U.S. Route 60. It later received the Interstate 64 designation, and, much later, State Route 168 was truncated south of the crossing.

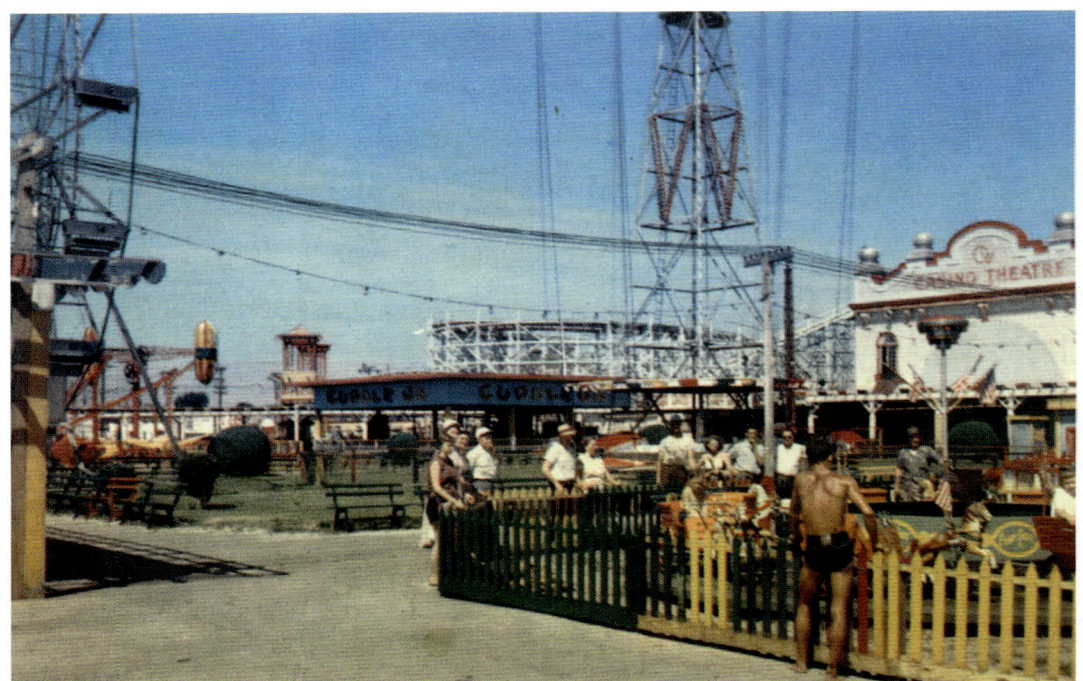

AFTER THE WAR: The post-Second World War period was Ocean View Amusement Park's best and most memorable to those still around who remember it well. More than 1 million visitors came to park annually from Easter to Labor Day at that time and it was as advertised bigger and better than its earlier iterations. Shown here in 1960, visitors could enjoy the rides, amusements and go for a swim all in the same place. What put Ocean View Amusement Park out of business was not the lack of fun and sun, it was the larger theme parks built outside of Hampton Roads, Busch Gardens Williamsburg and Kings Dominion in Doswell, just north of Richmond, among them. Cooper's park closed on Labor Day, 1978, and The Rocket was imploded the following year for the television movie *The Death at Ocean View Park*.